# The Vigilantes of Montana

## Popular Justice in the Rocky Mountains

Thomas J. Dimsdale

Skyhorse Publishing

First published 1866
First Skyhorse Publishing edition 2014

Skyhorse Publishing books may be purchased in bulk at special discounts for sales promotion, corporate gifts, fund-raising, or educational purposes. Special editions can also be created to specifications. For details, contact the Special Sales Department, Skyhorse Publishing, 307 West 36th Street, 11th Floor, New York, NY 10018 or info@skyhorsepublishing.com.

Skyhorse® and Skyhorse Publishing® are registered trademarks of Skyhorse Publishing, Inc.®, a Delaware corporation.

Visit our website at www.skyhorsepublishing.com.

10 9 8 7 6 5 4 3 2 1

Library of Congress Cataloging-in-Publication Data is available on file.

Cover design by Anthony Morais

Print ISBN: 978-1-62914-680-5
Ebook ISBN: 978-1-63220-175-1

Printed in the United States of America

# PREFACE.

The object of the writer in presenting this narrative to the public, is twofold. His intention is, in the first place, to furnish a correct history of an organization administering justice without the sanction of constitutional law; and secondly, to prove not only the necessity for their action, but the equity of their proceedings.

Having an intimate acquaintance with parties cognizant of the facts related, and feeling certain of the literal truth of the statements contained in this history, he offers it to the people of the United States, with the belief that its perusal will greatly modify the views of those even who are most prejudiced against the summary retribution of mountain law, and with the conviction that all honest and impartial men will be willing to admit both the wisdom of the course pursued and the salutary effect of the rule of the Vigilantes in the Territory of Montana.

It is also hoped that the history of the celebrated body, the very mention of whose name sounded as a death-knell in the ears of the murderers and

Road Agents, will be edifying and instructive to the general reader. The incidents related are neither trivial in themselves, nor unimportant in their results; and, while rivaling fiction in interest, are unvarnished accounts of transactions, whose fidelity can be vouched by thousands.

As a literary production, the author commits it to the examination of the critical without a sigh. If any of these author-slayers are inclined to be more severe in their judgment than he is himself, he trusts they will receive the reward to which their justice entitles them; and if they should pass it by, he cannot but think that they will exercise a sound discretion, and avoid much useless labor. With all its imperfections, here it is.

THOS. J. DIMSDALE.

# CHAPTER I.

## INTRODUCTORY—VIGILANCE COMMITTEES.

*" The teeth that bite hardest are out of sight. "*—PROV.

The end of all good government is the safety and happiness of the governed. It is not possible that a high state of civilization and progress can be maintained unless the tenure of life and property is secure; and it follows that the first efforts of a people in a new country for the inauguration of the reign of peace, the sure precursor of prosperity and stability, should be directed to the accomplishment of this object. In newly settled mining districts, the necessity for some effective organization of a judicial and protective character is more keenly felt than it is in other places, where the less exciting pursuits of agriculture and commerce mainly attract the attention and occupy the time of the first inhabitants.

There are good reasons for this difference. The first is the entirely dissimilar character of the populations; and the second, the possession of vast sums of money by uneducated and unprincipled people, in all places where the precious metals may be obtained at the cost of the labor necessary to exhume them from the strata in which they lie concealed.

In an agricultural country, the life of the pioneer settler is always one of hard labor, of considerable privation, and of more or less isolation, while the people who seek to clear a farm in the wild forest, or who break up the virgin soil of the prairies are usually of the steady and hard-working classes, needing little assistance from courts of justice to enable them to maintain rights which are seldom invaded; and whose differences, in the early days of the country, are, for the most part, so slight as to be scarcely worth the cost of a litigation more complicated than a friendly and, usually, gratuitous, arbitration—submitted to the judgment of the most respected among the citizens.

In marked contrast to the peaceful life of the tiller of the
soil, and to the placid monotony of his pursuits are the
turbulent activity, the constant excitement and the perpet-
ual temptations to which the dweller in a mining camp is
subject, both during his sojourn in the gulches, or, if he be
given to prospecting, in his frequent and unpremeditated
change of location, commonly called a "stampede." There
can scarcely be conceived a greater or more apparent difference than exists between the staid and sedate inhabi-
ants of rural districts, and the motley group of miners, professional men and merchants, thickly interspersed with shar-
pers, refugees, and a full selection from the dangerous classes
that swagger, armed to the teeth, through the diggings and
infest the roads leading to the newly discovered gulches,
where lies the object of their worship—Gold.

Fortunately the change to a better state of things is
rapid, and none who now walk the streets of Virginia
would believe that, within two years of this date, the great
question to be decided was, which was the stronger, right
or might?

And here it must be stated, that the remarks which truth
compels us to make, concerning the classes of individuals
which furnish the law defying element of mining camps,
are in no wise applicable to the majority of the people, who,
while exhibiting the characteristic energy of the American
race in the pursuit of wealth, yet maintain, under every disadvantage, an essential morality, which is the more creditable since it must be sincere, in order to withstand the temptations to which it is constantly exposed. "Oh, cursed thirst
of gold," said the ancient, and no man has even an inkling
of the truth and force of the sentiment, till he has lived
where gold and silver are as much the objects of desire,
and of daily and laborious exertion, as glory and promotion
are to the young soldier. Were it not for the preponderance of this conservative body of citizens, every camp in
remote and recently discovered mineral regions would be a
field of blood; and where this is not so, the fact is proof irresistible that the good is in sufficient force to control the
evil, and eventually to bring order out of chaos.

Let the reader suppose that the police of New York were

withdrawn for twelve months, and then let them picture the wild saturnalia which would take the place of the order that reigns there now. If, then, it is so hard to restrain the dangerous classes of old and settled communities, what must be the difficulty of the task, when, tenfold in number, fearless in character, generally well armed, and supplied with money to an extent unknown among their equals in the east, such men find themselves removed from the restraints of civilized society, and beyond the control of the authority which there enforces obedience to the law.

Were it not for the sterling stuff of which the mass of miners is made, their love of fair play, and their prompt and decisive action in emergencies, this history could never have been written, for desperadoes of every nation would have made this country a scene of bloodshed and a sink of iniquity such as was never before witnessed.

Together with so much that is evil, no where is there so much that is sternly opposed to dishonesty and violence as in the mountains; and though careless of externals and style, to a degree elsewhere unknown, the intrinsic value of manly uprightness is no where so clearly exhibited and so well appreciated as in the Eldorado of the west. Middling people do not live in these regions. A man or a woman becomes better or worse by a trip towards the Pacific. The keen eye of the experienced miner detects the imposter at a glance, and compels his entire isolation, or his association with the class to which he rightfully belongs.

Thousands of weak-minded people return, after a stay in the mountains, varying in duration from a single day to a year, leaving the field where only the strong of heart are fit to battle with difficulty, and to win the golden crown which is the reward of persevering toil and unbending firmness. There is no man more fit to serve his country in any capacity requiring courage, integrity, and self-reliance, than an "honest miner," who has been tried and found true by a jury of mountaineers.

The universal license that is, at first, a necessity of position in such places, adds greatly to the number of crimes, and to the facilities for their perpetration. Saloons, where poisonous liquors are vended to all comers, and consumed in quantities sufficient to drive excitable men to madness and to the commission of homicide, on the slightest provocation, are to be found in amazing numbers, and the villainous compounds there sold, under the generic name of whiskey, are more familiarly distinguished by the cognomens of "Tangleleg," "Forty-rod," "Lightning," "Tarantula-juice," etc., terms only too truly describing their acknowledged qualities.

The absence of good female society, in any due proportion to the numbers of the opposite sex, is likewise an evil of great magnitude; for men become rough, stern and cruel, to a surprising degree, under such a state of things.

In every frequent street, public gambling houses with open doors and loud music, are resorted to, in broad daylight, by hundreds—it might almost be said—of all tribes and tongues, furnishing another fruitful source of "difficulites," which are commonly decided on the spot, by an appeal to brute force, the stab of a knife, or the discharge of a revolver. Women of easy virtue are to be seen promenading through the camp, habited in the gayest and most costly apparel, and receiving fabulous sums for their purchased favors. In fact, all the temptations to vice are present in full display, with money in abundance to secure the gratification of the desire for novelty and excitement, which is the ruling passion of the mountaineer.

One "institution," offering a shadowy and dangerous substitute for more legitimate female association, deserves a more peculiar notice. This is the "Hurdy-Gurdy" house. As soon as the men have left off work, these places. are opened, and dancing commences. Let the reader picture to himself a large room, furnished with a bar at one end—where champagne at $12 (in gold) per bottle, and "drinks" at twenty-five to fifty cents, are wholesaled, (correctly speaking)—and divided, at the end of this bar, by a railing running from side to side. The outer enclosure is densely crowded (and, on particular occasions, the inner one also) with men in every variety of garb that can be seen on the continent. Beyond the barrier, sit the dancing women, called "hurdy-gurdies," sometimes dressed in uniform, but, more generally, habited according to the dictates of indi-

vidual caprice, in the finest clothes that money can buy,
and which are fashioned in the most attractive styles that
fancy can suggest. On one side is a raised orchestra. The
music suddenly strikes up, and the summons, "Take your
partners for the next dance," is promptly answered by some
of the male spectators, who paying a dollar in gold for a
ticket, approach the ladies' bench, and—in style polite, or
otherwise, according to antecedents—invite one of the ladies
to dance.

The number being complete, the parties take their places,
as in any other dancing establishment, and pause for the
performance of the introductory notes of the air.

Let us describe a first class dancer—"sure of a partner
every time"—and her companion. There she stands at the
head of the set. She is of middle height, of rather full and
rounded form; her complexion as pure as alabaster, a pair
of dangerous looking hazel eyes, a slightly Roman nose, and
a small and prettily formed mouth. Her auburn hair is
neatly banded and gathered in a tasteful, ornamented net, with
a roll and gold tassels at the side. How sedate she looks
during the first figure, never smiling till the termination of
"promenade, eight," when she shows her little white hands
in fixing her handsome brooch in its place, and settling her
glistening ear-rings. See how nicely her scarlet dress, with
its broad black band round the skirt, and its black edging,
sets off her dainty figure. No wonder that a wild mountaineer would be willing to pay—not one dollar, but all that
he has in his purse, for a dance and an approving smile
from so beautiful a woman.

Her cavalier stands six feet in his boots, which come to
the knee, and are garnished with a pair of Spanish spurs,
with rowels and bells like young water wheels. His buckskin leggings are fringed at the seams, and gathered at the
waist with a U. S. belt, from which hangs his loaded revolver and his sheath knife. His neck is bare, muscular and
embrowned by exposure, as is also his bearded face, whose
sombre hue is relieved by a pair of piercing dark eyes. His
long, black hair hangs down beneath his wide felt hat, and,
in the corner of his mouth, is a cigar, which rolls like the
lever of an eccentric, as he chews the end in his mouth.

After an amazingly grave salute, "all hands round" is shouted by the prompter, and off bounds the buckskin hero, rising and falling to the rhythm of the dance, with a clumsy agility and a growing enthusiasm, testifying his huge delight. His fair partner, with practiced foot and easy grace, keeps time to the music like a clock, and rounds to her place as smoothly and gracefully as a swan. As the dance progresses, he of the buckskins gets excited, and nothing but long practice prevents his partner from being swept off her feet, at the conclusion of the miner's delight, "set your partners," or "gents to the right." An Irish tune or a hornpipe generally finishes the set, and then the thunder of heel and toe, and some amazing demivoltes are brought to an end by the aforesaid, "gents to the right," and "promenade to the bar," which last closes the dance. After a treat, the barkeeper mechanically raps his blower as a hint to "weigh out," the ladies sit down, and with scarcely an interval, a waltz, polka, shottische, mazurka, varsovienne, or another quadrille commences.

All varieties of costume, physique and demeanor can be noticed among the dancers—from the gayest colors and "loudest" styles of dress and manner, to the snugly fitted black silk, and plain, white collar, which sets off the neat figure of the blue-eyed, modest looking Anglo-Saxon. Yonder, beside the tall and tastily clad German brunette, you see the short curls, rounded tournure and smiling face of an Irish girl; indeed, representatives of almost every dancing nation of white folks, may be seen on the floor of the Hurdy-Gurdy house. The earnings of the dancers are very different in amount. That dancer in the low necked dress, with the scarlet "waist," a great favorite and a really good dancer, counted fifty tickets into her lap before "The last dance, gentlemen," followed by, "Only this one before the girls go home," which wound up the performance. Twenty-six dollars is a great deal of money to earn in such a fashion; but fifty sets of quadrilles and four waltzes, two of them for the love of the thing, is very hard work.

As a rule, however, the professional "hurdies" are Teutons, and, though first rate dancers, they are, with some few exceptions, the reverse of good looking.

The dance which is most attended, is one in which ladies to whom pleasure is dearer than fame, represent the female element, and, as may be supposed, the evil only COMMENCES at the Dance House. It is not uncommon to see one of these syrens with an "outfit" worth from seven to eight hundred dollars, and many of them invest with merchants and bankers thousands of dollars in gold, the rewards and presents they receive, especially the more highly favored ones, being more in a week, than a well educated girl would earn in two years in an Eastern city.

In the Dance House you can see Judges, the Legislative corps, and every one but the Minister. He never ventures further than to engage in conversation with a friend at the door, and while intently watching the performance, lectures on the evil of such places with considerable force; but his attention is evidently more fixed upon the dancers than on his lecture. Sometimes may be seen gray haired men dancing, their wives sitting at home in blissful ignorance of the proceeding. There never was a dance house running, for any length of time, in the first days of a mining town, in which "shooting scrapes" do not occur; equal proportions of jealousy, whiskey and revenge being the stimulants thereto. Billiard saloons are everywhere visible, with a bar attached, and hundreds of thousands of dollars are spent there. As might be anticipated, it is impossible to prevent quarrels in these places, at all times, and, in the mountains, whatever weapon is handiest—foot, fist, knife, revolver, or deringer—it is instantly used. The authentic, and, indeed, LITERALLY exact accounts which follow in the course of this narrative will show that the remarks we have made on the state of society in a new mining country, before a controlling power asserts its sway, are in no degree exaggerated, but fall short of the reality, as all description must.

One marked feature of social intercourse, and (after indulgence in strong drink) the most fruitful source of quarrel and bloodshed is the all prevading custom of using strong language on every occasion. Men will say more than they mean, and the unwritten code of the miners, based on a wrong view of what constitutes manhood, teaches them to resent by force which should be answered by silent contempt.

Another powerful incentive to wrong doing is the absolute nullity of the civil law in such cases. No matter what may be the proof, if the criminal is well liked in the community, "Not Guilty" is almost certain to be the verdict of the jury, despite the efforts of the Judge and prosecutor. If the offender is a monied man, as well as a popular citizen, the trial is only a farce—grave and prolonged, it is true but capable of only one termination—a verdict of acquittal. In after days, when police magistrates in cities can deal with crime, they do so promptly. Costs are absolutely frightful, and fines tremendous. An assault provoked by drunkenness, frequently costs a man as much as thrashing forty different policemen would do, in New York. A trifling "tight" is worth from $20 to $50 in dust, all expenses told, and so on. One grand jury that we wot of, presented that it would be better to leave the punishment of offenders to the Vigilantes, who always acted impartially, and who would not permit the escape of proved criminals on technical and absurd grounds—than to have justice defeated, as in a certain case named. The date of that document is not ancient, and though, of course, refused and destroyed, it was the deliberate opinion, on oath, of the Grand Inquest, embodying the sentiment of thousands of good citizens in the community.

Finally, swift and terrible retribution is the only preventive of crime, while society is organizing in the far West. The long delay of justice, the wearisome proceedings, the remembrance of old friendships, etc., create a sympathy for the offender, so strong as to cause a hatred of the avenging law, instead of inspiring a horror of the crime. There is something in the excitement of continued stampedes that makes men of quick temperaments uncontrollably impulsive. In the moment of passion, they would slay all round them; but let the blood cool, and they would share their last dollar with the men whose life they sought, a day or two before.

Habits of thought rule communities more than laws, and the settled opinion of a numerous class is, that calling a man a liar, a thief, or a son of a b—h is provocation sufficient to justify instant slaying. Juries do not ordinarily bother themselves about the lengthy instruction they hear read by the court. They simply consider whether the deed is a crime against the Mountain Code; and if not, "not guilty" is the verdict, at once returned. Thieving, or any action which a miner calls MEAN, will surely be visited with condign punishment, at the hands of a Territorial jury. In such cases mercy there is none; but, in affairs of single combats, assaults, shootings, stabbings, and highway robberies, the civil law, with its positively awful expense and delay, is worse than useless.

One other main point requires to be noticed. Any person of experience will remember that the universal story of criminals, who have expiated their crimes on the scaffold, or who are pining away in the hardships of involuntary servitude— tells of habitual Sabbath breaking. This sin is so general in newly discovered diggings in the mountains, that a remonstrance usually produced no more fruit than a few jocular oaths and a laugh. Religion is said to be "played out," and a professing Christian must keep straight, indeed, or he will be suspected of being a hypocritical member of a tribe, to whom it would be very disagreeable to talk about hemp.

Under these circumstances, it becomes an absolute necessity that good, law-loving, and order-sustaining men should unite for mutual protection, and for the salvation of the community. Being united, they must act in harmony; repress disorder; punish crime, and prevent outrage, or their organization would be a failure from the start, and society would collapse in the throes of anarchy. None but extreme penalties inflicted with promptitude, are of any avail to quell the spirit of the desperadoes with whom they have to contend; considerable numbers are required to cope successfully with the gangs of murderers, desperadoes and robbers, who infest mining countries, and who, though faithful to no other bond, yet all league willingly against the law. Secret they must be, in council and membership, or they will remain nearly useless for the detection of crime, in a country where equal facilities for the transmission of intelligence are at the command of the criminal and the judiciary; and an organization on this footing is a VIGILANCE COMMITTEE.

Such was the state of affairs, when five men in Virginia, and four in Bannack, initiated the movement which resulted in the formation of a tribunal, supported by an omnipresent executive, comprising within itself nearly every good man in the Territory, and pledged to render impartial justice to friend and foe, without regard to clime, creed, race or politics. In a few short weeks it was known that the voice of justice had spoken, in tones that might not be disregarded. The face of society was changed, as if by magic; for the Vigilantes, holding in one hand the invisible, yet effectual shield of protection, and in the other, the swift descending and inevitable sword of retribution, struck from his nerveless grasp the weapon of the assassin; commanded the brawler to cease from strife; warned the thief to steal no more; bade the good citizen take courage, and compelled the ruffians and marauder who had so long maintained the "reign of terror" in Montana, to fly the Territory, or meet the just rewards of their crimes. Need we say that they were at once obeyed? yet not before more than one hundred valuable lives had been pitilessly sacrificed and twenty-four miscreants had met a dog's doom as the reward of their crimes.

To this hour, the whispered words, "Virginia Vigilantes," would blanch the cheek of the wildest and most redoubtable desperado, and necessitate an instant election between flight and certain doom.

The administration of the lex talionis by self-constituted authority is, undoubtedly, in civilized and settled communities, an outrage on mankind. It is there, wholly unnecessary; but the sight of a few of the mangled corpses of beloved friends and valued citizens; the whistle of the desperado's bullet, and the plunder of the fruits of the patient toil of years spent in weary exile from home, in places where civil law is as powerless as a palsied arm, from sheer lack of ability to enforce its decrees—alter the basis of the reasoning, and reverse the conclusion. In the case of the Vigilantes of Montana, it must be also remembered that the Sheriff himself was the leader of the Road Agents, and his deputies were the prominent members of the band.

The question of the propriety of establishing a Vigilance Committee, depends upon the answers which ought to be given to the following queries: Is it lawful for citizens to slay robbers or murderers, when they catch them; or ought they to wait for policemen, where there are none, or put them in penitentiaries not yet erected?

Gladly, indeed, we feel sure, would the Vigilantes cease from their labor, and joyfully would they hail the advent of power, civil or military, to take their place; but, till this is furnished by Government, society must be preserved from demoralization and anarchy; murder, arson and robbery must be prevented or punished, and road agents must die. Justice, and protection from wrong to person or property, are the birth-right of every American citizen, and these must be furnished in the best and most effectual manner that circumstances render possible. Furnished, however, they must be by constitutional law, undoubtedly, wherever practical and efficient provision can be made for its enforcement. But where justice is powerless as well as blind; the strong arm of the mountaineer must wield her sword; for "self preservation is the first law of nature."

## CHAPTER II

### THE SUNNY SIDE OF MOUNTAIN LIFE.

"The friends thou hast, and their adoption tried,
Grapple them to thy soul with hooks of steel."—SHAKS.

In the preceding chapter, it was necessary to show to the reader the dark side of the cloud; but it has a golden lining, and though many a cursory observer, or disappointed speculator, may deny this fact, yet thousands have seen it, and know to their heart's content that it is there. Yes! Life in the mountains has many charms. The one great blessing is perfect freedom. Untrammelled by the artificial restraints of more highly organized society, character devel-

opes itself so fully and so truly, that a man who has a friend,
knows it, and there is a warmth and depth in the attachment
which unites the dwellers in the wilderness, that is worth
years of the insipid and uncertain regard of so-called, polite
circles, which, too often, passes by the name of friendship,
and, sometimes, insolently apes the attributes, and dishonors
the fame of love itself. Those who have slept at the same
watch-fire, and traversed together many a weary league,
sharing hardship and privations, are drawn together by ties
which civilization wots not of. Wounded or sick, far from
home, and depending for life itself, upon the ministration and
tender care of some fellow traveller, the memory of these
deeds of mercy and kindly fellowship often mutually rendered, is as an oasis in the desert, or as a crystal stream to
the fainting pilgrim.

As soon as towns are built, society commences to organize, and there is something truly cheering in the ready hos-
pitality, the unfeigned welcome, and the friendly toleration
of personal peculiarities which mark the intercourse of the
dwellers in the land of gold. Every one does what pleases
him best. Forms and ceremonies are at a discount, and
generosity has its home in the pure air of the Rocky Mountains. This virtue, indeed, is as inseparable from mountaineers of all classes, as the pick and shovel from the pros-
pector. When a case of real destitution, is made public, if
any well known citizens will but take a paper in his hand
and go round with it, the amount collected would astonish
a dweller in Eastern cities, and it is a fact that gamblers and
saloon keepers are the very men who subscribe the most lib-
erally. Mountaineers think little of a few hundreds of dollars, when the feelings are engaged, and the number of instances in which men have been helped to fortunes and presented with valuable property by their friends, is truly astonishing.

The Mountains also may be said to circumscribe and
bound the paradise of amiable and energetic women. For
their labor they are paid magnificently, and they are treated
with a deference and liberality unknown in other climes.
There seems to be a law, unwritten but scarcely ever trans-
gressed, which assigns to a virtuous and amiable woman, a

power for good which she can never hope to attain else-where. In his wildest excitement, a mountaineer respects a woman, and anything like an insult offered to a lady, would be instantly resented, probably with fatal effect, by any bystander. Dancing is the great amusement with persons of both sexes, and we might say, of all ages. The comparative disproportion between the male and female ele-ments of society, ensures the possessor of personal charms of the most ordinary kind, if she be good natured, the greatest attention, and the most liberal provision for her wants, whether real or fancied.

If two men are friends, an insult to one is resented by both, an alliance offensive and defensive being a necessary condition of friendship in the mountains. A popular citi-zen is safe everywhere, and any man may be popular that has anything useful or genial about him.

"Putting on style," or the assumption of aristocratic airs, is the detestation of everybody. No one but a person lack-ing sense attempts it. It is neither forgotten nor forgiven, and KILLS a man like a bullet. It should also be remembered that no people more admire and respect upright moral con-duct, than do the sojourners in mining camps, while at the same time none more thoroughly despise hypocrisy in any shape. In fact, good men and good women may be as moral and as religious as they choose to be, in the mining countries, and as happy as human beings can be. Much they will miss that they have been used to, and much they will receive that none offered them before.

Money is commonly plentiful; if prices are high, remuner-ation for work is liberal, and, in the end, care and industry will achieve success and procure competence. We have travelled far and seen much of the world, and the result of our experience is a love for our mountain home, that time and change of scene can never efface.

# CHAPTER III.

### SETTLEMENT OF MONTANA.

"I hear the tread of pioneers,
    Of nations yet to be ;
The first low wash of waves, where soon
    Shall roll a human sea.—WHITTIER.

Early in the Spring of 1862, the rumor of new and rich discoveries on Salmon River, flew through Salt Lake City, Colorado, and other places in the Territories. A great stampede was the consequence. Faith and hope were in the
ascendant among the motley crew that wended their toilsome way by Fort Hall and Snake river, to the new Eldorado. As the trains approached the goal of their desires, they
were informed that they could not get through with wagons,
and shortly after came the discouraging tidings that the new
mines were overrun by a crowd of gold-hunters from California, Oregon, and other western countries ; they were also
told, that finding it impossible to obtain either claims or
labor, large bands of prospectors were already spreading over
the adjacent territory ; and finally, that some new diggings
had been discovered at Deer Lodge.

The stream of emigration diverged from the halting place,
where this last welcome intelligence reached them. Some,
turning towards Deer Lodge, crossed the mountains, between
Fort Lemhi and Horse Prairie Creek, and, taking a cut-off
to the left, endeavored to strike the old trail from Salt Lake
to Bitter Root and Deer Lodge Valleys. These energetic
miners crossed the Grasshopper Creek, below the Canon,
and finding good prospects there, some of the party remained,
with a view of practically testing their value. Others went
on to Deer Lodge ; but finding that the diggings were
neither so rich nor so extensive as they had supposed, they
returned to Grasshopper Creek—afterwards known as the

Beaver Head Diggings—so named from the Beaver Head
River, into which the creek empties. The river derives its
appellation from a rock, which exactly resembles, in its out-
line, the head of a Beaver.

From this camp—the rendezvous of the emigration—started, from time to time, the bands of explorers who first discovered and worked the gulches east of the Rocky Mountains, in the world renowned country now the Territory of
Montana. Other emigrants, coming by Deer Lodge, struck
the Beaver Head diggings; then the first party from Minnesota arrived; after them, came a large part of the Fisk
company who had travelled under Government escort, from
the same State, and a considerable number drove through
from Salt Lake City and Bitter Root, in the early part of
the winter, which was very open.

Among the later arrivals were some desperadoes and
outlaws, from the mines west of the mountains. In this
gang were Henry Plummer, afterwards the SHERIFF, Charley Reeves, Moore and Skinner. These worthies had no
sooner got the "lay of the country," than they commenced
operations. Here it may be remarked, that if the professed
servants of God would only work for their master with the
same energy and persistent devotion, as the servants of the
Devil use for their employer, there would be no need of a
Heaven above, for the earth itself would be a Paradise.

---

## CHAPTER IV.

### THE ROAD AGENTS.

"Thieves for their robbery have authority
When judges steal themselves."—SHAKESPEARE

It may easily be imagined that life in Bannack, in the early
days of the settlement, was anything but pleasant. The
ruffians, whose advent we have noticed, served as a nucleus,
around which the disloyal, the desperate, and the dishonest

gathered, and quickly organizing themselves into a band, with captain, lieutenants, secretary, road agents, and outsiders, became the terror of the country. The stampede to the Alder Gulch, which occurred early in June, 1863, and the discovery of the rich placer diggings there, attracted many more of the dangerous classes, who, scenting the prey from afar, flew like vultures to the battle field.

Between Bannack and Virginia, a correspondence was constantly kept up, and the roads throughout the Territory were under the serveillance of the "outsiders" before mentioned. To such a system were these things brought, that horses, men and coaches were marked in some understood manner, to designate them as fit objects for plunder, and thus the liers in wait had an opportunity of communicating the intelligence to the members of the gang, in time to prevent the escape of the victims.

The usual arms of a road agent were a pair of revolvers, a double-barrelled shot-gun, of large bore, with the barrels cut down short, and to this they invariably added a knife or dagger. Thus armed and mounted on fleet, well trained horses, and being disguised with blankets and masks, the robbers awaited their prey in ambush. When near enough, they sprang out on a keen run, with levelled shot-guns, and usually gave the word, "Halt! Throw up your hands you sons of b——s!" If this latter command were not instantly obeyed, there was the last of the offender; but, in case he complied, as was usual, one or two sat on their horses, covering the party with their guns, which were loaded with buck-shot, and one, dismounting, disarmed the victims, and made them throw their purses on the grass. This being done, and a search for concealed property being effected, away rode the robbers, reported the capture and divided the spoils.

The confession of two of their number one of whom, named Erastus Yager alias Red, was hung in the Stinkingwater Valley, put the Committee in possession of the names of the prominent men in the gang, and eventually secured their death or voluntary banishment. The most noted of the road agents, with a few exceptions were hanged by the Vigilance Committee, or banished. A list of the place and date of execution of the principle members of the band is here presented. The remainder of the red calendar of crime and retribution will appear after the account of the execution of Hunter:

### NAMES, PLACE AND DATE OF EXECUTION.

George Ives, Nevada City, Dec. 21st 1863; Erastus Yager (Red) and G. W. Brown, Stinkingwater Valley, January 4th, 1864; Henry Plummer, Ned Ray and Buck Stinson, Bannack City, January 10th, 1864; George Lane, (Clubfoot George,) Frank Parish, Haze Lyons, Jack Gallagher and Boone Helm, Virginia City, January 14th, 1864; Steven Marsland, Big Hole Ranche, January 16th, 1864; William Bunton, Deer Lodge Valley, January 19th 1864; Cyrus Skinner, Alexander Carter, and John Cooper, Hell Gate, January 25th, 1864; George Shears, Frenchtown, January 24th, 1864; Robert Zachary, Hell Gate, January 25th, 1864; William Graves alias Whiskey Bill, Fort Owens, January 26th, 1864; William Hunter, Gallatin Valley, February 3d, 1864; John Wagoner, (Dutch John) and Joe Pizanthia Bannack City, January, 11th, 1864.

Judge Smith and J. Thurmond, the counsel of the road agents, were banished. Thurmond brought an action, at Salt Lake, against Mr. Fox, charging him with aiding in procuring his banishment. After some peculiar developments of justice in Utah, he judiciously withdrew all proceedings, and gave a receipt in full of all past and future claims on the Vigilance Committee, in which instance he exhibited a wise discretion—

"I'ts no for naething the gled whistles."

The Bannack branch of the Vigilantes also sent out of the country, H. G. Sessions, convicted of circulating bogus dust, and one H. D. Moyer, who furnished a room at midnight, for them to work in, together with material for their labor. A man named Kustar was also banished for recklessly shooting through the windows of the hotel opposite his place of abode.

The circumstances attending the execution of J. A. Slade, and the charges against him, will appear in full in a subsequent part of this work. This case stands on a footing distinct from all the others.

Moore and Reeves were banished, as will afterwards appear, by a miners' jury, at Bannack, in the winter of 1863, but came back in the Spring. They fled the country when the Vigilantes commenced operations, and are thought to be in Mexico.

Charley Forbes was a member of the gang; but being wounded in a scuffle, or a robbery, a doctor was found and taken to where he lay. Finding that he was incurable, it is believed that Moore and Reeves shot him, to prevent his divulging what he knew of the band; but this is uncertain. Some say he was killed by Moore and Reeves, in Red Rock Canon.

The headquarters of the marauders was Rattlesnake Ranche. Plummer often visited it, and the robbers used to camp, with their comrades, in little wakiups above and below it, watching, and ready for fight, flight or plunder. Two rods in front of this building was a sign post, at which they used to practice with their revolvers. They were capital shots. Plummer was the quickest hand with his revolver of any man in the mountains. He could draw the pistol and discharge the five loads in three seconds. The post was riddled with holes, and was looked upon as quite a curiosity, until it was cut down, in the summer of 1863.

Another favorite resort of the gang was Dempsey's Cottonwood Ranche. The owner knew the character of the robbers, but had no connection with them; and, in those days, a man's life would not have been worth fifteen minutes purchase, if the possessor had been foolish enough even to hint at his knowledge of their doings. Daley's, at Ramshorn Gulch, and ranches or wakiups on the Madison, the Jefferson, Wisconsin Creek, and Mill Creek, were also constantly occupied by members of the band.

By discoveries of the bodies of the victims, the confessions of the murderers before execution, and reliable information sent to the Committee, it was found that one hundred and two people had been certainly killed by those miscreants in various places, and it was believed, on the best information, that scores of unfortunates had been murdered and buried, whose remains were never discovered, nor their fate definitely ascertained. All that was known, was that they started, with greater or less sums of money, for various places, and were never heard of again.

CHAPTER V.

THE DARK DAYS OF MONTANA.

"Will all Neptune's Ocean wash this blood
Clean from my hand ?"—MACBETH.

Henry Plummer, a sketch of whose previous career will appear in a subsequent part of this narrative, came to Montana Territory from Orofino. He and Reeves had there got into a difficulty with another man, and had settled the matter in the way usual in the trade—that is to say, they shot him.

Plummer—who, it seems, had for a long time contemplated a visit to the States—made at once for the River, intending to go down by boat; but finding that he was too late, he came back to Gold Creek, and there met Jack Cleveland, an old acquaintance, and former partner in crime. They made arrangements to pass the winter together at Sun River Farm. Plummer was to attend to the chores about the house, and Jack Cleveland was to get the wood. The worthy couple true to their instincts, did not long remain in harmony, but quarrelled about a young lady, whom Plummer afterwards married. Neither would leave, unless the other went also, and at last they both started, in company, for Bannack.

This town originated from the "Grasshopper Diggings," which were first discovered in the month of July, by John White and a small party of prospectors, on the Grasshopper Creek, a tributary of the Beaverhead. The discoverer, together with Rodolph Dorsett, was murdered by Charley Kelly, in the month of December, 1863, near the Milk Ranche, on the road from Virginia City to Helena. Wash

Stapleton and his party came in a short time after, and were soon joined by others, among whom were W. B. Dance, S. T. Hauser, James Morley, Drury Underwood, F. M. Thomson, N. P. Langford, James Fergus, John Potter, Judge Hoyt and Dr. Hoyt, Chas. St. Clair, David Thompson, Buz Caven, Messrs. Burchett, Morelle, Harby, J. M. Castner, Pat Bray and brother, Sturges, Col. McLean, R. C. Knox, and other well known citizens of Montana. The name, "Bannack," was given to the settlement, from the Bannack Indians, the lords of the soil. It was the first "mining camp" of any importance, discovered on the eastern slope of the Mountains, and as the stories of its wonderful richness went abroad, hundreds of scattered prospectors flocked in, and before the following Spring, the inhabitants numbered upwards of a thousand.

It is probable that there never was a mining town of the same size that contained more desperadoes and lawless characters, than did Bannack, during the winter of 1862-3. While a majority of the citizens were of the sterling stock, which has ever furnished the true American pioneers, there were great numbers of the most desperate class of roughs and road agents, who had been roving though the mountains, exiles from their former haunts in the mining settlements, from which they had fled to avoid the penalties incurred by the commission of many a fearful crime. These men no sooner heard of the rich mines of Bannack, than they at once made for the new settlement, where, among strangers, ignorant of their crimes, they would be secure from punishment, at least until their true character should become known.

During their journey to Bannack, Cleveland often said, when a little intoxicated, that Plummer was his MEAT. On their arrival at their destination, they were, in Mountain phrase, "strapped;" that is, they were without money or means; but Cleveland was not thus to be foiled; the practice of his profession furnishing him with ample funds, at the cost of a short ride and a pistol cartridge. In February, 1863, a young man named George Evans, having a considerable sum of money on his person, was hunting stock belonging to William Bates, beyond Buffalo Creek, about eight miles from Bannack, and this man, it is believed, was shot by Cleveland, and robbed, as the murderer—who had no money at the time—was seen riding close to the place, and the next day he had plenty. Evans' partner, Ed. Hibbert, got a horse from J. M. Castner, and searched for him in vain, returning impressed with the belief that he had frozen to death. In a short time, a herder named Duke, a partner of Jemmy Spence, was also hunting cattle, when he found Evans' clothes tucked into a badger hole. A body, which, however, was never fully identified, was jound naked in the willows, with a shot wound in the right armpit. It seems as if the victim had seen a man about to shoot, and had raised his arm deprecatingly.

Shortly after this, Cleveland came in to Goodrich's saloon, and said he was CHIEF; that he knew all the d——d scoundrels from the "other side," and would get even on some of them. A difficulty arose between him and Jeff. Perkins, about some money which the latter owed in the lower country. Jeff. assured him that he had settled the debt, and thereupon Jack said, "Well, if it's settled, it's all right;" but he still continued to refer to it, and kept reaching for his pistol. Plummer, who was present, told him that if he did not behave himself, he would take him in hand, for that Jeff. had settled the debt, and he ought to be satisfied. Jeff. went home for his derringers, and while he was absent, Jack Cleveland boastingly declared that he was afraid of none of them. Plummer jumped to his feet instantly, saying, "You d——d son of a b——h, I am tired of this," and, drawing his pistol, he commenced firing at Cleveland. The first ball lodged in the beam overhead, where it still remains. The second struck him below the belt, and he fell to his knees, grasping wildly at his pistol, and exclaiming, "Plummer, you won't shoot me when I'm down;" to which Plummer replied, "No you d——d son of a b——h; get up," and, as he staggered to his feet, he shot him a little above the heart. The bullet, however, glanced on the rib, and went round his body. The next entered below the eye, and lodged in his head. The last missile went between Moore and another man, who was sitting on the bench. As may be supposed the citizen discov-

ered that business called him outside immediately; and,
met George Ives, with a pistol in his hand, followed by
Reeves, who was similarly accoutred for the summary ad-
justment of "difficulties."

Singular enough, it must appear to the inhabitants of settled communities, that a man was being shaved in the saloon
at the time, and neither he nor the operator left off business
—CUSTOM IS EVERYTHING, and fire-eating is demonstrably an
acquired habit.

Ives and Reeves each took Plummer by the arm, and
walked down street, asking as they went along: "Will the
d——d strangling sons of b——s hang you now?"

Hank Crawford was, at this time, boarding with L. W.
Davenport, of Bannack, and was somewhat out of health.
His host came into the room, and said that there was a
man shot somewhere up town, in a saloon.  Crawford immediately went to where the crowd had gathered, and found
that such was the fear of the desperadoes, that no one
dared to lift the head of the dying man.  Hank said aloud,
that it was out of the question to leave a man in such a
condition, and asked, "Is there no one that will take him
home ?"  Some answered that they had no room; to which he
replied, that he had not, either, but he would find a place for
him ; and, assisted by three others, he carried him to his own
lodging—sending a messenger for the doctor.

The unfortunate man lived about three hours.  Before his
decease, he sent Crawford to Plummer for his blankets.
Plummer asked Crawford what Jack had said about him;
Crawford told him, "nothing."  "It is well for him," said
Plummer, "or I would have killed the d——d son of a
b——h in his bed."  He repeated his question several times,
very earnestly.  Crawford then informed him that, in answer to numerous inquiries by himself and others, about
Cleveland's connections, he had said, "Poor Jack has got
no friends.  He has got it, and I guess he can stand it."
Crawford had him decently buried, but he knew, from that
time, that Plummer had marked him for destruction, fear-
ing that some of Cleveland's secrets might have transpired,
in which case he was aware that he would surely be hung at
the first opportunity.

No action was taken about this murder for some time. It required a succession of horrible outrages to stimulate the citizens to their first feeble parody of justice. Shooting, duelling, and outrage, were from an early date, daily occurrences, in Bannack; and many was the foul deed done, of which no record has been preserved. As an instance of the free and easy state of society at this time, may be mentioned a "shooting scrape" between George Carrhart and George Ives, during the winter of '62-3. The two men were talking together in the street, close to Carrhart's cabin. Gradually they seemed to grow angry, and parted, Ives exclaiming aloud, "You d——d son of a b——h, I'll shoot you," and ran into a grocery for his revolver. Carrhart stepped into his cabin, and came out first, with his pistol in his hand, which he held by his side, the muzzle pointing downwards. George Ives came out, and turning his back on Carrhart, looked for him in the wrong direction—giving his antagonist a chance of shooting him in the back, if he desired to do so. Carrhart stood still till Ives turned, watching him closely. The instant Ives saw him, he swore an oath, and raising his pistol, let drive, but missed him by an inch or so, the bullet striking the wall of the house, close to which he was standing. Carrhart's first shot was a miss-fire, and a second shot from Ives struck the ground. Carrhart's second shot flashed right in Ives's face, but did no damage, though the ball could hardly have missed more than a hairs' breadth. Carrhart jumped into the house, and reaching his hand out, fired at his opponent. In the same fashion, his antagonist returned the compliment. This was continued till Ives's revolver was emptied—Carrhart having one shot left. As Ives walked off to make his escape, Carrhart shot him in the back, near the side. The ball went through, and striking the ground in front of him, knocked up the dust ahead of him. Ives was not to be killed by a shot, and wanted to get another revolver, but Carrhart ran off down the street. Ives cursed him for a coward "shooting a man in the back." They soon made up their quarrels, and Ives went and lived with Carrhart, on his ranche, for the rest of the winter.

Accidents will happen in the best regulated families, and

we give a specimen of "casualties" pertaining to life in
Bannack during this delightful period. Dr. Biddle, of Minnesota, and his wife, together with Mr. and Mrs. Short, and
their hired man, were quietly sitting round their camp fire
on Grasshopper Creek, when J. M. Castner, thinking that
a lady in the peculiar situation of Mrs. Biddle would need
the shelter of a house, went over to the camp, and sitting
down, made his offer of assistance, which was politely acknowledged, but declined by the lady, on the ground that
their wagon was very comfortably fitted up. Scarcely were
the words uttered, when crack! went a revolver, from the
door of a saloon, and the ball went so close to Castner's ear,
that it stung for two or three days. It is stated that he shif-
ted the position of his head with amazing rapidity. Mrs.
Biddle nearly fainted and became much excited, trembling
with terror. Castner went over to the house, and saw Cyrus
Skinner in the act of laying his revolver on the table, at the
same time requesting a gentleman who was playing cards
to count the balls in it. He at first refused, saying he was
busy; but, being pressed, said, after making a hasty inspection, "Well, there are only four." Skinner replied, "I nearly frightened the —— out of a fellow, over there." Castner laid his hand on his shoulder, and said, "My friend, you
nearly shot Mrs. Biddle." Skinner declared that he would
not have killed a woman "for the world," and swore that
he thought it was a camp of Indians, which would, in his
view, have made the matter only an agreeable pastime.
He asked Castner to drink, but the generous offer was declined. Probably the ball stuck in his throat. The Doctor
accepted the invitation. These courtesies were like an invitation from a Captain to a Midshipman, "No compulsion,
only you must."

A little episode may here be introduced, as an illustration
of· an easy method of settling debts, mentioned by Shakespeare. The sentiment is the Earl of Warwick's. The practical enforcement of the doctrine is to be credited in this
instance, to Haze Lyons, of the Rocky Mountains, a self-
constituted and energetic Receiver-General of all moneys
and valuables not too hot or too heavy for transportation by

man or horse, at short notice. The "King Maker" says:
"When the debt grows burdensome, and cannot be discharged
A sponge will wipe out all, and cost you nothing."
The substitute for the "sponge" above alluded to, is, usually,
in cases like the following, a revolver, which acts effectually, by "rubbing out" either the debt or the creditor, as
circumstances may render desirable. Haze Lyons owed a
board bill to a citizen of Bannack, who was informed that
he had won $300 or $400 by gambling the night before,
and accordingly asked him for it. He replied, "You son
of a b——h, if you ask me for that again, I'll make it un-
healthy for you." The creditor generously refrained from
further unpleasant inquiries, and the parties met again for
the first time, face to face, at the gallows, on which Haze
expiated his many crimes.

The next anecdote is suggestive of one, among many ways
of incidentally expressing dislike of a man's "style" in business matters. Buck Stinson had gone security for a friend,
who levanted; but was pursued and brought back. A
mischievous boy had been playing some ridiculous pranks,
when his guardian, to whom the debt mentioned was due,
spoke to him severely, and ordered him home. Buck at once
interfered, telling the guardian that he should not correct
the boy. On receiving for answer that it certainly would
be done, as it was the duty of the boy's protector to look
after him, he drew his revolver, and thrusting it close to
the citizen's face, saying, "G——d d——n you, I don't like
you very well, any how," was about to fire, when the latter
seized the barrel and threw it up. A struggle ensued, and
finding that he couldn't fire, Stinson wrenched the weapon
out of his opponent's hand, and struck him heavily across
the muscles of the neck, but failed to knock him down. The
bar-keeper interfering, Stinson let go his hold, and swore
he would shoot him; but he was quieted down. The gentleman being warned, made his way home at the double-quick,
or faster, and put on his revolver and bowie, which he wore
for fifteen days. At the end of this time, Plummer per-
suaded Stinson to apologize, which he did, and thereafter
behaved with civility to that particular man.

The wild lawlessness and the reckless disregard for life

which distinguished the outlaws, who had by this time concentrated at Bannack, will appear from the account of the first "Indian trouble." If the facts here stated do not justify the formation of a Vigilance Committee in Montana, then may God help Uncle Sam's nephews when they venture west of the River, in search of new diggings. In March, 1863, Charley Reeves, a prominent "clerk of St. Nicholas," bought a Sheep-eater squaw; but she refused to live with him, alleging that she was ill-treated, and went back to her tribe, who were encamped on the rise of the hill, south of Yankee Flat, about fifty yards to the rear of the street. Reeves went after her, and sought to force her to come back with him, but on his attempting to use violence, an old chief interfered. The two grappled. Reeves, with a sudden effort, broke from him, striking him a blow with his pistol, and, in the scuffle, one barrel was harmlessly discharged.

The next evening, Moore and Reeves, in a state of intoxication, entered Goodrich's saloon, laying down two double-barrelled shot-guns and four revolvers, on the counter, considerably to the discomfiture of the bar-keeper, who, we believe, would have sold his position very cheap, for cash, at that precise moment, and it is just possible that he might have accepted a good offer "on time." They declared, while drinking, that if the d——d cowardly white folks on Yankee Flat, were afraid of the Indians, they were not, and that they would soon "set the ball a rolling." Taking their weapons, they went off to the back of the houses, opposite the camp, and levelling their pieces, they fired into the tepee, wounding one Indian. They returned to the saloon and got three drinks more, boasting of what they had done, and accompanied by William Mitchell, of Minnesota, and two others, they went back, determined to complete their murderous work. The three above named then deliberately poured a volley into the tepee, with fatal effect. Mitchell, whose gun was loaded with an ounce ball and a charge of buckshot, killed a Frenchman named Brissette, who had run up to ascertain the cause of the first firing—the ball striking him in the forehead, and the buckshot wounding him in ten different places. The Indian chief, a lame Indian boy, and a pappoose, were also killed; but the number of the parties who were wounded has never been ascertained. John Burnes escaped with a broken thumb, and a man named Woods was shot in the groin, of which wound he has not yet entirely recovered. This unfortnuate pair, like Brissette, had come to see the cause of the shooting, and of the yells of the savages. The murderers being told that they had killed white men, Moore replied, with great SANG FROID, ";The d——d sons of b——s had no business there."

---

## CHAPTER VI

### THE TRIAL.

Desponding fear, of feeble fancies full,
Weak and unmanly, loosens every power.—THOMSON.

The indignation of the citizens being aroused by this atrocious and unprovoked massacre, a mass meeting was held the following morning to take some action in the premises. Charley Moore and Reeves hearing of it, started early in the morning, on foot, towards Rattlesnake, Henry Plummer preceeding them on horseback. Sentries were then posted all round the town, to prevent egress, volunteers were called for, to pursue the criminals, and Messrs. Lear, Higgings, O. J. Rockwell and Davenport at once followed on their track, coming up with them where they had hidden, in a thicket of brush, near the creek. The daylight was beginning to fade, and the cold was intense when a reinforcement arrived, on which the fugitives came out, delivered themselves up, and were conducted back to Bannack.

Plummer was tried and honorably acquitted, on account of Cleveland's threats. Mitchell was banished, but he hid around the town for awhile, and never went away. Reeves and Moore were next tried. Mr. Rheem had promised the evening before to conduct the prosecution, and Judge Smith had undertaken the defense, when on the morning of the

trial, Mr. Rheem announced that he was retained for the
defense. This left the people without any lawyer or prosecutor. Mr. Coply at last undertook the case, but his talents
not lying in that direction, he was not successful as an advocate. Judge Hoyt, from St. Paul, was elected Judge, and
Hank Crawford, Sheriff. Owing to the peculiarly divided
state of public opinion, it seemed almost impossible to select
an impartial jury from the neighborhood, and therefore a
messenger was sent to Godfrey's Canon, where N. P. Langford, R. C. Knox, A. Godfrey, and others, were engaged in
erecting a saw-mill, requesting them to come down to Bannack and sit on the jury. Messrs. Langford and Godfrey
came down at once, to be ready for the trial the next day.
The assembly of citizens numbered about five or six hundred, and to them the question was put, "Whether the prisoners should be tried by the people EN MASSE, or by a selected jury." Some leading men advocated the first plan. N.
P. Langford and several prominent residents took the other
side, and argued the necessity for a jury. After several
hours' discussion, a jury was ordered, and the trial proceeded. At the conclusion of the evidence and argument, the
case was given to the jury without any charge. The Judge
also informed them that if they found the prisoners guilty,
they must sentence them. At the first ballot, the vote
stood: For death, 1; against it, 11. The question of the
prisoners' GUILT admitted of no denial. N. P. Langford
alone voted for the penalty of death. A sealed verdict of
banishment and confiscation of property was ultimately
handed to the Judge, late in the evening. Moore and Reeves
were banished from the Territory, but were permitted to
stay at Deer Lodge till the Range would be passable.

In the morning, the Court again met, and the Judge informed the people that he had received the verdict, which
he would now hand back to the foreman to read. Mr. Langford accordingly read it aloud.

From that time forward, a feeling of the bitterest hostili-
ty was manifested by the friends of Moore, Reeves and
Mitchell toward all who were prominently connected with
the proceedings.

During the trial, the roughs would swagger into the space

allotted for the Judge and Jury, giving utterance to clearly understood threats, such as, "I'd like to see the G—d d——d Jury that would dare to hang Charley Reeves or Bill Moore," etc., etc., which doubtless had fully as much weight with the Jury as the evidence had. The pretext of the prisoners that the Indians had killed some whites, friends of theirs, in '49, while going to California, was accepted by the majority of the jurors as some sort of justification; but the truth is, they were afraid of their lives—and, it must be confessed, not without apparent reason.

To the delivery of this unfortunate verdict may be attributed the ascendancy of the roughs. They thought the people were afraid of them. Had the question been left to old Californians or experienced miners, Plummer, Reeves and Moore would have been hanged, and much bloodshed and suffering would have been thereby prevented. No organization of the Road Agents would have been possible.

## CHAPTER VII.

### PLUMMER VERSUS CRAWFORD.

"I had rather chop this hand off at a blow
And with the other fling it at thy face,
Than bear so low a sail, to strike to the."
SHAKSPEARE—HENRY VI.

Crawford, who was appointed Sheriff at the trial of Moore and Reeves, tendered his resignation on two or three different occasions; but was induced to continue in office by the strongest representations of his friends. They promised to stand by him in the execution of his duty, and to remunerate him for his loss of time and money. The arms taken from Plummer, Reeves and Mitchell were sold by Crawford to defray expenses,

Popular sentiment is shifting and uncertain as a quicksand. Shortly after this, "Old Tex," one of the gang, col-

lected a miners' meeting, and at it, it was resolved to give
the thieves their arms, Plummer and Tex claiming them as
their property. The Sheriff had to go and get them, pay--
ing, at the same time, all expenses, including in the list even
the board of the prisoners. For his services not a cent was
ever paid to him. Popular institutions are of devine origin.
Government by the people EN MASSE is the acme of ab--
surdity.

Cleveland had three horses at the time of his death. One
was at a Ranch at Bannack, and two were down on Big
Hole. Crawford called two meetings, and was authorized
to seize Cleveland's property and sell it, in order to reim-
burse himself for his outlay, which was both considerable
in amount and various in detail, and repay himself for his
outlay and expenses of various kinds. He went to old Tex
who said that Jack Cleveland had a partner, named Terwilliger, (another of the gang) who was absent, and that he
had better leave them till he came back. One day Crawford wanted to go to Beaverhead, and wished to take one of
the horses to ride. Tex said it would be wrong to do so.
In a day or two after, Crawford saw the horse in town, and
asking Tex if it was not the animal. He said "No, it was
not; but Crawford, doubting his statement, inquired of a
man that he knew was perfectly well informed on the subject, and found that it was as he supposed, and that the
ranchman had brought it in for Tex to ride during the journey he contemplated, with the intention of meeting Terwilliger. Crawford ordered the horse back, and desired that
it should not be given to any one. The man took it as directed. When the men were banished, Plummer went to
the Ranch, took the horse and rode it, when escorting the
culprits out of town. He then brought it back. Crawford
who had charge of the horse, asked Hunter if Tex had taken
it. He said "no."

The next evening, Crawford and some acquaintances went
down to the bakery to take a drink, and there met Plummer, who accused him of ordering the horse to be kept from
him, which he denied, and said he never mentioned his
name. Hunter being called by Plummer confirmed the statement. He also observed, that he thought that as Plummer,

had killed the man, he need not wish to take his money and his goods also. Plummer then remarked that Bill Hunter did not stand to what he had said, and left the house. He had dared Crawford to remain and face Hunter's testimony, expecting to raise a row and shoot him. Crawford accepted the challenge, and, surrounded by his friends, with their hands on their six shooters, awaited his coming. If he had moved his hand to his pistol, he would have died on the spot, and knowing this, he cooled off.

The next day he sent word to Crawford, by an old mountaineer, that he had been wrongly informed, and that he wished to meet him as a friend. He replied that he had been abused without cause, and that, if he wanted to see him, he must come himself, as he was not going to accept of such apologies by deputy. Plummer sent word two or three times, to Hank, in the same way, and received the same reply; till at last some of the boys brought them together, and they shook hands, Plummer declaring that he desired his friendship ever after.

In a few days, Hank happened to be in a saloon, talking to a man who had been fighting, when a suspicious looking individual came up to him, and asked what he was talking about. He replied that it was none of his business. The man retorted with a challenge to fight with pistols. Hank said, "You have no odds of me with a pistol." The fellow offered to fight with fists. Hank agreed, and seeing that the man had no belt on, took off his own, and laid his pistol in, on the bar. The man stepped back into a dark corner, and Crawford going up, slapped him across the face. He instantly leveled a six shooter at Crawford, which he had concealed; but Hank was too quick, and catching him by the throat and hand, disarmed him. Plummer joined the man, and together, they wrested the pistol from his hand, and made a rush at him. Hank and Harry Flegger, however, kept the pistol in spite of them. Harry fetched his friend out, saying, "Come on Hank; this is no place for you; they are set on murdering you, any way." He then escorted him home. The owner of the saloon told Crawford, afterwards, that it was all a plot. That the scheme was to entice him out to fight with pistols, and that the gang of Plummer's friends were ready with double-barrelled shot-guns, to kill him, as soon as he appeared.

Everything went on quietly for a few days, when Hank found he should have to start for Deer Lodge, after cattle. Plummer told him that he was going to Benton. Hank asked him to wait a day or two, and he would go with him; but Plummer started on Monday morning, with George Carrhart, before Hank's horses came in. When the animals were brought in, Hank found that private business would detain him, and accordingly sent his butcher in his place. The next day Plummer, finding that he was not going, stopped at Big Hole, and came back. Hank afterwards learned that Plummer went out to catch him on the road, three different times, but, fortunately, missed him.

During the week, Bill Hunter came to Hank, and pretended that he had said something against him. To this Hank replied, that he knew what he was after, and added, "If you want anything, you can get it right straight along." Not being able "to get the drop on him," (in mountain phrase) and finding that he could not intimidate him, he turned and went off, never afterwards speaking to Hank.

On the following Sunday, Plummer came into a saloon where Hank was conversing with George Purkins, and, addressing the latter, said, "George, there's a little matter between you and Hank that's got to be settled." Hank said, "Well, I don't know what it can be," and laughed. Plummer observed, "You needn't laugh, G—d d——n you. It's got to be settled." Turning to Purkins, he stated that he and Crawford had said he was after a squaw, and had tried to court "Catharine." He commenced to abuse Purkins and telling him to "come out," and that he was "a cowardly son of a b——h." He also declared that he could "lick" both him and Hank Crawford. George said that he was a coward, and no fighting man, and that he would not go out of doors with any body. Plummer gave the same challenge to Hank, and received for a reply, that he was not afraid to go out with any man, and that he did not believe one man was made to scare another. Plummer said, "come on," and started ahead of Hank towards the street. Hank walked quite close up to him, on his guard all the time, and Plummer at once said, "Now pull your pistol." Hank refused, saying, I'll pull no pistol; I never pulled a pistol on a man, and you'll not be the first." He then offered to fight him in any other way. "I'm no pistol shot," he added, "and you would not do it if you hadn't the advantage." Plummer said, "If you don't pull your pistol, I'll shoot you like a sheep." Hank quietly laid his hand on his shoulder, and, fixing his eyes on him, said slowly and firmly, "If that's what you want, the quicker you do it, the better for you," and turning round, walked off. Plummer dared not shoot without first raising a fuss, knowing that he would be hung. During the altercation above narrated, Hank had kept close to Plummer ready for a struggle, in case he offered to draw his pistol, well knowing that his man was the best and quickest shot in the mountains; and that if he had accepted his challenge, long before he could have handled his own revolver, three or four balls would have passed through his body. The two men understood one another, at parting. They looked into each other's eyes. They were mountaineers, and each man read, in his oppenent's face, "Kill me, or I'll kill you." Plummer believed that Hank had his secret, and one or the other must therefore die.

Hank went, at once, to his boarding house, and taking his double-barrelled shot gun, prepared to go out, intending to find and kill Plummer at sight. He was perfectly aware that all attempts at pacification would be understood as indications of cowardice, and would render his death a mere question of the goodness of Plummer's ammunition. Friends, however, interferred, and Hank could not get away till after they left, late in the evening.

By the way, is it not rather remarkable, that if a man has a few friends round him, and he happens to become involved in a fight, the aforesaid sympathizers, instead of restraining his antagonist, generally hold HIM, and wrestle all the strength out of him, frequently enabling his opponent to strike him while in the grasp of his officious backers? A change of the usual programme would be attended with beneficial results, in nine cases out of ten. Another suggestion we have to make, with a view to preventing actual hostilities, and that is, that when a man raves and tears, shouting, "let go," "let me at him," "hold my shirt while I pull off my coat," or makes other bellicose requests, an instant compliance with his demands will at once prevent a fight. If two men, also, are abusing one another, in loud and foul language, the way to prevent blows is to sieze hold of them and commencing to strip them for a fight, form a ring. This is commonly a settler. No amount of coin could coax a battle out of them. Such is our experience of all the loud mouthed brigade. Men that mean "fight" may hiss a few muttered anathemas, through clenched teeth; but they seldom talk much, and never bandy slang.

Hank started and hunted industriously for Plummer, who was himself similarly employed, but they did not happen to meet.

The next morning, Hank's friends endeavored to prevail upon him to stay within doors until noon; but it was of no avail. He knew what was before him, and that it must be settled, one way or the other. Report came to him, that Plummer was about to leave town, which at once put him on his guard. The attempt to ensnare him into a fatal carelessness was too evident.

Taking his gun, he went up town, to the house of a friend —Buz Caven. He borrowed Buz's rifle, without remark, and stood prepared for emergencies. After waiting some time, he went down to the butcher's shop which he kept, and saw Plummer frequently; but he always had somebody close beside him, so that, without endangering another man's life, Hank could not fire.

He finally went out of sight, and sent a man to compromise, saying they would agree to meet as strangers. He would never speak to Crawford, and Crawford should never address him. Hank was to wary to fall into the trap. He sent word back to Plummer that he had broken his word once, and that his pledge of honor was no more than the wind, to him; that one or the other had to suffer or leave.

A friend came to tell Hank that they were making arrangements to shoot him in his own door, out of a house on the other side of the street. Hank kept out of the door, and about noon, a lady, keeping a restaurant, called to him to come and get a dish of coffee. He went over without a gun.

While he was drinking the coffee, Plummer, armed with a double-barrelled gun, walked opposite to his shop door, watching for a shot. A friend, Frank Ray, brought Hank a rifle. He instantly leveled at Plummer, and fired. The ball broke his arm. His friends gathered round him, and he said, some son of a b——h has shot me." He was then carried off. He sent Hank a challenge to meet him in fifteen days; but he paid no attention to a broken armed man's challenge, fifteen days ahead. In two days after, while Hank was in Meninghall's store, George Carrhart came in. Hank saw there was mischief in his look, and went up to him at once, saying, "Now, George, I know what you want. You had better go slow." Stickney got close to him on the other side, and repeated the caution. After a while he avowed that he came to kill him; but, on hearing his story, he pulled open his coat, showing his pistol ready in the band of his pants, and declared at the same time that he would be his friend. Another party organized to come down and shoot Crawford, but failed to carry out their intention. Some of the citizens, hearing of this, offered to shoot or hang Plummer, if Crawford would go with them; but he refused, and said he would take care of himself. On the 13th of March, he started for Wisconsin, riding on horseback to Fort Benton. He was followed by three men, but they never came up with him, and taking boat at the river, he arrived safely at home. It was his intention to come out in the Fall, and his brothers sent him money for that purpose; but the coach was robbed, and all the letters taken. The money, unfortunately, shared the fate of the mail. Crawford was lately living at Virginia City—having returned shortly after his marriage in the States.

The account of the troubles of one man, which we have given above, has been inserted with the object of showing the state of society which could permit such openly planned and persistent outrages, and which necessitated such a method of defense. Crawford, or any of the others, might as well have applied to the Emperor of China, for redress or protection, as to any civil official.

The ball which struck Plummer in the arm ran down his bone, and lodged in the wrist. After his execution, it was found brightened by the constant friction of the joint. His pistol hand being injured for belligerent purposes, though the limb was saved by the skill of the attendant physician —Plummer practiced assiduously at drawing and shooting with his left; attaining considerable proficiency; but he never equalled the deadly activity and precision he had acquired with the other hand, which he still preferred to use.

## CHAPTER VIII.

### A CALENDAR OF CRIMES.

The murderer's curse, the dead man's fixed still glare,
And fears and death's cold sweat, they all are there.

Others connected with the mock trial which we have described, fared badly, being waylaid and cruelly beaten. Mr. Ellis, the principal witness was dogged every time he went to, or returning from his claim, and finally was compelled to return to the States. He was followed to Fort Benton, a distance of three hundred miles, escaping death at the hands of his pursuers by slipping away secretly down the river, and hiding till the steamer came past, when springing joyfully from his place of concealment, and hailing her, he was taken on board.

N. P. Langford was an especial object of hatred to them. They had counted on his favoring them, at the trial, because he voted for a jury; but when they found that his ballot was cast for the death penalty, they vowed vengeance against him, and a gentleman, his particular friend. The latter could never go to his claim without a loaded gun and a revolver. Once, the roughs had the plot all completed for the assassination of Mr. Langford; but accident revealed their preparations and intentions, and, through the timely warning of a friend, the conspiracy failed. The combination of the comrades of the two gentlemen, which embraced the order loving of the community, was too strong to be openly defied by the roughs. The danger of sudden surprise and assassinnation was, however, continued.

One day, as Langford's friends were sauntering down Main street, he saw Plummer approaching. He immediately drew a small bowie knife from his belt, and began to whittle a billet of wood, which he picked up for the purpose. Soon he came face to face with Plummer, who, looking with suspicious intelligence at the weapon, asked: "Why do you begin to whittle when you meet me?" The citizen regarding him with a stern and determined look, promptly answered: "Mr. Plummer, you know what opinion I hold concerning you and your friends, and I don't never intend to let you get the advantage of me. I don't want to be shot down like a dog."

Finding that Mitchell had not gone away from town, a great many citizens thought it would be the height of injustice to keep Moore and Reeves away at Hell Gate, where the snow prevented the passage of the mountains, and, on Sunday, a miners' meeting was called, at which their sentence was remitted, by vote, and they accordingly came back.

An attempt had also been made, before this to rob the store of Messrs. Higgins & Worden, of Deer Lodge; but the proprietors got word in time to hide the safe.

The Walla Walla Express was robbed by the band of Road Agents. Plummer directed this affair, and it is thought Long John had some share in it. The men actually engaged in it are not known.

A. Mr. Davenport and his wife were going to Benton, from Bannack, intending to proceed by steamboat to the States. While taking a lunch at Rattlesnake, a man masked in black suddenly came out of the willows, near which they were camped, and demanded their money. Davenport said he had none; the fellow laughed, and replied that his wife had, and named the amount. A slight application of a Colt's corkscrew, which was pointed at Davenport's head, brought forth his money, and he was ordered, on pain of death, not to go back to Bannack at once; but to leave his wife somewhere ahead. This Davenport promised, and performed, after which he returned, and obtained some money from the citizens to assist him in his necessity. His wife proceeded to the States, where she arrived in safety. Davenport never knew who robbed him.

The house of a Frenchman, named Le Grau, who kept a bakery and blacksmith shop at the back of Main street, Bannack, was broken into, and everything that could be found was stolen, after which the robbers threw the curtains into a heap and tried to burn down the house, but they failed in this. The greater part of the owner's money was, fortunately, hidden, and that they missed.

We have before spoken of Geo. Carrhart. He was a remarkably handsome man, well educated, and it has been asserted that he was a member of one of the Western Legislatures. His manners were those of a gentleman, when he was sober; but an unfortunate lover of whiskey had destroyed him. On one or two occasions, when inebriated, he had ridden up and down the street, with a shot-gun in his hand, threatening everybody. He was extremely generous to a friend, and would make him a present of a horse, an interest in a Ranch, or indeed, of anything that he thought he needed. His fondness for intoxicating liquors threw him into bad company, and caused his death.

One day, while sleeping in Skinner's saloon, a young man of acknowledged courage, named Dick Sap, was playing "poker" with George Banefield, a gambler, whose love of money was considerably in excess of his veneration for the eighth commandment. For the purpose of making a "flush," this worthy stole a card. Sap at once accused him of cheating, on which he jumped up, drew his revolver, and leveled at Sap, who was unarmed. A friend supplied the necessary weapon, and quick as thought, Sap and Banefield exchanged all their shots, though, strange to say, without effect, so far as they were personally concerned.

The quarrel was arranged after some little time, and then it was found that Buz Caven's dog, "Toodles," which was under the table, had been struck by three balls, and lay there dead. A groan from Carrhart attracted attention, and his friends looking at him, discovered that he had been shot through the bowels, accidentally, by Banefield. Instantly

Moore called to Reeves and Forbes, who were present, "Boy's they have shot Carrhart; let's kill them," and raising his pistol, he let fly twice at Sap's head. Sap threw up his hands, having no weapon, and the balls came so close that they cut one little finger badly, and just grazed the other hand. The road agents fired promiscuously into the retreating crowd, one ball wounding a young man, Goliath Reilly, passing through his heel. Banefield was shot below the knee, and felt his leg numbed and useless. He, however, dragged himself away to a place of security, and was attended by a skillful physician; but, refusing to submit to amputation, he died of mortification.

In proof of the insecurity of life and property in places where such desperadoes as Plummer, Stinson, Ray and Skinner make their headquarters, the following incident may be cited:

Late in the Spring of '63, Winnemuck, a warrior chief of the Bannacks, had come in with his band, and had camped in the brush, about three-fourth of a mile above the town. Skinner and the roughs called a meeting, and organized a band for the purpose of attacking and murdering the whole tribe. The leaders, however, got so drunk that the citizens became ashamed, and drooped off by degrees, till they were so few that the enterprise was abandoned. A half-breed had in the meantime, warned Winnemuck, and the wily old warrior lost no time in preparing for the reception of the party. He sent his squaws and pappooses to the rear, and posted his warriors, to the number of three or four hundred, on the right side of a canyon, in such a position that he could have slaughtered the whole command at his ease. This he fully intended to do, if attacked, and also to have sacked the town and killed every white in it. This would have been an achievement requiring no extraordinary effort, and had not the drunkenness of the outlaws defeated their murderous purpose, would undoubtedly have been accomplished. In fact, the men whom the Vigilantes afterwards executed, were ripe for any villainy, being Godless, fearless, worthless, and a terror to the community.

In June of the same year, the report came in that Joe Carrigan, William Mitchell, Joe Brown, Smith, Indian Dick,

and four others had been killed by the Indians, whom they
had pursued to recover stolen stock, and that overtaking
them, they had dismounted and fired into their tepees. The
Indians attacked them when their pieces were emptied,
killed the whole nine, and took their stock.

Old Snag, a friendly chief, came into Bannack with his
band, immediately after this report. One of the tribe—a
brother-in-law of Johnny Grant, of Deer Lodge—was fired
at by Haze Lyons, to empty his revolver, for luck, on general principles, or for his pony—it is uncertain which. A number of citizens, thinking it was an Indian fight, ran out, and
joined in the shooting. The savage jumped from his horse,
and, throwing down his blanket, ran for his life, shouting
"Good Indian." A shot wounded him in the hip. (His
horse's leg was broken.) But, though badly hurt, he climbed
up the mountain and got away, still shouting as he ran,
"Good Indian," meaning that he was friendly to the whites.
Carroll, a citizen of Bannack, had a little Indian girl living
with him, and Snag had called in to see her. Carroll witnessed the shooting we have described, and running in, he
informed Snag, bidding him and his son ride off for their
lives. The son ran out and jumped on his horse. Old Snag
stood in front of the door, on the edge of the ditch, leaning
upon his gun, which was in a sole leather case. He had his
lariet in his hand, and was talking to his daughter, Jemmy
Spence's squaw, named Catherine. Buck Stinson, without
saying a word, walking to within four feet of him, and drawing his revolver, shot him in the side. The Indian raised
his right hand and said, Oh! don't." The answer was a
ball in the neck, accompanied by the remark, enveloped in
oaths, "I'll teach you to kill whites," and then again he shot
him through the head. He was dead when the first citizen
attracted by the firing, ran up. Carroll, who was standing
at the door, called out, "Oh don't shoot into the house;
you'll kill my folks." Stinson turned quickly upon him and
roared out, with a volley of curses, topped off with the cus-
tomary expletive form of address adopted by the roughs,
"Put in your head, or I'll shoot the top of it off." Cyrus
Skinner came up and scalped the Indian. The band scattered in flight. One who was behind, being wounded,

plunged into the creek, seeking to escape, but was killed as he crawled up the bank, and fell among the willows. He was also scalped. The remainder of them got away, and the chief's son, checking his horse at a distance, waved to the men who had killed his father to come on for a fight, but the bullets beginning to cut the ground about him, he turned his horse and fled.

While the firing was going on, two ladies were preparing for a grand ball supper in a house adjoining the scene of the murder of Snag. The husband of one of them being absent, cutting house logs among the timber, his wife, alarmed for his safety, ran out with her arms and fingers extended with soft paste. She jumped the ditch at a bound, her hair streaming in the wind, and shouted aloud, "Where's Mr. ———? Will nobody fetch me my husband?" We are happy to relate that the object of her tender solicitude turned up uninjured, and if he was not grateful for this display of affection, we submit to the ladies, without any fear of contradiction, that he must be a monster.

The scalp of old Snag, the butchered chief, now hangs in a Banking House, in Salt Lake City.

We have recorded a few, among many, of the crimes and outrages that were daily committed in Bannack. The account is purposely literal and exact. It is not pleasant to write of blasphemous and indecent language, or to record foul and horrible crimes; but as the anatomist must not shrink from the corpse, which taints the air, as he investigates the symptoms and examines the results of disease, so, the historian must either tell the truth for the instruction of mankind, or sink to the level of a mercenary pander, who writes, not to inform the people, but to enrich himself.

# CHAPTER IX.

### PERILS OF THE ROAD.

"I'll read you matter deep and dangerous,
As full of peril and adventurous spirit,
As to o'erwalk a current, roaring loud,
On the unsteadfast footing of a spear."—SHAK.

On the 14th day of November, 1863, Sam. T. Hauser, and
N. P. Langford started for the States, in company with sev-
en or eight freighters. Owing to some delay in their preparations, they were not ready to start at the hour proposed
(twelve o'clock M.) and after considerable urging, they prevailed upon one of the freighters to delay his departure till
five o'clock P. M. representing to him that by driving during
part of the night, they would be enable to overtake the rest
of the train at Horse Prairie, where they were to camp for
the night. These arrangements were all made at the store
of George Chrisman, where Plummer had his office, and consequently their plans for departure were all known to this
arch-villain.

During that afternoon, it was reported in Bannack that a
silver lode had been discovered, and Plummer, whose residence in Nevada had given him some reputation as a judge
of silver ores, was requested to go out and examine it.
Plummer had, on several occasions, been sent for to go out
and make minute examinations, and it had never been sur-
mised that his errands on these occasions were different from
what they purported to be. This notice to Plummer that a
"silver lode" had been discovered, was the signal that the
occasion demanded the presence of the chief of the gang,
who was needed to head some marauding expedition that
required a skillful leader, and promised a rich booty as the
reward of success. Plummer always obeyed it, and in this
instance, left Bannack a little while after noon, taking a

northerly direction, towards Rattlesnake; but, after getting out of town, he changed his course and went south, towards Horse Prairie.

Before leaving Bannack, he presented Mr. Hauser with a wollen scarf, telling him that he would "find it useful on the journey these cold nights."

The two gentlemen did not complete their arrangements for starting till half past seven in the evening; and, as they were about leaving Hauser's cabin, a splash, caused by the fall of some heavy body in the water, and calls for assistance were heard from the brow of the hill, south of Bannack. Upon going to the spot, it was found that Henry Tilden, in attempting to cross the Bannack Ditch, had missed the bridge, and his horse had fallen upon him in the water. On being relieved from his dangerous situation, he went to the house of Judge (now Governor) Edgerton, and reported that he had been robbed by three men—one of whom was Plummer—between Horse Prairie and Bannack. After he had detailed the circumstances, the greatest anxiety was felt for the safety of Messrs. Langford and Hauser, who, it was generally supposed had started at five o'clock on the same road.

The unconscious wayfarers, however, knew nothing of the matter, but they were, nevertheless, on the alert all the time. Hauser had that morning communicated to his friend Langford, his suspicion that they were being watched, and would be followed by the road agents, with the intention of plundering them, and while Langford was loading his gun with twelve revolver balls in each barrel, George Dart asked him why he was 'filling the gun-barrel so full of lead;" to which Langford replied, that if they had any trouble with the road agents, it would be on that night. So well satisfied were they that an attack upon them, was contemplated, that they carried their guns in their hands, ready cocked, throughout the whole journey to Horse Prairie, a distance of twelve miles, but they saw nothing of the ruffians who robbed young Tilden.

It is supposed that Plummer and his gang had concluded that the non-appearance of the party was owing to the knowledge of what had happened in the afternoon, and that they were not coming out at all, that night. This is the more probable, from the fact that Tilden arrived home in time to have communicated the story of his robbery to them before they started, and the freighter with whom they took passage had told them that morning, in the presence of Plummer, that he would leave them behind if they were not ready to start by five o'clock p. m. It is not to be thought that Plummer would have risked a chance of missing them, by robbing Tilden of so small an amount as $10, unless he had felt sure that they would start at the time proposed. It is also likely that, as his intended victims did not make their appearance, he feared that the citizens of Bannack might turn out in search of the Road Agents who had attacked Tilden, and that it would be prudent to return home by a circuitous route, which he did. One thing is certain, when they missed them, Plummer went, in hot haste, to Langford's boarding house, to inquire whether he was gone, and on receiving an answer in the affirmative, rode off at once in pursuit.

In the wagon with Langford and Hauser, was a third passenger—a stranger to the rest of the party—who had sent forward his blankets by one of the vehicles which left at noon, and on his arrival at camp, he found them appropriated by some of the party, who had given up all ideas of seeing the others before morning, and had laid down for the night.

Rather than disturb the sleepers, Langford directed his fellow traveller, who was in delicate health, to occupy the wagon with Hauser, while he himself took a buffalo robe and made a bedstead of mother earth.

The night was a cold one, and becoming chilled through Langford arose and at first walked briskly up and down by the camp, in order to warm himself. After awhile, he turned his steps towards the creek, which was about one hundred and fifty yards distant, but with the instinctive caution engendered by a residence in the mountains, he armed himself with his trusty "double-barrell," and then, with his thoughts wandering to other scenes and other days, he slowly sauntered by the rippling waters.

His musings were brought to a sudden close by the murmur of voices, born on the breeze, accompanied by the well known tramp of horses at speed. The banks of the rivulet were lined with willows, and lay in deep shadow, except where an opening in the thicket disclosed the prairie that lay beyond, sleeping peacefully in the moonlight. Drawing aside the bushes he saw three mounted men in the act of passing one of these avenues, at the gallop. Roused to a sense of danger, he cocked his gun and followed them down stream, to a place where an interval between the thickets that lined both sides of the creek gave him a good sight of the night rangers, and stood in full view, his piece lying in the hollow of his hand, ready for instant service.

As soon as he emerged from the shelter of the willows, and the horsemen became aware of his presence, they stopped for a few moments, and then bore away down the valley, determined to see the end of the matter, and having the brush for cover, while his friends were still within hail, if needed, the watcher pushed on for about two hundred yards and wading to the other bank, he had no sooner reached the top, than he saw four men at that moment mounting their horses. No sooner did they observe him than they drove their spurs into their horses' flanks, and started on a run for Bannack. These men were Plummer, Buck Stinson, Ned Ray and George Ives, who, on their return to the town by another road, after the robbery of Tilden, having found, as before related, that Langford and Hauser had really gone— followed at once upon their track.

But for the providential circumstances connected with the chance appropriation of the blankets, and the consequent sleeping of Langford on the ground, together with his accidental appearance with his gun in his hand, as if on guard —the whole party would have been murdered, as it was known to their pursuers that they had a considerable amount of treasure with them.

The scarf which Plummer presented to Hauser was given for the purpose of enabling the cunning robber to identify his man by night.

It is a somewhat singular coincidence that Plummer was hung on the next birth day of Hauser, (the 10th of January, 1864.)

The party proceeded on their journey without interruption, and on their arrival at Salt Lake City, they were besieged by their acquaintances with inquiries concerning several parties who were known to have preceded them on the road thither by about a week; but the unfortunate objects of their solicitude never reached their destination, or were afterwards heard of. They sleep in bloody graves; but where, how, and when they met their death, at the hands of the Road Agents, will probably never be known. The fate that could not be avoided was, nevertheless avenged.

----

# CHAPTER X.

### THE REPULSE.

"Though few the numbers—theirs the strife,
That neither spares nor speaks for life."—BYRON.

In the present and succeeding chapters, will be found accounts of actual experiences with Road Agents, in the practice of their profession. The exact chronological order of the narrative has, in these cases, been broken in upon, that the reader may have a correct notion of what an attack by Road Agents usually was. We shall show at a future time what it too often became when bloodshed was added to rapine. As the facts related are isolated, the story is not injured by the slight anachronism.

About three weeks after the occurrences recorded in the last chapter, M. S. Moody, (Milt Moody) with three wagons started, in company with a train of packers, for Salt Lake City. Among the later were John McCormick, Billy Sloan, J. S. Rockfellow, J. M. Bozeman, Henry Branson and M. V. Jones.

In the entire caravan there was probably from $75,000 to $80,000 in gold, and it must not be supposed that such a splendid prize could escape the lynx-eyed vigilance of the Road Agents.

Plummer engaged Dutch John and Steve Marshland for the job, and his selection was not a bad one, so far as Dutch John was concerned, for a more courageous, stalwart or reckless desperado never threw spurs on the flanks of a cayuse, or cried "Halt!" to a true man.  Steve Marshland was a bold fellow when once in action; but he preferred what mountaineers call a "soft thing," to an open onslaught. This unprofessional weakness not only saved the lives of several whom we are proud to call friends, but ensured his own and his friends capture and death, at the hands of the Vigilantes.

In Black Tail Deer Canyon, the party were seated at breakfast, close to a sharp turn in the road, when they heard two men conversing, close at hand, but hidden by the brush. Says the "First Robber," "You take my revolver and I'll take yours, and you come on right after me." Every man found his gun between his knees in less than no time, and not a few discovered that their revolvers were cocked.  Pulsation became more active, and heads were "dressed" towards the corner.  In a few moments, Dutch John and Steve Marshland rode round the bend, with their shot-guns ready.  On seeing the party prepared to receive them, they looked confused, and reined up.  Steve Marshland recognized Billy Sloan, and called out, "How do you do, Mr. Sloan?" to which Billy replied, "Very well, THANK YOU." The last two words have been a trouble to Sloan ever since, being too figurative for his conscience.  By way of excuse for their presence, the Road Agents asked if the party had seen any horses, and whether they had any loose stock, saying that they had been informed by some half-breeds that the animals which they claimed to be lost had been with their train.  A decided negative being vouchsafed, they rode on.

The Robbers did not expect to come upon them so soon, and were not masked.  But for this fact, and the sight of the weapons on hand for use, if required, the train would have been relieved of the responsibility attaching to freighting treasure in those days, without any delay.

Little did the party imagine that the safety of their property and their lives hung upon a thread, and that, the evening before, the "prudence" of Steve Marshland had saved six or eight of the party from unexpected death. Yet so it was. Wagner and Marshland had followed their trail, and hitching their steeds to the bush, with their double-barrelled guns loaded with buckshot, and at full cock, they crawled up to within fifteen feet of the camp, and leisurely surveyed them by the light of the fire. The travellers lay around in perfect ignorance of the proximity of the Road Agents; their guns were everywhere but where they ought to be, and without a sentry to warn them of the approach of danger, they carelessly exposed themselves to death, and their property to seizure.

Wagner's proposal was that he and Marshland should select their men, and kill four with their shot-guns; that then they should move quickly around, and keep up a rapid fire with their-revolvers, shouting loudly at the same time, to make them believe that they were attacked by a large concealed force. There was no fear of their shooting away all their charges, as the arms of the men who would inevitably fall would be at their disposal, and the chances were a hundred to one that the remainder would take to flight, and leave their treasure—for a considerable time, at all events —within reach of the robbers. Steve, however, "backed down," and the attack was deferred till the next day.

It was the custom of the packers to ride ahead of the train towards evening, in order to select a camping place, and it was while the packers were thus separated from the train that the attack on the wagons took place.

On top of the Divide, between Red Rock and Junction, the robbers rode up to the wagons, called on them to halt, and gathering the drivers together, Dutch John sat on his horse, covering them with his shot-gun, while Steve dismounted and searched both them and their wagons.

Moody had slipped a revolver into his boot, which was not detected; $100 in greenbacks, which were in his shirt pocket, were also unnoticed. The material wealth of Kit Erskine and his comrade driver, appeared to be represented by half a plug of tobacco, for the preservation of which Kit pleaded; but Steve said it was "Just what he wanted," and appropriated it forthwith.

After attending to the men, Steve went for the wagons, which he searched, cutting open the carpet sacks, and found $1,500 in treasury notes; but he missed the gold, which was packed on the horses, in cantinas. In the hind wagon was a sick man, named Kennedy, with his comrade, Lank Forbes; but the nerves of the first mentioned gentleman was so unstrung that he could not pull trigger, when Steve climbed up and drew the curtain. Not so with Forbes. He let drive and wounded Steve in the breast. With an oath and a yell, Steve fell to his knees, but recovered, and jumping down from the wagon again fell, but rose and made, afoot, for the tall timber, at an amazing speed. The noise of the shot frightened Dutch John's horse, which reared as John discharged both barrels at the teamsters, and the lead whizzed past, just over their heads, Moody dropped his hand to his boot, and seizing the revolver, opened fire on Dutch John, who endeavored to increase the distance between him and the wagons, to the best of his horse's ability.

Three balls were sent after him, one of which took effect in his shoulder. Had Moody jumped on Marshland's horse and pursued him, he could have killed him easily, as the shot gun was at his saddle bow. These reflections, and suggestions, however, occur more readily to a man sitting in an easy chair, than to the majority of the unfortunate individuals who happen to be attacked by masked highwaymen.

John's wound and Marshland's were proof conclusive of their guilt, when they were arrested. John made for Bannack and was nursed there. Steve Marshland was taken care of at Deer Lodge.

The packers wandered what had become of the wagons, and, though their anxiety was relieved, yet their astonishment was increased, when, about 8 o'clock P. M. Moody rode up and informed them that his train had been attacked by Road Agents, who had been repulsed and wounded.

Steve's horse, arms and equipage, together with twenty pounds of tea, found lying on the road, which had been stolen from a Mormon train, previously, were, as an acquaintance of ours expresses it, "confiscated."

J. S. Rockfellow and two others rode back, and striking the trail of Steve, followed it till eleven P. M. When afterwards arrested, this scoundrel admitted that they were within fifteen feet of him at one time.

On the ground, they found scattered along the trail of the fugitive robber, all the stolen packages, and envelopes, containing Treasury notes; so that he made nothing by his venture, except frozen feet; and he lost his horse, arms and traps. J. X. Beidler met Dutch John, and bandaged up his frozen hands, little knowing who his frigid acquaintance was. He never tells this story without observing, "That's just my darned luck;" at the same time polishing the butt of his "Navy" with one hand, and scratching his head with the other, his gray eye twinkling like a star before rain, with mingled humor and intelligence.

Lank Forbes claimed the horse and accoutrements of Steve as the lawful spoil of his revolver, and the reward of his courage. A demurrer was taken to this by Milt Moody, who had done the agreeable to Dutch John, and the drivers put in a mild remonstrance on their own behalf, on the naval principle that all ships in sight share in the prize captured. They claimed that their "schooners," were entitled to be represented by the "steersmen." The subject afforded infinite merriment to the party at every camp. At last a Judge was elected, a jury was empannelled, and the attorneys harangued the judicial packers. The verdict was that Lank should remain seized and possessed of the property taken from the enemy, upon payment of $20 to each of the teamsters, and $30 to Milt, and thereupon the court adjourned. The travellers reached Salt Lake City in safety.

# CHAPTER XI.

### THE ROBBERY OF PEABODY & CALDWELL'S COACH.

"On thy dial write, 'Beware of thieves.'"—O. W. HOLMES.

Late in the month of October, 1863, the sickness of one of the drivers making it necessary to procure a substitute, William Rumsey was engaged to take the coach to Bannack. In the stage, as passengers, were Messrs. Mattison, Percival and Wilkinson. After crossing the hills in the neighborhood of Virginia City, it began to snow furiously, and the storm continued without abatement, till they arrived within two miles of John Baker's Ranch, on Stinkingwater, a stream which ows its euphonious appellation to the fact that the mountaineers who named it found on its banks the putrifying corpses of Indians, suspended horizontally according to their usual custom, from a frame work of poles.

The corral at the station was found to be empty, and men were despatched to hunt up the stock. The herdsmen came back at last with only a portion of Peabody & Caldwell's horses, the remainder belonging to A. J. Oliver & Co. This detained them two hours, and finding that they could do no better, they hitched up the leaders, that had come in with the coach, and putting on two of Oliver's stock for wheelers, they drove through to Bob Dempsey's on a run, in order to make up for lost time.

At this place they took on board another passenger, Dan McFadden, more familiarly known as "Bummer Dan." The speed was maintained all the way to Point of Rocks, then called Copeland's Ranch. There they again changed horses, and being still behind time, they went at the gallop to Bill Bunton's Ranch, on Rattlesnake, at which place they arrived about sunset.

Here they discovered that the stock had been turned loose an hour before their arrival, the people stating that they did not expect the coach after its usual time was so long passed. Rumsey ordered them to send a man to gather up the team, which was done, and, at dark, the fellow came back, saying that he could not find them anywhere. The consequence was that they were obliged to lie over for the night. This was no great affliction; so they spent the time drinking whiskey, in mountain style—Bill Bunton doing the honors and sharing the grog. They had sense enough not to get drunk, being impressed with a seasonable conviction of the probability of the violation of the rights of property, if such should be the case. The driver had lost a pair of gauntlet gloves at the same place, before. At daylight, all arose, and two herders went out for the stock. One of them came back about 8 o'clock, and said that the stock was gone. A little before nine o'clock, the other herder came in with the stock that had hauled the coach over the last route.

The only way they could manage was to put on a span of the coach horses, with two old "plugs" for the wheel. The whole affair was a plan to delay the coach, as the horses brought in were worn down stock, turned out to recruit, and not fit to put in harness. During the previous evening, Bob Zachary, who seemed a great friend of Wilkinson's, told them that he had to go on horseback to Bannack, and to take a spare horse with him, which he wanted him to ride. The offer was not accepted at that time, but in the morning Bob told him that he must go, for he could not bring the horse along by himself. The miserable team being brought out and harnessed up, Oliver's regular coach, and an extra one came in sight, just at the creek crossing. Soon Rumsey shouted, "all aboard," the other stages came up, and all the passengers of the three vehicles turned in, on the mutual consolation principle, for a drink. Rumsey who sat still on the box, called, "All aboard for Bannack," and all took their seats but Wilkinson, who said he had concluded to go with Bob Zachary, Bill Bunton came out with the bottle and the glass, and gave Rumsey a drink, saying that he had not been in with the rest, telling him at the same time that he was going to Bannack himself, and that he wanted them to wait till he had got through with the rest of the passengers, for that then he would go with them. While Bunton was in the house, Rumsey had been professionally swinging the whip, and found his arm so lame from the exercise of the day before, that he could not use it. He thereupon asked the boys if any of them were good at whipping? but they all said "No." It was blustering, cold and cloudy—blowing hard; they let down the curtains. Finally, Bunton appeared and Rumsey said, "Billy, are you good at whipping?" To which he answered, "Yes," and getting up, whipped away, while Rumsey drove. A good deal of this kind of work was to be done, and Bunton said he was "a d——d good whipper." They crossed the creek and went on the table land at a run. The horses, however, soon began to weaken, Bunton whipping heavily, his object being to tire the stock. Rumsey told him to "ease up on them," or they would not carry them through. Bunton replied that the wheelers were a pair that had "played out" on the road, and had been turned out to rest. He added that if they were put beyond a walk they would fail. They went on, at a slow trot, to the gulch, and there fell into a walk, when Bunton gave up the whip, saying that Rumsey could do the little whipping, necessary, and got inside. He sat down on a box beside Bummer Dan. Percival and Madison were on the fore seat, with their backs to the driver.

The stage moved on for about four minutes after this, when the coachman saw two men wrapped in blankets, with a hood over their heads, and a shot-gun apiece. The moment he saw them, it flashed through his mind, "like gunpowder," (as he afterwards said,) that they were Road Agents, and he shouted at the top of his voice, "Look! look! boys! See what's a coming! Get out your arms!" Each man looked out of the nearest hole, but Matteson, from his position was the only man that had a view of them. They were on full run for the coach, coming out of a dry gulch, ahead, and to the left of the road, which ran into the main canyon. He instantly pulled open his coat, threw off his gloves, and laid his hand on his pistol, just as they came up to the leaders, and sang out, "Up wid your hands," in a feigned voice and dialect. Rumsey pulled up the horses; and they again shouted, "Up with your hands, you ———" (See formula.) At that, Bill Bunton cried, imploringly, "Oh! for God's sake, men don't kill one." (He was stool-pitching a little, to teach the rest of the passengers what to do.) "For God's sake don't kill me. You can have all the money I've got." Matteson was just going for his pistol, when the Road Agents again shouted, "Up wid you'r hands," etc., "and keep them up." Bunton went at his prayers again, piteously exclaiming, "Oh! for God's sake, men, dont' kill me. I'll come right to you. You can search me; I've got no arms." At the same time he commenced getting out on the same side of the coach as they were.

The Road Agents then roared out, "Get down, every ——— of you, and hold up your hands, or we'll shoot the first of you that puts them down." The passengers all got down in quick time. The robbers then turned to Rumsey, and said, "Get down, you ———" (as usual) "and take off the passengers' arms." This did not suit his fancy, so he replied, "You must be d——d fools to think I'm going to get down and let this team run away. You don't want the team; it won't do you any good." Get down, you ———," said the spokesman, angrily. "There's a man that has shown you he has no arms; let him take them," suggested Billy. (Bunton had turned up the skirts of his coat to prove that he had no weapons on.) Bunton, who knew his business, called out, "I'll hold the horses! I'll hold the horses!" The Road Agent who did the talking, turned to him, saying, "Get up, you long-legged ———, and hold them." Bunton at once went to the leaders, behind the two Road Agent, and they wheeling round to Billy Rumsey, ordered him down from the box. He tied the lines round the handle of the brake and got down, receiving the following polite reminder of his duty, "Now, you ———, take them arms off."

"Needs must, when the Devil drives," says the proverb, so off went Billy to Bummer Dan, who had on two "Navies," one on each side. Rumsey took them, and walked off diagonally, thinking that he might get a shot at them; but they were too knowing, and at once ordered him to throw them on the ground. He laid them down, and going back to Matteson, took his pistol off, laying it down besides the others, the robbers yelling to him, "Hurry up, you ———." He then went to Percival, but he had no arms on.

The Road Agents next ordered him to take the passengers' money, and to throw it on the ground with the pistols. Rumsey walked over to Percival, who taking out his sack, handed it to him. While he was handing over, Bill Bunton took out his own purse, and threw it about half way to Rumsey, saying, "There's a hundred and twenty dollars for you—all I have in the world; only don't kill me."

Billy next went to Bummer Dan, who handed out two purses from his pocket. Rumsey took them, and threw them on the ground besides the pistols. The next man was Matteson; but as he dropped his hands to take out his money, the leader shouted, "Keep up your hands, you ——. Take his money." Rumsey approached him, and putting his hand into his left pocket, found there a purse and a porte monnaie. Seizing the opportunity, he asked—in a whisper—if there was anything in the porte monnaie. He said "No." Rumsey turned to the robbers and said, "You don't want this, do you?" holding up the porte monnaie. Matteson told them that there was nothing in it but papers. They surlily answered, "We don't want that." On examining the other pocket, the searcher found a purse, which he threw out on the ground with the pistols.

They then demanded of Rumsey whether he had all; and on his answering "Yes," turning to Matteson the leader said, "Is that all you've got?" "No," said he, "there's another in here." He was holding up his hands when he spoke, and he nudged the pocket with his elbow.) The Road Agent angrily ordered Rumsey to take it out, and not leave "Nothing." He did as he was bidden, and threw the purse on the ground, after which he started for the coach, and had his foot on the hub of the wheel, when the robbers yelled out, "Where are you going, you ——?" "To get on the coach, you fool," said the irate driver, "You've got all there is." He instantly retorted, "Go back there and get that big sack," and added pointing to Bummer Dan, "You'r the man we're after. Get that strap off your shoulder, you d——d Irish ——." Bummer Dan had a strap over his shoulder, fastened to a large purse, that went down into his pants. He had thrown out two little sacks before. Seeing that there was no chance of saving his money, he

commenced unbuckling the strap, and when Rumsey got to
him he had it off. Billy took hold of the tab to pull it out,
but it would not come; whereupon he let go and stepped
back. Dan commenced to unbutton his pants, the "Cap"
ordering Rumsey to jerk it off, or he would shoot him in a
minute. While he was speaking, Rumsey saw that Dan had
another strap round his body, under his shirt. He stepped
back again, saying, "You fools! you're not going to kill a
man who is doing all he can for you. Give him time."
They ordered him to hurry up, calling him "An awkward
——," and telling him that they hadn't any more time to
lose. Dan had by this time got the belt loose, and he handed
Rumsey a big, fringed bag, containing two other sacks. He
received it, and tossed it beside the pistols.

The Road Agents finished the proceedings by saying, "Get
aboard, every —— of you; and get out of this; and if
we ever hear a word from one of you, we'll kill you surer
than h—l."

They all got aboard, with great promptitude, Bunton
mounting beside the driver, (he did not want to get inside
then,) and commenced to whip the horses, observing that
that was a d——d hot place for him, and he would get out
of it as soon as he could. Rumsey saw, at a turn of the road
by looking over the coach, that the Road Agents had dismounted, one holding the horses, while the other was picking up the plunder, which amounted to about $2,800.

The coach went on to Bannack, and reported the robbery
at Peabody's Express Office. George Hilderman was in
Peabody's when the coach arrived. He seemed as much
surprised as any of them. His business was to hear what
would happen, and to give word if the passengers named
either of the robbers, and then, on their return, they would
have murdered them. It was at this man's place that Geo.
Ives and the gang with him were found. He was banished
when Ives was hung. Had he been caught only a little
time afterwards, he would have swung with the rest, as his
villainies were known.

The Road Agents had a private mark on the coach, when
it carried money, and thus telegraphed it along the road.
Rumsey told in Bannack whom he suspected; but he was

wrong. Bummer Dan and Percival knew them, and told Matteson; but neither of them ever divulged it until the men were hung. They were afraid of their lives. Frank Parish confessed his share in this robbery. George Ives was the other.

## CHAPTER XII.

### THE SETTLEMENT OF VIRGINIA CITY AND THE MURDER OF DILLINGHAM.

Early in June, 1863, Alder Gulch was discovered by Tom Cover, Bill Fairweather, Barney Hughes, Edgar and some others. It was a sheer accident. After a long and unsuccessful tour, they came thither on their way to Bannack, and one of them took a notion to try a pan of dirt. A good prospect was obtained, and the lucky "panner" gave his name to the far famed "Fairweather District."

Tom Cover and some others of the party returned to Bannack for provisions, and for the purpose of communicating the discovery to their friends. A wild stampede was the consequence.

One poor fellow, while in the willows at Beaverhead, being mistaken for a beaver, was accidentally shot by his comrade. He lived several days, and was carefully nursed by his slayer, who was greatly grieved at the occurrence. The stampeders came in with pack animals. Colonel McLean brought the first vehicle to the Gulch. The stampede reached the Gulch on the 6th of June. The course of the stream was marked by the alders, that filled the Gulch so densely as to prevent passage, in many places. Some people camped on the edge of the brush, about three-fourths of a mile above the town, accidentally set it on fire, and with a tremenduous roar, the flames swept down the creek, and burned up the entire undergrowth.

Almost immediately after the first great rush from Bannack—in addition to the tents, brush wakiups and extempore fixings for shelter—small log cabins were erected. The first of these was the Mechanical Bakery, now standing near the lower end of Wallace street. Morier's saloon went up at about the same time, and the first dwelling house was built by John Lyons. After this beginning, houses rose as if by magic. Dick Hamilton, Root & Davis, J. E. McClurg, Hall & Simpson, N. Story and O. C. Matthews, were among the first merchants. Dr Steele was first President of the Fairweather District. Dr. G. G. Bissel was the first Judge of the Miners' Court. The duty of the Recorder's Office was, we believe, performed by James Furgus.

Among the citizens were S. S. Short, Sweney and Rogers, (discoverers,) Johnny Green, Nelson Ptomey, Judge Potter of Highland, Jem Galbraith, Judge Smith, (afterwards banished,) W. F. Bartlett, C. Crouch, Bixter & Co., Tom Conner, William Cadwell, W. Emerick, Frank Heald, Frank Woody, Marcellus Lloyd, Washburne Stapleton, John Sharp, Jerry Nowlan, E. C. Stickney, Frank Watkins, T. L. Luce, (Mechanical Bakery,) Robinson and Cooley, the first bakers, (open air,) Hugh O'Neil, of fistic fame, Jem Vivian, Jack Russell, the first man who panned out "wages" in the Grasshopper Creek, Sargent Tisdale, W. Nowlan, of the Bank, Tom Duffy, John Murphy, Jem Patton, Jno. Kane, Pat Lynch, John Robertson, Worcester Wymans and Charley Wymans, Barney Gilson, and many others.

The first name given to the present capital of Montana, was "Varina," in honor of Jeff. Davis's wife, but it was soon changed to "Virgina." Dr. (Judge) G. G. Bissel was the first man that wrote it Virginia. Being asked to head a legal document with "Varina," he bluntly said he would see them d——d first, for that was the name of Jeff. Davis's wife; and, accordingly, as he wrote it, so it remained. From this little circumstance it will be seen that politics were anything but forgotten on the banks of Alder Creek; but miners are sensible men, in the main, and out in the mountains, a good man makes a good friend, even where political opinions are widely different. The mountaineer holds his own like a vice, and he extends the same privilege to others. The theory is, "You may drive your stake where you darned please; only, if you try to jump my claim, I'll go for you, sure."

That is the basis of the mountain man's creed, in love, law, war, mining, and in fact, in everything regulated by principle.

Of course a number of the roughs came over when the Gulch was settled, prominent among whom was Cyrus Skinner. Per contra, "X," was among the early inhabitants, which fact reminds us of the line in Cato's soliloquy,

"My bane and antidote are both before me."

The celebrated "Rogues" Antidote," aforesaid, has, however, survived all the renowned Road Agents of the period alluded to. The true Western man is persistent, tough, and hard to abolish. Fierce, flighty spirits, like Lord Byron —when they get into trouble—say :

"Better perish by the shock,
Than moulder piece-meal on the rock."

The motto of the Mountaineer, put into similar shape, would read :

Never say die, but brave the shock,
While there's a shell-fish on the rock.

Which sentiment, though equally forcible, we reluctantly admit, is, perhaps, a shade less poetical; but it is nevertheless, good philosophy, which, with all respect for his lordship, is the reverse of what should be said of the teaching derivable from the beautiful lines of that erring genius.

As a proof of the address and tact of Plummer, and of the terrible state of society, it may be mentioned that he got himself elected Sheriff, at Bannack, despite of his known character, and immediately appointed two of his Road Agents; Buck Stinson and Ned Ray, as Deputies. Nor did he remain contented with that; but he had the effrontery to propose to a brave and good man, in Virginia that he should make way for him there, and as certain death would have been the penalty for a refusal, he consented. Thus Plummer was actually Sheriff of both places at once. This politic move threw the unfortunate citizens into his hands completely, and by means of his robber deputies—whose legal functions cloaked many a crime—he ruled with a rod of iron.

The marvellous riches of the great Alder Gulch attracted

crowds from all the West, and afterwards from the East, also; among whom were many diseased with crime to such an extent that for their cure, the only available prescription was a stout cord and a good drop.

Plummer had appointed as his Deputies, Jack Gallagher, Buck Stinson and Ned Ray. The head Deputy was a man of another stripe, entirely, named Dillingham, who had accurate knowledge of the names of the members of the Road Agent Band, and was also acquainted with many of their plans, though he himself was innocent. He told a man named Dodge, who was going to Virginia with Wash Stapleton and another, that Buck Stinson, Haze Lyons and Charley Forbes intended to rob them. Dodge, instead of keeping his council, foolishly revealed the whole affair to the robbers, who, of course, were much struck at the news. Hays ejaculated, "——, is that so ?" The three men at once concluded to murder Dillingham.

At Rattlesnake, Haze Lyons came to Wash Stapleton, who was on the road between Bannack and Virginia, and asked him if he had heard about the intended robbery, adding that he had followed Dillingham that far, and that he had come to kill him, but he said that he feared that he had heard about it, and had got out of the country. Wash who says he has felt more comfortable, even when sleeping in church—at once replied, "No ; this is the first I've heard of it. I have only $100 in greenbacks, and they may as well take them, if they want them, and let me go." The other swore it was all a d——d lie, and they separated.

The robbers went on to Virginia. Jack Gallagher came to X, and wanted a pony for his friend Stinson to ride down the Gulch. At first his request was refused, the owner saying that he wanted to ride it down the Gulch, himself. Jack insisted, and promising that he would be back in half an hour, X lent it to him. He was away for two hours, and the proprietor was "as hot as a wolf," when he came back. The truth was that they had been consulting and fixing the programme for the murder, which was arranged for the next day, they having discovered that Dillingham was in the gulch.

In the morning, Buck Stinson, Haze Lyons and Charley

Forbes might be seen engaged in a grand "Medicine talk," in the neighborhood of a brush wakiup, where Dr. Steele was holding court, and trying the right to a bar claim, the subject of a suit between F. Ray and D. Jones. Dillingham was standing close by the impromptu Hall of Justice, when the three Road Agents came up. "We want to see you," said Haze; Stinson walked a pace or two ahead of the others. Haze was on one side and Forbes was behind. "Bring him along! Make him come!" said Buck Stinson, half turning and looking over his shoulder. They walked on about ten paces, when they all stopped, and the three faced towards Dillingham. "———— you, take back those lies," said Haze, and instantly the three pulled their pistols and fired, so closely together that eye-sight was a surer evidence of the number of shots discharged than hearing. There was a difference, however; Haze fired first; his ball taking effect in the thigh. Dillingham put his hand to the spot, and groaned. Buck Stinson's bullet went over his head; but Charley Forbes' shot passed through his breast. On receiving the bullet in the chest, Dillingham fell like an empty sack. He was carried into a brush wakiup, and lived but a very short time.

Jack Gallagher, being Deputy Sheriff, settled the matter very neatly and effectively (for his friends.) He rushed out, as per agreement, and took their pistols, putting them together and reloading Buck Stinson's, so that no one knew (that would tell) whose pistols fired the fatal shots.

The men were, of course, arrested. Red tape is an institution not yet introduced among miners. A captain of the guard, elected by the people, and a detail of miners, took charge of the prisoners, who were lodged in a log building, where John Mings' store now stands.

A people's court was organized and the trial commenced. It was a trial by the people EN MASSE. For our own part, knowing as we do the utter impossibility of all the voters hearing half the testimony; seeing, also, that the good and the bad are mingled, and that a thief's vote will kill the well considered verdict of the best citizen, in such localities and under such circumstances, verdicts are as uncertain as the direction of the wind on next Tibb's Eve. We often hear of the justice of the masses—"in the LONG run;" but a man may get hung "in the SHORT run"—or may escape the rope he has so remorselessly earned, which is, by a thousand chances to one, the more likely result of a mass trial. The chance of a just verdict being rendered is almost a nullity. Prejudice, or selfish fear of consequences, and not reason, rules the illiterate, the lawless, and the uncivilized. These latter are in large numbers in such places, and if they do right, it is by mistake. We are of Tenterden's opinion in the matter of juries, (in cases like these.) "Gentlemen of the Jury," said his Lordship, to eleven hard looking followers of a consequential foreman, in an appalling state of watch-chain and shirt frill, "Allow me to congratulate you upon the soundness of your verdict; it is highly creditable to you." "My Lord," replied the pursy and fussy little bald-pated and spectacled foreman, "The ground on which we based our verdict, was—" "Pardon me, Mr. Foreman," interrupted the Judge, "Your verdict is perfectly correct; the ground on which it is based is most probably entirely untenable." The favors of the dangerous classes are bestowed, not on the worthy, but on the popular, who are their uncommissioned leaders. Such favors are distributed like sailors' prize money, which is nautically supposed to be sifted through a ladder. What goes through is for the officers; what sticks on the rounds is for the men.

James Brown and H. P. A. Smith, were in favor of a trial by twelve men; but E. R. Cutler opposed this, for he knew that the jury would have been impanneled by a Road Agent Sheriff. A vote was taken on the question, by "Ayes" and "Noes;" but this failing, two wagons were drawn up, with an interval between them. Those in favor of a trial by a jury of twelve went through first. Those who preferred a trial by the people traversed the vehicular defile afterwards. The motion of a jury for the whole prevailed.

Judge G. G. Bissell was appointed President by virtue of his office. He stated that it was an irregular proceeding, but that if the people would appoint two reliable men to sit with him, he would carry it through. This was agreed to, Dr. Steel and Dr. Rutar being chosen as associates.

Three Doctors were thus appointed Judges, and naturally enough directed the "medicine talk" on the subject.

E. R. Cutler, a blacksmith, was appointed Public Prosecutor; Jem Brown was elected assistant; Judge H. P. A. Smith was for the defense, and the whole body of the people were Jurors. We may add that the jury box was Alder Gulch, and that the throne of Justice was a wagon, drawn up at the foot of what is now Wallace street.

The trial commenced by the indictment of Buck Stinson and Haze Lyons, and continued till dark, when the court adjourned. The prisoners were placed under a strong guard at night. They were going to chain them, but they would not submit. Charley Forbes said he "would suffer death first." This (of course?) suited the guard of miners, and, quick as a flash, down came six shot guns in a line with Charley's head. The opinion of this gentlemen on the subject of practical concatenation underwent an instantaneous change. He said, mildly, "Chain me." The fetters were composed of a light logging chain and padlocks.

All was quiet during the rest of the night; but Haze sent for a "leading citizen," who, covered by the guns of the guard, approached and asked him what he wanted. "Why," said he, "I want you to let these men off. I am the man that killed Dillingham. I came over to do it, and these men are innocent. I was sent here by the best men in Bannack to do it." Upon being asked who they were, he named some of the best citizens, and then added, "Henry Plummer told me to shoot him." The first half of the statement was an impossible falsehood, many of the men knowing nothing of the affair for several days after. The last statement was exactly true.

After breakfast, the trial was resumed, and continued till near noon. The attorneys had by this time finished their pleas, and the question was submitted to the people, "GUILTY, OR NOT GUILTY?" A nearly unanimous verdict of "Guilty," was returned. The question as to the punishment to be inflicted was next submitted by the President, and a chorus of voices from all parts of the vast assembly, shouted, "Hang them." Men were at once appointed to build a scaffold and to dig the graves of the doomed criminals.

## CHAPTER XII.

In the meantime, Charley Forbes' trial went on.  An effort was made to save Charley on account of his good looks and education, by producing a fully loaded pistol, which they proved (?) was his.  It was, however, Buck Stinson's, and had been "set right" by Gallagher.  The miners had got weary, and many had wandered off, when the question was put; but his own masterly appeal, which was one of the finest efforts of eloquence ever made in the mountains, saved him.

Forbes was a splendid looking fellow—straight as a ramrod; handsome, brave and agile as a cat, in his movements. His friends believed that he excelled Plummer in quickness and dexterity at handling his revolver.  He had the scabbard sewn to the belt, and wore the buckle always exactly in front, so that his hand might grasp the butt, with the forefinger on the trigger and the thumb on the cock, with perfect certainty, whenever it was needed, which was pretty often.

Charley told a gentleman of the highest respectability that he killed Dillingham, and he used to laugh at the "softness" of the miners who acquitted him.  He moreover warned the gentleman mentioned that he would be attacked on his road to Salt Lake; but the citizen was no way scary, and said, "You can't do it, Charley; your boys are scattered and we are together, and we shall give you ———, if you try it." The party made a sixty mile drive the first day, and thus escaped molestation.  Charley had corresponded with the press, some articles on the state and prospects of the Territory having appeared in the California papers, and were very well written.

Charley was acquitted by a nearly unanimous vote.  Judge Smith burst into tears, fell on his neck and kissed him, exclaiming, "My boy! my boy!"  Hundreds pressed round him, shaking hands and cheering, till it seemed to strike them all at once, that there were two men to hang, which was even more exciting, and the crowd "broke" for the "jail."

A wagon was drawn up by the people to the door, in which the criminals were to ride to the gallows. They were then ordered to get into the wagon, which they did, several of their friends climbing in with them.

At this juncture, Judge Smith was called for, and then, amidst tremendous excitement and confusion; Haze Lyons crying and imploring mercy; a number of ladies, much affec-. ted, begged earnestly to "Save the poor young boys' lives." The ladies admit the crying; but declare that they wept in the interest of fair play. One of them saw Forbes kill Dillingham, and felt that it was popular murder to hang Stinson and Lyons, and let off the chief desperado, because he was good looking. She had furnished the sheet with which the dead body was covered.

We cannot blame the gentle hearted creatures; but we deprecate the practice of admitting the ladies to such places. They are out of their path. Such sights are unfit for them to behold, and in rough and masculine business of every kind, women should bear no part. It unsexes them and destroys the most lovely parts of their character. A woman is a queen in her own home; but we neither want her as a blacksmith, a plough-woman, a soldier, a lawyer, a doctor, nor in any such professions or handicraft. As sisters, mothers, nurses, friends, sweethearts and wives, they are the salt of the earth, the sheet anchor of society, and the humanizing and purifying element in humanity. As such, they cannot be too much respected, loved and protected. But from Blue Stockings, Bloomers, and strong-minded she-males, generally, "Good Lord, deliver us."

A letter (written by other parties to suit the occasion) was produced, and a gentleman—a friend of Lyons—asked that "The letter which Haze had written to his mother, might be read." This was done, amid cries of "Read the letter," "—— the letter;" while others who saw how it would turn out, shouted, "Give him a horse and let him go to his mother." A vote was taken again, after it had all been settled, as before mentioned—the first time by ayes and noes. Both parties claimed the victory. The second party was arranged so that the party for hanging should go up-hill, and the party for clearing should go down-hill. The down-hill men claimed that the prisoners were acquitted; but the up-hills would not give way. All this time, confusion confounded reigned around the wagon. The third vote was differently managed. Two pairs of men were chosen. Between one pair passed those who were for carrying the sentence into execution, and between the other pair marched those who were for setting them at liberty. The latter party ingeniously increased their votes by the simple but effectual expedient of passing through several times, and finally, an honest Irish miner, who was not so weak-kneed as the rest, shouted out, "Be ——, there's a bloody naygur voted three times." The descendant of Ham broke for the willows at top speed, on hearing this announcement. This vote settled the question, and Gallagher, pistol in hand, shouted, "Let them go, they're cleared." Amidst a thousand confused cries of, "Give the murderers a horse," "Let them go," "Hurrah!" etc., one of the men, seeing a horse with an Indian saddle, belonging to a Blackfoot squaw, seized it, and mounting both on the same animal, the assassins rode at a gallop out of the gulch. One of the guard remarked to another—pointing at the same time to the gallows—"There is a monument of disappointed Justice."

While all this miserable farce was being enacted, the poor victim of the pardoned murderers lay stark and stiff on a gambling table, in a brush wakiup, in the gulch. Judge Smith came to X, and asked if men enough could not be found to bury Dillingham. X said there were plenty, and, obtaining a wagon, they put the body into a coffin, and started up the "Branch," towards the present graveyard on Cemetery Hill, where the first grave was opened in Virginia, to receive the body of the murdered man. As the party proceeded, a man said to Judge Smith; "Only for my dear wife and daughter, the poor fellows would have been hanged." A citizen, seeing that the so-called ladies had not a tear to shed for the victim, promptly answered, "I take notice that your dear wife and daughter have no tears for poor Dillingham; but only for two murderers." "Oh," said the husband, "I cried for Dillingham." "Darned well you thought of it," replied the mountaineer. A party of eight or ten were around the grave, when one asked who would perform the burial service. Some one said, "Judge, you have been doing the talking for the last three days, and you had better pray." The individual addressed knelt down and made a long and appropriate prayer; but it must be stated that he was so intoxicated that kneeling, was, at least, as much a convenience as it was a necessity. Some men never "experience religion" unless they are drunk. They pass through the convivial and the narrative stages, into the garrulous, from which they sail into the religious, and are deeply affected. The scene closes with the lachrymose or weeping development, ending in pig like slumbers. Any one thus moved by liquor is not reliable.

---

## CHAPTER XIII.

### THE ROBBERY OF THE SALT LAKE MAIL COACH BY GEORGE IVES, BILL GRAVES alias WHISKEY BILL, AND BOB ZACHARY.

"Which is the villain? Let me see his eyes,
That when I note another man like him
I may avoid him."—SHAKSPEARE.

At the latter end of the month of November, 1863, Oliver's Salt Lake coach, driven by Thos. C. Caldwell, left Virginia for Salt Lake City, carrying as passengers Leroy Southmayde and Captain Moore. There was also a discharged driver named Billy. At about three P. M., they reached Loraine's Ranch, where George Ives rode up and stopped. He wanted to get a change of horses, but could not obtain them. He then ordered grain for his horse, standing beside Southmayde all the time. Suddenly he said, "I have heard of Tex; he is at Cold Spring Ranch," and then ordered his horse. Steve Marshland was in his company.

Between Loraine's and Cold Spring Ranch, they passed the coach, and sure enough there the three were, in conversation at the Ranch, as the stage drove up.

ᴐᵗTex, alias Jem Crow, afterwards stated that they told him they were going to rob the stage that night. Old Tex was watching the coach when it started from Virginia, and Captain Moore observing him and knowing his character, told Southmayde that he did not like to see him there. Circumstances and conclusive testimony have since proved that he was the spy, and being furnished with a fleet horse, he rode across the country, at full speed, heading the coach, as before described.

They drove on to the point of Rocks, and there they lay over till morning. At Stone's Ranch, the Road Agents made a circuit and passed the coach unobserved. Ives had been joined, in the meanwhile, by Whiskey Bill and Bob Zachary. About 11 A. M., the travelers overtook the three Road Agents. Each one had his shot gun lying over his left arm, and they appeared, from behind, like hunters. As the stage came up, they wheeled their horses, at once, and presented their pieces. Bill Graves drew a bead on Tom Caldwell; Ives covered Southmayde, while Bob Zachary, keeping his gun pointed at the coach, watched Captain Moore and Billy.

Southmayde had the opportunity of looking down the barrels of Ives's gun, and could almost see the buckshot getting ready for a jump. As a matter of taste, he thinks such a sight anything but agreeable or edifying, and if his luck should bring him in the vicinity of Road Agents in pursuit of their calling, he confidentially informs us that he would prefer a side view of the operation, as he would then be able to speak dispassionately of the affair. To report without "Fear, favor or affection," is rather hard when the view is taken in front, at short range. Without "Favor or affection" can be managed; but the observance of the first condition would necessitate an indifference to a shower of "cold pewter," possessed only by despairing lovers of the red-cover novellette class, and these men never visit the mountains; alkali, sage brush fires, and "beef-straight" having a decidedly "material" tendency, and being very destructive of sentiment. Ives called out, "halt! throw up your hands," and then bade Zachary "Get down and look after those fellows."

Accordingly Bob dismounted, and leaving his horse, he walked, gun in hand, up to Southmayde. While engaged in panning out Southmayde's dust, he trembled from head to foot (and that not with cold.)

The appearance of the Road Agents, at this moment, was striking, and not at all such as would be desired by elderly members of the "Peace party." Each man had on a green and blue blanket, covering the body entirely. Whiskey Bill wore a "plug" hat, (the antitype of the muff on a soupplate usually worn in the East.) His sleeves were rolled up above the elbow; he had a black silk handkerchief over his face, with holes for sight and air, and he rode a gray horse, covered from the ears to the tail with a blanket, which, however, left the head and legs exposed to view. George Ives' horse was blanketed in the same way. It was a dappled gray, with a roached mane. He himself was masked with a piece of a gray blanket, with the necessary perforations. Zachary rode a blue-gray horse, belonging to Bob Dempsey, ("All the country" was their stable)—blanketed like the others—and his mask was a piece of a Jersey shirt.

Ives was on the off side of the driver, and Graves on the near side. When Zachary walked up to Southmayde, he said, "Shut your eyes." This Southmayde respectfully declined, and the matter was not pressed. Bob then took Leroy's pistol and money, and threw them down.

While Southmayde was being robbed, Billy, feeling tired, put down his hands; upon which Ives instantly roared out, "Throw them up, you ———." It is recorded that Billy obeyed with alacrity, though not with cheerfulness.

Zachary walked up to Captain Moore and made a similar request. The Captain declared with great solemnity, as he handed him his purse, that it was "All he had in the world;" but it afterwards appeared that a sum of $25 was not included in that estimate of his terrestial assets; for he produced this money when the Road Agents had disappeared.

Continuing his search, the relieving officer came to Billy, and demanded his pistol, which was immediately handed over. Ives asked, "Is it loaded," and being answered in the negative, told Bob to give it back to the owner. Tom Caldwell's turn came next. He had several small sums belonging to different parties, which he was carrying for them to their friends, and also he had been commissioned to make some purchases. As Bob approached him, he exclaimed, "My God! what do you want with me; I have nothing." Graves told Zachary to let him alone, and inquired if there was anything in the mail that they wanted. Tom said he did not think that there was. Zachary stepped upon the brake bar and commenced an examination, but found nothing. As Caldwell looked at Zachary while he was thus occupied, Ives ordered him not to do that. Tom turned and asked if he might look at him. Ives nodded.

Having finished his search, Zachary picked up his gun, and stepped back. Ives dismissed the "parade" with the laconic command, "Get up and 'skedaddle.' "

The horses were somewhat restive, but Tom held them fast, and Southmayde, with a view to reconnoitering, said in a whisper, "Tom, drive slow." Ives called out, "Drive on." Leroy turned round on his seat, determined to find out who the robbers were, and looked carefully at them for nearly a minute, which Ives at last observing, he yelled out, "If you don't turn round, and mind your business, I'll shoot the top of your head off." The three robbers gathered together, and remained watching, till the coach was out of sight.

Leroy Southmayde lost $400 in gold, and Captain Moore delivered up $100 in Treasury Notes, belonging to another man..

The coach proceeded on its way to Bannack without further molestation, and on its arrival there, Plummer was in waiting, and asked, "Was the coach robbed to-day?" and being told that it had been, as Southmayde jumped down, he took him by the arm, and knowing him to be Sheriff, Southmayde was just about to tell him all about it, when Judge G. G. Bissell gave Leroy a slight nudge, and motioned for him to step back, which he did, and the Judge told him to be very careful what he told that man, meaning Plummer; Southmayde closed one eye as a private signal of comprehension, and rejoined Plummer, who said, "I think I can tell you who it was that robbed you." Leroy asked, "Who?"

Plummer replied, "George Ives was one of them." South-mayde said, "I know; and the others were Whiskey Bill and Bob Zachary; and I'll live to see them hanged before three weeks." Plummer at once walked off, and though Leroy was in town for three days, he never saw him after-wards. The object of Plummer's accusation of Ives was to see whether Southmayde really knew anything. Some time after, Judge Bissell—who had overheard Southmayde tell-ing Plummer who the thieves were—remarked to him, "Le-roy, your life is not worth a cent."

On the second day after, as Tom, was returning, he saw Graves at the Cold Spring Ranch, and took him on one side asking him if he had heard of the "little robbery." Graves replied that he had, and asked him if he knew who were the perpetrators. Tom said, "No," adding, "And I wouldn't for the world; for if I did, and told of them, I shouldn't live long." "That's a fact, Tom," said Graves, "You wouldn't live fifteen minutes." I'll tell you of a circumstance as hap-pened to me about bein' robbed in Californy:

One night about ten o'clock, me and my partner was ridin' along, and two fellers rode up and told us to throw up our hands, and give up our money. We did it pretty quick I guess. They got $2,000 in coined gold from us. I told 'em, "Boys," sez I, "It's pretty rough to take all we've got." So the feller said it was rather rough, and he gave us back $40. About a week after, I seen the two fellers dealin' Faro. I looked pretty hard at them, and went out. One of the chaps follered me, and sez he, "Ain't you the man that was robbed the other night?" "No," sez I, for I was afraid to tell him the truth. Sez he, "I want you to own up; I know you're the man. Now I'm agoing to give you $4,000 for keeping your mouth shut," and he did, ——. Now you see, Tom, that's what I got for keepin' my mouth shut. I saved my life, and got $4,000.

Ives made for Virginia City, and there told, in a house of ill-fame, that he was the Bamboo chief that made Tom Cald-well throw up his hands, and that, ——, he would do it again. He and a Colorado driver, who was a friend of Cald-well's went together to Nevada. Each of them had a shot-gun. Ives was intoxicated. The driver asked Ives whom did he suppose to be the robbers; to which he quickly replied, "I am the Bamboo chief that robbed it," etc., etc., as before mentioned. The man then said, "Don't you think Tom knows it?" "Of course I do," said George. As they came back to town, the driver saw Tom, and waved to him to keep back, which he did, and sent a man to inquire the reason of the signal. The messenger brought him back information of what had passed, and told him to keep out of Ives' way, for he was drunk and might kill him.

The same evening, Tom and his friend went to the Cold Spring Ranch together, on the coach, and the entire particulars came out, in conversation. The driver finished the story by stating that he sat on his horse, ready to shoot Ives, if he should succeed in getting the "drop" on Caldwell.

Three days after, when Southmayde was about to return from Bannack, Buck Stinson and Ned Ray came into the Express Office, and asked who were for Virginia. On being told that there were none but Southmayde, they said, "Well, then, we'll go." The Agent came over and said to Leroy, "For God's sake, don't go; I believe you'll be killed." Southmayde replied, "I have got to go; and if you'll get me a double-barrelled shot gun, I will take my chances." Oliver's Agent accordingly provided Leroy Southmayde, Tom Caldwell, and a young lad about sixteen years of age, who was also going by the coach to Virginia, with a shot gun each. Leroy rode with Tom. They kept a keen eye on a pair of Road Agents, one driving and the other watching.

The journey was as monotonous as a night picket, until the coach reached the crossing of the Stinkingwater, where two of the three men that robbed it (Bob Zachary and Bill Graves) were together, in front of the station, along with Aleck Carter. Buck Stinson saw them, and shouted, "Ho! you ——— Road Agents." Said Leroy to Tom Caldwell, "Tom, we're gone up." Said Tom, "That's so."

At the Cold Spring Station, where the coach stopped for supper, the amiable trio came up. They were, of course fully armed with gun, pistols and knife. Two of them set down their guns at the door, and came in. Aleck Carter had his gun slung at his back. Bob Zachary feigning to be drunk, called out, "I'd like to see the —— man that don't like Stone." Finding that, as far as could be ascertained, everybody present, had a very high opinion of Stone, he called for a treat to all hands, which having been disposed of, he bought a bottle of whiskey and behaved "miscellaneously" till the coach started.

After going about a quarter of a mile, they wheeled their horses and called "Halt." The instant the word left their lips, Leroy dropped his gun on Aleck Carter; Tom Caldwell, and the other passenger each picked his man, and drew a bead on him, at the same moment. Aleck Carter called out, "We only want you to take a drink; but you can shoot and be ——, if you want to." Producing the bottle, it was handed round; but Leroy and Tom only touched their lips to it. Tom believed it to be poisoned. After politely inquiring if any of the —— wanted any more, they wheeled their horses, saying, "We're off for Pete Daley's," and clapped spurs to their horses, and headed for the Ranch, going on a keen run.

Before leaving Cold Spring Ranch, Leroy Southmayde told Tom that he saw through it all, and would leave the coach; but Tom said he would take Buck up beside him, and that surely the other fellow could watch Ray. Buck did not like the arrangement; but Tom said, "You're an old driver, and I want you up with me, ——."

The two passengers sat with their shot guns across their knees, ready for a move on the part of eithers of the robbers.

At Lorraine's Ranch, Leroy and Caldwell went out a little way from the place, with the bridles in their hands, and talked about the "situation." They agreed that it was pretty rough, and were debating the propriety of taking to the brush, and leaving the coach, when their peace of mind was in no way assured by seeing that Buck Stinson was close to them, and must have overheard every word they had uttered. Buck endeavored to allay their fears by saying there was no danger. They told him that they were armed, and that if they were attacked, they would make it a warm time for some of them; at any rate, they would "get" three or four of them. Buck replied, "Gentlemen, I pledge you my word, my honor, and my life, that you will not be attacked between this and Virginia."

The coach went on, directly the horses were hitched up, and Buck commenced roaring out a song, without intermission, till at last he became tired, and then, at his request, Ray took up the chorus. This was the signal to the other three to keep off. Had the song ceased, an attack would have been at once made ; but, without going into Algebra, they were able to ascertain that such a venture had more peril than profit, and so they let it alone. The driver, Southmayde and the young passenger were not sorry when they alighted safe in town. Ned Ray called on Southmayde and told him that if he knew who committed the robbery he should not tell ; for that death would be his portion if he did.

## CHAPTER XIV.

### THE OPENING OF THE BALL—GEORGE IVES.

They mustered in their simple dress,
For wrongs to seek a stern redress.

As a matter of course, after the failure of Justice in the case of the murderers of Dillingham, the state of society, bad as it was rapidly deteriorated, until a man could hardly venture to entertain a belief that he was safe for a single day. We have been repeatedly shown places where bullets used to come through the chinks between the logs separating one of the stores in town from a saloon. Wounded men lay almost unnoticed about the city, and a night or day without shooting, knifing or fighting would have been recognized as a small and welcome instalment of the milenium. Men dared not go. from Virginia to Nevada or Summit after dark. A few out of the hundreds of instances must suffice. A Dutchman, known as Dutch Fred, was met by one of the band, who ordered him to throw up his hands, as usual. Finding he had $5 in Treasury Notes with him, the robber told him he would take them at par, and added with a volley of curses, "If ever you come this way with only $5, I'll shoot you; —— you, I'll shoot you anyhow," and raising his pistol, he shot him in the arm. Another man was robbed of two or three dollars, about two or three miles below Nevada, and was told that if ever he came with as little money again they would kill him.

George Ives was a young man of rather prepossessing appearance, probably twenty-seven years old. His complexion and hair were light, and his eyes blue. He wore no whiskers. His height was nearly six feet, and he wore a soldier's overcoat and a light felt hat. The carriage of this renowned desperado was sprightly, and his coolness was imperturbable. Long practice in confronting danger had made him absolutely fearless. He would face death with an indifference that had become constitutional, and the spirit of reckless bravado with which he was animated made him the terror of the citizens. He would levy black mail under the guise of a loan and as a matter of sport, and to show the training of his horse, he would back the animal into the windows of a store, and then ride off laughing. In looking at Ives a man would, at first sight, be favorably impressed; but a closer examination by any one skilled in physiognomy, would detect in the lines of the mouth and in the strange, fierce and sinister gleam of the eye, the quick spirit which made him not only the terror of the community, but the dread of the band of ruffians with whom he was associated.

As before mentioned, he was with Henry Plummer when he started to rob Langford and Hauser; he assisted at the robbery of the coaches in October and November, and, after that, he figured as a highwayman with Aleck Carter, down on Snake River, under the alias of Lewis.

In company with a friend, he visited his comrades, Hunter and Carter, at Brown's Gulch, and on their way back, among the hills which form, as it were, the picket line of the Ramshorn Mountains, the two met Anton M. Holter, now a citizen of Virginia. They politely invited him to replenish their exchequers by a draft on his own, which, under the circumstances, he instantly did; but he was able at the moment to honor only a small check. They read him a lecture upon the impropriety of travelling with so small a sum in his possession, and then, as an emphatic confirmation of their expressed displeasure, George drew his revolver, and, aiming at his head, sent a ball through his hat, grazing his scalp. A second shot, with more deliberate aim, was only prevented by the badness of the cap. After this failure, this "Perfect gentleman" went his way, and so did Holter, doubtless blessing the cap maker.

Tex was a frequent companion of Ives, who was also intimate with Plummer, and George used frequently to show their letters, written in cypher, to unskilled if not unsuspecting citizens. He spent a life of ceaseless and active wickedness up to the very day of his capture.

Perhaps the most daring and cold blooded of all his crimes was the murder which he committed near the Cold Spring Ranch. A man had been whipped for larceny near Nevada, and to escape the sting of the lash, he offered to give information about the Road Agents. Ives heard of it, and meeting him purposely between Virginia and Dempsey's, he deliberately fired at him with his double-barrelled gun. The gun was so badly loaded, and the man's coat so thickly padded that the buckshot did not take effect, upon which he coolly drew his revolver and, talking to him all the time, shot him dead. This deed was perpetrated in broad daylight, on a highway—a very Bloomingdale Road of the community—and yet, there, in plain view of Daley's and the Cold Spring Ranch, with two or three other teams in sight, he assassinated his victim, in a cool and business like manner, and when the murdered man had fallen from his horse, he took the animal by the bridle and led it off among the hills.

Ives then went to George Hilderman and told him that he should like to stay at his wakiup for a few days, as he had killed a man near Cold Spring Ranch, and there might be some stir and excitement about it.

In about half an hour after, some travellers arrived at the scene of murder. The body was still warm, but lifeless, and some of the neighbors from the surrounding ranches dug a lonely grave in the beautiful valley, and there, nameless, uncoffined and unwept, the poor victim :

> "Life's fitful fever over,
> Sleeps well."

The passer-by may even now notice the solitary grave, where he lies, marked as it still is by the upheaved earth, on the left side of the road as he goes down the valley, about a mile on the Virginia side of the Cold Spring Ranch.

All along the route the ranchmen knew the Road Agents, but the certainty of instant death in case they revealed what they knew enforced their silence, even when they were really desirous of giving information or warning.

Nicholas Tbalt had sold a span of mules to his employers, Butschy & Clark, who paid him the money. Taking the gold with him, he went to Dempsey's Ranch to bring up the animals. Not returning for some time, they concluded that he had run away with the mules, and were greatly grieved that a person they had trusted so implicitly should deceive them. They were, however, mistaken. Faithful to his trust, he had gone for the mules, and met his death from the hand of George Ives, who shot him, robbed him of his money, and stole his mules. Ives first accused Long John of the deed; but he was innocent of it, as was also Hilderman, who was a petty thief and hider, but neither murderer nor Road Agent. His gastronomic feats at Bannack had procured him the name, the American Pie-Eater. Ives contradicted himself at his execution, stating that Aleck Carter was the murderer; but in this he wronged his own soul. His was the bloody hand that committed the crime. Long John said, on his examination at the trial, that he did not see the shots fired, but that he saw Nicholas coming with the mules, and George Ives going to meet him; that Ives rode up shortly after with the mules, and said that the Dutchman would never trouble anybody again.

The body of the slaughtered young man lay frozen, stiff and stark, among the sage brush, whither it had been dragged, unseen of man; but the eye of Omniscience rested on the blood-stained corpse, and the fiat of the Eternal Judge ordered the wild bird of the mountains to point out the spot, and, by a miracle, to reveal the crime. It was the finger of God that indicated the scene of the assassination, and it was His will stirring in the hearts of the honest and indignant gazers on the ghastly remains of Tbalt that organized the party which, though not then formally enrolled as a Vigilance Committee, was the nucleus and embryo or the order—the germ from which sprang that goodly tree, under the shadow of whose wide-spreading branches the citizens of Montana can lie down and sleep in peace.

Nicholas Tbalt was brought into Nevada on a wagon, after being missing for ten days. William Herren came to Virginia and informed Tom Baume, who at once went down to where the body lay. The head had been pierced by a ball, which had entered just over the left eye. On searching the clothes of the victim, he found in his pocket a knife which he had lent him in Washington Gulch, Colorado, two years before, in presence of J. X. Beidler and William Clark.

The marks of a small lariat were on the dead man's wrists and neck. He had been dragged through the brush, while living, after being shot, and when found lay on his face, his right arm bent across his chest and his left grasping the willows above him.

William Palmer was coming across the Stinkingwater Valley, near the scene of the murder, ahead of his wagon, with his shot-gun on his shoulder. A grouse rose in front of him, and he fired. The bird dropped dead on the body of Tbalt. On finding the grouse on the body, he went down to the wakiup, about a quarter of a mile below the scene of the murder, and seeing Long John and George Hilderman there, he told them that there was the body of a dead man below, and asked them if they would help him to put the corpse into his wagon, and that he would take it to town, and see if it could be identified. They said "No; that is nothing. They kill people in Virginia every day, and there's nothing said about it, and we want to have nothing to do with it."

The man lay for half a day exposed in the wagon, after being brought up to Nevada. Elk Morse, William Clark and Tom Baume got a coffin made for him; took him up to the burying ground above Nevada; interred him decently, and, at the foot of the grave, a crotched stick was placed, which is, we believe still standing.

The indignation of the people was excited by the spectacle. The same afternoon, three or four of the citizens raised twenty-five men, and left Nevada at 10 P. M. The party subscribed an obligation before starting, binding them to mutual support, etc., and then travelled on, with silence and speed, towards the valley of the Stinkingwater. Calling at a Ranch on their way, they obtained an accession to their numbers, in the person of the man who eventually brought Ives to bay, after he had escaped from the guard who had him in charge. Several men were averse to taking him with them, not believing him to be a fit man for such an errand; but they were greatly mistaken, for he was both honest and reliable, as they afterwards found.

Avoiding the travelled road, the troop rode round by the bluff, so as to keep clear of Demsey's Ranch. About six miles further on, they called at a cabin and got a guide, to pilot them to the rendezvous.

At about half-past three in the morning, they crossed Wisconsin Creek, at a point some seven miles below Dempsey's, and found that it was frozen, but that the ice was not strong enough to carry the weight of man and horse, and they went through one after another, at different points, some of the riders having to get down, in order to help their horses, emergining half drowned on the other side, and continuing their journey, cased in a suit of frozen clothes, which, as one of them observed, "Stuck to them like death to a dead nigger." Even the irrepressible Tom Baumé was obliged to take a sharp nip on his "quid," and to summon all his fortitude to his aid to face the cold of his ice-bound "rig."

The leader called a halt about a mile further on, saying, "Every one light from his horse, hold him by the bridle, and make no noise till day break." Thus they stood motionless for an hour and a half. At the first peep of day the word was given, "Boys, mount your horses, and not a word pass, until we are in sight of the wakiup." They had not travelled far when a dog barked. Instantly they put spurs to their horses, and breaking to the right and left, formed the "surround," every man reining up with his shot-gun bearing on the wakiup. The leader jumped from his horse, and seeing eight or ten men sleeping on the ground in front of the structure, all wrapped up in blankets, sang out, "The first man that raises will get a quart of buckshot in him, before he can say Jack Robinson." It was too dark to see who they were, so he went on to the wakiup, leaving his horse in charge of one of the party, half of whom had dismounted and the others held the horses. "Is Long John here?" he asked. "Yes," said that longitudinal individual. "Come out here; I want you." "Well," said he, "I guess I know what you want me for." "Probably you do; but hurry up; we have got no time to lose." "Well, said John, "Wait till I get my moccasins on, won't you?" "Be quick about it then," observed his captor. Immediately after he came out of the wakiup, and they waited about half an hour before it was light enough to see distinctly. The captain took four of his men and Long John, and walked to the place where the murder had been committed, leaving the remainder of the troop in charge of the other men. They went up to the spot, and there Long John was charged with the murder. Palmer showed the position in which the body was found. He said, "I did not do it, boy's." He was told that his blood would be held answerable for that of Nicholas Tbalt; for that, if he had not killed him, he knew well who had done it, and had refused to help to put his body into a wagon. "Long John," said one of the men, handling his pistol as he spoke, "You had better prepare for another world." The leader stepped between and said, "This won't do; if there is anything to be done, let us all be together." Long John was taken aside by three of the men, and sat down. They looked up, and there, in the faint light—about a quarter of a mile off—stood Black Bess, the mule bought by X. Beidler in Washington Gulch. Pointing to the animal, they said, "John, whose mule is that?" "That's the mule that Nick rode down here," he answered. "You know whose mule that is, John. Things look dark. You had better be thinking of something else now." The mule was sent for, and brought before him, and he was asked where the other two mules were. He said he did not know. He was told

that he had better look out for another world, for that he
was played out in this. He said, "I did not commit that
crime. If you give me a chance, I'll clear myself." "John,"
said the leader, "You never can do it; for you knew of a
man lying dead for nine days, close to your house, and never reported his murder; and you deserve hanging for that.
Why didn't you come to Virginia and tell the people?" He
replied that he was afraid and dared not do it. "Afraid of
what?" asked the captain. "Afraid of the men round here."
"Who are they?" "I dare not 'tell who they are. There's
one of them round here." "Where?" "There's one of them
here at the wakiup, that killed Nick." "Who is he?"
"George Ives." "Is he down at the wakiup?" "Yes."
"You men stand here and keep watch over John, and I'll
go down." Saying this he walked to the camp.

On arriving at the wakiup, he paused, and picking out the
man answering to the description of George Ives, he asked
him, "Is your name George Ives?" "Yes," said that worthy.
"I want you," was the laconic reply. "What do you want
me for?" was the natural query. "To go to Virginia
City," was the direct but unpleasing rejoinder. "All right,"
said George, "I expect I have to go." He was at once giv-
en in charge of the guard.

So innocent were some of the troop, that they had adopted the "Perfect gentleman" hypothesis, and laid down their
arms in anger, at the arrest of this murderous villain. A
little experience prevent any similar exhibition of such a
weakness, in the future.

Two of the party went over to Tex, who was engaged in
the highly necessary operation of changing his shirt. "I
believe we shall want you too," said one of them; Tex denu-
ded himself of his under garment, and throwing it towards
Tom Baume, exclaimed, "There's my old shirt and plenty of
graybacks. You'd better arrest them too." He was politely informed that he himself, but neither the shirt nor its
population, was the object of this "unconstitutional restraint," and was asked if the pistols lying on the ground
were his, which he admitted, and was thereupon told that
they were wanted, also, and that he must consider himself
"under arrest"—a technical, yet simple, formula adopted by

mountaineers, to assure the individual addressed that his brains will, without further warning, be blown out, if he should attempt to make a "break." Tex dressed himself and awaited further developments.

There appeared to be a belief on the part of both Tex and Ives that they should get off; but when they saw the party with Long John, they appeared cast down, and said no more.

The other men who were lying round the wakiup, when the scouting party rode up, were Aleck Carter, Bob Zachary, Whiskey Bill, Johnny Cooper, and two innocent strangers, whose prolonged tenure of life can only be accounted for by the knowledge of the circumstance that they were without money at the time. Of the fact of the connection of the others with the band, the boys were ignorant, and were drinking coffee with them, laying down their guns within the reach of the robbers, on their bed clothes. Had the Road Agents possessed the nerve to make the experiment, they could have blown them to pieces. One of the party, pointing to Aleck Carter, said to the leader, "There's one good man among them, any way. I knew him on the 'other side,' " (west of the Mountains.) The captain's view of the state of things was not altered by this flattering notice. He sang out, in a tone of voice that signified "something's up," "Every man take his gun and keep it." In after expeditions, he had no need to repeat the command. Five men were sent into the wakiup, and the rest stood round it. The result of their search was the capture of seven dragoon and navy revolvers, nine shot-guns and thirteen rifles. These were brought out, and in laying them down, one of them went off close to Tom Baume's head. Leroy Southmayde's pistol—taken from him at the time of the robbery of the coach—was one of the weapons. It was recognized at the trial of Ives, by the number upon it. About half an inch of the muzzle had been broken off, and it had then been fixed up smoothly.

All being now ready, the party started for Dempsey's, and George, who was mounted on his spotted bob-tailed pony, went along with them. He had determined to escape and in order to carry out his design, he expressed a wish to try the speed of his horse against the others, and challenged several to race with him. This was foolishly permitted, and, but for the accidental frustration of his design to procure a remount of unsurpassed speed, a score of names might have been added to the long list of his murdered victims.

At Dempsey's Ranch there was a bridge in course of construction, and two of the men riding ahead, saw George Hilderman, standing on the center, at work. He was asked if his name was George Hilderman, and replied "Yes," whereupon he was informed that he was wanted to go up to Virginia City. He inquired whether they had any papers for him, and being told that they had not any, he declared that he would not leave the spot; but the leader coming up, told him to go "Without any foolishness," in a manner that satisfied him of the inutility of resistence, and he prepared to accompany them; but not as a volunteer, by any means. He said he had no horse. Tom Baume offered him a mule. Then he had no saddle. The same kind friend found one, and he had to ride with them. His final effort was couched in the form of a declaration that the beast would not go. A stick was lying on the ground, and he received an instruction, as the conventions word it, either to "whip and ride," or "walk and drive." This practically speaking, reconciled him to the breach of the provisions of Magna Charta and the Bill of Rights involved in his arrest, and he jogged along, if not comfortably, yet, at all events, in peace.

In the meantime, the arch villain in custody of the main body was playing his ROLE with much skill and with complete success. He declared his entire innocence of the awful crime with which he was charged, and rather insinuated than expressed his wish that he might be taken to Virginia, where his friends were, and that he might be tried by civil authorities, (Plummer to empannel the jury,) and incidentally remarked that he should not like to be tried at Nevada, for that he once killed a dog there, which had scared his horse, and for that reason, they had prejudices against him, which might work him serious injury in the event of his trial at that place.

There is no doubt that the seeming alacrity with which

he apparently yielded to the persuasions of his captors, threw them off their guard, and he was permitted to ride unarmed, but otherwise unrestrained, along with the escort.

So large a troop of horsemen never yet rode together, mounted on fleet cayuses, on the magnificent natural roads of Montana, without yielding to the temptation presented to try the comparative merits of their horses, and our company of partizan police were no exception to this rule. Scrub races were the order of the day, until, in one of them, Geo. Ives, who was the winner, attracted the attention of the whole party, by continuing his race at the top of his horse's speed; but not until he was at least ten rods ahead of the foremost rider, did the guard (?) realize the fact that the bird had flown from the open cage. Twenty-four pairs of spurs were driven home, into the flanks of twenty-four horses, and with a clatter of hoofs never since equalled on that road, except when the deluded cavalry of Virginia rode down the valley : ·

"To see the savage fray ;"

or at the reception given to the Hon. J. M. Ashley and party—they swept on like a headlong rout.

For awhile, the fugitive gained gradually, but surely, on his pursuers, heading for Daley's Ranch, where his own fleet and favorite mare was standing bridled and saddled, ready for his use, (so quickly did intelligence fly in those days.) Fortune, however, declared against the robber. He was too hotly pursued to be able to avail himself of the chance. His pursuers seeing a fresh horse from Virginia and a mule standing there, leaped on their backs and continued the chase. Ives turned his horses' head towards the mountains round Bivens' Gulch, and across the plain, in that race for life, straining every nerve, flew the representatives of crime and justice. Three miles more had been passed, when the robber found that his horses' strength was failing, and every stride diminishing. The steeds of Wilson and Burtchey were in no better condition; but the use of arms might now decide the race, and springing from his horse, he dashed down a friendly ravine, whose rocky and boulder strewn sides might offer some refuge from his relentless foes. Quick as thought, the saddles of his pursuers were empty, and the trial of speed was now to be continued on foot. On arriving at the edge of the ravine, Ives was not visible ; but it was evident that he must be concealed within a short distance. Burtchey quickly "surrounded" the spot, and sure enough, there was Ives crouching behind a rock. Drawing a bead on him, Burtchey commanded him to come forth, and with a light and careless laugh he obeyed. The wily Bohemian was far to astute, however, to be thus overreached, and befor Ives could get near enough to master his gun, a stern order to "stand fast," destroyed his last hope, and he remained motionless until assistance arrived, in the person of Wilson.

Two hours had elapsed between the time of the escape and the recapture and return of the prisoner. A proposition was made to the captain to raise a pole and hang him there, but this was negatived. After gaily chatting with the boys, and treating them, the word was given to "Mount," and in the centre of a hollow square, Ives began to realize his desperate situation.

Tidings of the capture flew fast and far. Through every nook and dell of the inhabited parts of the Territory, wildly and widely spread the news. Johnny Gibbons, who afterwards made such sly and rapid tracks for Utah, haunted with visions of vigilance committees, joined the party before they reached the canyon at Alder Creek, and accompanied them to Nevada. At that time he was a part owner of the Cottonwood Ranch, (Dempsey's,) and kept the band well informed of all persons who passed with large sums of money.

The sun had sunk behind the hills when the detachment reached Nevada, on the evening of the 18th of December, and a discussion arose upon the question whether they should bring Ives to Virginia, or detain him for the night at Nevada. The "conservatives" and "radicals" had a long argument developing an "irrepressible conflict;" but the radicals, on a vote, carried their point—rejecting Johnny Gibbon's suffrage on the ground of mixed blood. It was thereupon determined to keep Ives at Nevada until morning, and then to determine the place of trial.

The prisoners were separated and chained. A strong

guard was posted inside and outside of the house, and the night came and went without developing anything remarkable. But all that weary night, a "solitary horseman might have been seen" galloping along the road at topmost speed, with frequent relays of horses, on his way to Bannack City. This was Lieut. George Lane alias Club-Foot, who was sent with news of the high-handed outrage that was being perpetrated in defiance of law, and with no regard whatever to the constituted authorities. He was also instructed to suggest that Plummer should come forthwith to Nevada; demand the culprit for the civil authorities, enforce that demand by what is as fitly called HOCUS POCUS as HABEAS CORPUS, and see that he had a fair (?) trial.

As soon as it was determined that Ives should remain at Nevada, Gibbons dashed up the street to Virginia, meeting a lawyer or two on the way—

"Where the carrion is, there will the vultures," etc.

At the California Exchange, Gibbons found Messrs. Smith and Ritchie, and a consultation between client, attorney and PROCH EIN AMI, resulted in Lane's mission to Bannack, as one piece of strategy that faintly promised the hoped for rewards. All of Ives' friends were notified to be at Nevada early the next morning.

The forenoon of the 19th saw the still swelling tide of miners, merchants and artizans wending their way to Nevada, and all the morning was spent in private examinations of the prisoners, and private consultations as to the best method of trial. Friends of the accused were found in all classes of society; many of them were assiduously at work to create a sentiment in his favor, while a large multitude were there, suspicious that the right man had been caught; and resolved, if such should prove to be the case, that no loop-hole of escape should be found for him, in any technical form of the law.

Although on the eve of "Forefathers' Day," there was in the atmosphere the mildness and the serenity of October. There was no snow, and but little ice along the edges of sluggish streams; but the Sun, bright and genial, warmed the clear air, and even thawed out the congealed mud in the middle of the streets. Little boys were at play in the streets, and fifteen hundred men stood in them, impatient for action, but waiting without a murmur, in order that everything might be done decently and in order.

Messrs. Smith, Richie, Thurmond and Colonel Wood were Ives' lawyers, with whom was associated Mr. Alex. Davis, then a comparative stranger in Montana.

Col. W. F. Sanders, at that time residing at Bannack City, but temporarily sojourning at Virginia, was sent for to conduct the prosecution, and Hon. Charles S. Bagg was appointed his colleague, at the request of Judge Wilson, Mr. Bagg being a miner, and, then, little known.

In settling upon the mode of trial, much difference of opinion was developed; but the miners finally determined that it should be held in presence of the whole body of citizens, and reserved to themselves the ultimate decision of all questions; but lest something should escape their attention, and injustice thereby be done to the public, or to the prisoner, a delegation composed of twelve men from each district (Nevada and Junction) was appointed to hear the proof, and to act as an advisory jury. W. H. Patton, of Nevada, and W. Y. Pemberton, of Virginia, were appointed amanuenses. An attempt to get on the jury twelve men from Virginia was defeated, and late in the afternoon, the trial began and continued till nightfall. The three prisoners, George Ives, George Hilderman and Long John (John Franck) were chained with the lightest logging chain that could be found—this was wound round their legs, and the links were secured with padlocks.

In introducing testimony for the people, on the morning of the 21st, the miners informed all concerned that the trial must close at three P. M. The announcement was received with great satisfaction.

It is unnecessary to describe the trial, or to recapitulate the evidence. Suffice it to say that two alibis, based on the testimony of George Brown and honest Whiskey Joe, failed altogether. Among the lawyers, there was, doubtless, the usual amount of brow-beating and technical insolence, intermingled with displays of eloquence and learning; but not the rhetoric of Blair, the learning of Coke, the metaphysics of Alexander, the wit of Jerrold, or the odor of Oberlin, could dull the perceptions of those hardy Mountaineers, or mislead them from the stern and righteous purpose of all this labor, which was to secure immunity to the persons and property of the community, and to guarantee a like protection to those who should cast their lot in Montana in time to come.

The evidence was not confined to the charge of murder; but showed, also, that Ives had been acting in the character of a robber, as well as that of a murderer; and it may well be doubted whether he would have been convicted at all, if developments damaging to the reputations and dangerous to the existence of some of his friends had not been made during the trial, on which they absented themselves mysteriously, and have never been seen since. There was an instinctive and unerring conviction that the worst man in the community was on trial; but it was hard work, after all the proof and all this feeling, to convict him.

Prepossessing in his appearance; brave, beyond a doubt; affable in his manners; jolly and free among his comrades, and with thousands of dollars at his command; bad and good men alike working upon the feeling of the community, when they could not disturb its judgment—it seemed, at times, that all the labor was to end in disastrous failure.

The crowd which gathered around that fire in front of the Court, is vividly before our eyes. We see the wagon containing the Judge, and an advocate pleading with all his earnestness and eloquence for the dauntless robber, on whose unmoved features no shade of despondency can be traced by the fitful glare of the blazing wood, which lights up, at the same time, the stern and impassive features of the guard, who, in every kind of habiliments, stand in various attitudes, in a circle surrounding the scene of Justice. The attentive faces and compressed lips of the Jurors show their sense of the vast responsibility that rests upon them, and of their firm resolve to do their duty. Ever and anon a brighter flash than ordinary reveals the expectant crowd of miners, thoughtfully and steadily gazing on the scene, and listening intently to the trial. Beyond this close phalanx, fretting and shifting around its outer edge, sways with quick and uncertain motion, the wavering line of desperadoes and sympathizers with the criminal; their haggard, wild and alarmed countenances showing too plainly that they tremble at the issue which is, when decided to drive them in exhile from Montana, or to proclaim them as associate criminals, whose fate could neither be delayed nor dubious. A sight like this will ne'er be seen again in Montana. It was the crisis of the fate of the Territory. Nor was the position of prosecutor, guard, juror, or Judge, one that any but a brave and law-abiding citizen would chose, or even except. Marked for slaughter by desperadoes, these men staked their lives for the welfare of society. A mortal strife between Colonel Sanders and one of the opposing lawyers was only prevented by the prompt action of wise men, who corraled the combatants on their way to fight. The hero of that hour of trial was avowedly W. F. Sanders. Not a desperado present but would have felt honored by becoming his murderer, and yet, fearless as a lion, he stood there confronting and defying the malice of his armed adversaries. The citizens of Montana, many of them his bitter political opponents, recollect his actions with gratitude and kindly feeling. Charles S. Bagg is also remembered as having been at his post when the storm blew loudest.

The argument of the case having terminated, the issue was, in the first place, left to the decision of the twenty-four who had been selected for that purpose, and they thereupon retired to consult.

Judge Byam, who shouldered the responsibility of the whole proceeding, will never be forgotten by those in whose behalf he courted certain, deadly peril, and probable death.

The Jury were absent, deliberating on their verdict, but little less than half an hour, and on their return, twenty-three made a report that Ives was proven guilty; but one member—Henry Spivey—declined to give in any finding, for unknown reasons.

The crisis of the affair had now arrived. A motion was made, "That the report of the committee be received, and it discharged from further consideration of that case," which Mr. Thurmond opposed; but upon explanation, deferred pressing his objections until the motion should be made to adopt the report, and to accept the verdict of the Commit-

tee as the judgment of the people there assembled; and thus
the first formal motion passed without opposition.

Before this, some of the crowd were clamerous for an ad-
journment, and now Ives' friends renewed the attempt; but
it met with signal failure.

Another motion, "That the assembly adopt as their verdict the report of the Committee," was made, and called
forth the irrepressible and indefatigable Thurmond and Col.
J. M. Wood; but it carried, there being probably not more
than one hundred votes against it.

Here it was supposed by many that the proceedings
would end for the present, and that the Court would adjourn until the morrow, as it was already dark.  Col. Sanders, however, mounted the wagon, and, having recited that
Ives had been declared a murderer and a robber by the people there assembled, moved, "That George Ives be forthwith
hung by the neck until he is dead"—a bold and business-
like movement which excited feeble opposition, was carried
before the defendant seemed to realize the situation; but
a friend or two and some old acquaintances having gained
admission to the circle within which Ives was guarded, to
bid him farewell, awakened him to a sense of the condition
in which he was placed, and culprit and counsel sought to
defer the execution.  Some of his ardent counsel shed tears,
of which lachrymose effusions it is well to say no more than
that they were copious.  The vision of a long and scaly
creature, inhabiting the Nile, rises before us in connection
with this acqueous sympathy for an assassin.  Quite a number of his old chums were, as Petroleum V. Nasby says:
"Weeping profoosly."  Then came moving efforts to have
the matter postponed until the coming morning, Ives giving
assurances, upon his HONOR, that no attempt at rescue or
escape would be made; but already, Davis and Hereford
were seeking a favorable spot for the execution.

Our Legislative Assembly seem to have forgotten that
Mr. A. B. Davis had any of these arduous labors to perform
but none who were present will ever forget the fearless activity which he displayed all through those trials.  A differently constituted body may yet sit in Montana, and vote
him his five hundred dollars.

The appeals made by Ives and Thurmond for a delay of the execution, were such as human weakness cannot well resist. It is most painful to be compelled to deny even a day's brief space, during which the criminal may write to mother and sister, and receive for himself such religious consolation as the most hardened desire, under such circumstances; but that body of men had come there deeply moved by repeated murders and robberies, and meant "business." The history of former trials was there more freshly and more deeply impressed upon the minds of men than it is now, and the result of indecision was before their eyes. The most touching appeal from Ives, as he held the hand of Col. Sanders, lost its force when met by the witheringly sarcastic request of one of the crowd, "Ask him how long a time he gave the Dutchman." Letters were dictated by him and written by Thurmond. His will was made, in which the lawyers and his chums in iniquity were about equally remembered, to the entire exclusion of his mother and sisters, in Wisconsin. Whether or not it was a time for tears, it was assuredly a time of tears; but neither weakness nor remorse moistened the eyes of Ives. He seemed neither haughty nor yet subdued; in fact, he was exactly imperturbable. From a place not more than ten yards from where he sat during the trial, he was led to execution.

The prisoner had repeatedly declared that he would never "Die in his boots," and he asked the sergeant of the guard for a pair of moccasins, which were given to him; but after a while, he seemed to be chilled, and requested that his boots might again be put on. Thus, George Ives "Died in his boots."

During the whole trial, the doubting, trembling, desperate friends of Ives exhausted human ingenuity to devise methods for his escape, trying intimidation, weak appeals to sympathy, and ever and anon exhibiting their abiding faith in "Nice, sharp quillets of the law." All the time, the roughs awaited with a suspense of hourly increasing painfulness, the arrival of their boasted chief, who had so long and so successfully sustained the three inimical characters of friend of their clan, friend of the people, and guardian of the laws.

Not more anxiously did the Great Captain at Waterloo, sigh for "Night or Blucher,'' than did they for Plummer. But, relying upon him, they deferred all other expedients; and when the dreaded end came, as come it must, they felt that the tide in the affairs of villains had not been taken at its flood, and, not without a struggle, they yielded to the inevitable logic of events, and because they could not help it they gave their loved companion to the gallows.

Up to the very hour at which he was hanged, they were confident of Plummer's arrival in time to save him. But events were transpiring throughout the Territory which produced intense excitement, and rumor on her thousand wings was ubiquitious in her journeying on absurd errands.

Before Lane reached Bannack news of Ives' arrest had reached there, with the further story that the men of Alder Gulch were wild with excitement, and ungovernable from passion; that a Vigilance Committee had been formed; a number of the best citizens hanged, and that from three hundred to five hundred men were on their way to Bannack City to hang Plummer, Ray, Stinson, George Chrisman, A. J. McDonald and others. This last "bulletin from the front" was probably the offspring of Plummer's brain. It is also likely that Lane and perhaps, Ray and Stinson, helped in the hatching of the story. Suffice it to say that Plummer told it often, shedding crocodile tears that such horrible designs existed in the minds of any, as the death of his, as yet, unrobbed friends, Chrisman, McDonald and Pitt.

His was a most unctious sorrow, intended at that crisis, to be seen of men in Bannack, and quite a number of the good citizens clubbed together to defend each other from the contemplated assault, the precise hour for which Plummers' detectives had learned, and all night long many kept watch and ward to give the attacking party a warm reception.

There is no doubt that Plummer believed that such a body of men were on their way to Bannack City, after him, Ray, Stinson and company. The coupling of the other names with theirs was his own work, and was an excellent tribute paid in a backhanded way, to their integrity and high standing in the community.

"Conscience doth make cowards of us all."
and Lane found Plummer anxious to look after his own
safety, rather than that of George Ives.

The rumors carried day by day from the trial, to the
band in different parts of the Territory, were surprising in
their exactness, and in the celerity with which they were
carried; but they were changed in each community, by
those most interested; into forms best suited to subserve the
purposes of the robbers; and, in this way, did they beguile
into sympathy with them and their misfortunes, many fair,
honest men.

Ives' trial for murder, though not the first in the Territory, differed from any that had preceded it.

Before this memorable day, citizens, in the presence of a
well disciplined and numerous band of desperadoes, had
spoken of their atrocities with bated breath; and witnesses
upon their trial had testified in whispering humbleness.
Prosecuting lawyers, too, had, in their arguments, often startled the public with such novel propositions as, "Now, gentlemen, you have heard the witnesses, and it is for you to
say whether the defendant is or is not guilty; if he is guilty,
you should say so; but if not, you ought to acquit him. I
leave this with you, to whom it rightfully belongs." But
the counsel for the defense were, at least, guiltless of uttering these last platitudes; for a vigorous defense hurt no one
and won hosts of friends—of a CERTAIN KIND. But on Ives'
trial, there was given forth no uncertain sound. Robbery
and honesty locked horns for the mastery, each struggling
for empire; and each stood by his banner until the contest
ended—fully convinced of the importance of victory. Judge
Byam remained by the prisoner from the time judgment
was given, and gave all the necessary directions for carrying
it into effect. Robert Hereford was the executive officer.

An unfinished house, having only the side-walls up, was
chosen as the best place, near at hand, for carrying into
effect the sentence of death. The preparations, though entirely sufficient, were both simple and brief. The butt of a
forty-foot pole was planted inside the house, at the foot of
one of the walls, and the stick leaned over a cross beam.
Near the point, was tied the fatal cord, with the open noose

dangling fearfully at its lower end. A large goods box was the platform. The night had closed in, with a bright, full moon, and around that altar of Vengeance, the stern and resolute faces of the guard were visible, under all circumstances of light and shade conceivable. Unmistakable determination was expressed in every line of their bronzed and weather-beaten countenances.

George Ives was led to the scaffold in fifty-eight minutes from the time that his doom was fixed. A perfect Bable of voices saluted the movement. Every roof was covered, and cries of "Hang him!" "Don't hang him!" "Banish him!" "I'll shoot!" "—— their murdering souls!" "Let's hang Long John!" were heard all around. The revolvers could be seen flashing in the moonlight. The guard stood like a rock. They had heard the muttered threats of a rescue from the crowd, and with grim firmness—the characteristic of the miners when they mean "business"—they stood ready to beat them back. Woe to the mob that should surge against that living bulwark. They would have fallen as grass before the scythe.

As the prisoner stepped on to the fatal platform, the noise ceased, and the stillness became painful. The rope was adjusted, and the usual request was made as to whether he had anything to say. With a firm voice he replied, "I am innocent of THIS crime; Aleck Carter killed the Dutchman."

The strong emphasis on the word "this" convinced all around, that he meant his words to convey the impression that he was guilty of other crimes. Up to this moment he had always accused Long John of the murder.

Ives expressed a wish to see Long John, and the crowd of sympathizers yelled in approbation; but the request was denied, for an attempt at a rescue was expected.

All being ready, the word was given to the guard, "Men do your duty." The click of the locks rang sharply, and the pieces flashed in the moonlight, as they came to the "Aim;" the box flew from under the murderer's feet, with a crash, and George Ives swung in the night breeze, facing the pale moon that lighted up the scene of retributive justice.

As the vengeful click! click! of the locks sounded their note of deadly warning to the intended rescuers, the crowd stampeded in wild affright, rolling over one another in heaps, shrieking and howling with terror.

When the drop fell, the Judge, who was standing close beside Ives, called out, "His neck is broken; he is dead." This announcement, and the certainty of its truth—for the prisoner never moved a limb—convinced the few resolute desperadoes who knew not fear, that the case was hopeless, and they retired with grinding teeth, and with muttered curses issuing from their lips.

It is astonishing what a wonderful effect is produced upon an angry mob by the magic sound referred to. Hostile demonstrations are succeeded by a mad panic; rescuers turn their undivided attention to their own corporal salvation; eyes that gleamed with anger, roll wildly with terror; the desire for slaughter gives way to the fear of death, and courage hands the craven fear his scepter of command. When a double-barrelled shot-gun is pointed at a traveller by a desperado, the feeling is equally intense; but its development is different. The organ of "acquisitiveness" is dormant; "combativeness" and "destructiveness" are inert; "caution" calls "benevolence" to do its duty; a very large lump rises into the way-farer's throat; cold chills follow the downward course of the spine, and the value of money, as compared with that of bodily safety, instantly reaches the minimum point. Verily, "All that a man hath will he give for his life." We have often smiled at the fiery indignation of the great untried, when listening to their account of what they would have done, if a couple of Road Agents ordered them to throw up their hands; but they failed to do anything towards convincing us that they would not have sent valor to the rear at the first onset, and appeared as the very living and breathing impersonations of discretion. We felt certain that were they "loaded to the guards" with the gold dust, they would come out of the scrape as poor as Lazarus, and as mild and insinuating in demeanor as a Boston mamma with six marriageable daughters.

At last the deed was done. The law abiding among the citizens breathed more freely and all felt that the worst man in the community was dead—that the neck of crime was broken, and that the reign of terror was ended.

The body of Ives was left hanging for an hour. At the expiration of this period of time, it was cut down, carried into a wheel-barrow shop, and laid out on a work bench. A guard was then placed over it till morning, when the friends of the murderer had him decently interred. He lies in his narrow bed, near his victim—the murdered Tbalt—to await his final doom, when they shall stand face to face at the grand tribunal, where every man shall be rewarded according to his deeds.

George Ives, though so renowned a desperado, was by no means an ancient practitioner in his profession. In 1857–58, he worked as a miner, honestly and hard, in California, and though wild and reckless, was not accused of dishonesty. His first great venture in the line of robbery was the stealing of Government mules, near Walla Walla. He was employed as herder, and used to report that certain of his charge were dead, every time that a storm occurred. The officer of the Post believed the story, and inquired no further. In this way George ran off quite a decent herd, with the aid of his friends. In Elk City, he startled his old employer, in the mines of California by riding his horse into his saloon, and when that gentlemen seized the bridle, he drew his revolver, and would certainly have killed him, but fortunately he caught sight of the face of his intended victim in time, and returning his pistol he apologized for his conduct. When leaving the city, he wished to present his splendid gray mare to his friend, who had for old acquaintance sake supplied his wants; but the present, though often pressed upon this gentleman, was as often refused; for no protestations of Ives' could convince him that the beautiful animal was fairly his property. He said that he earned it honestly by mining. His own account of the stealing of the Government mules, which we have given above, was enough to settle that question definitively. It was from the "other side" that Ives came over to Montana—then a part of Idaho—and entered with full purpose upon the career which ended at Nevada, so fatally and shamefully for himself, and so happily for the people of this Territory.

A short biographical sketch of Ives and of the rest of the gang will appear at the end of the present work.

The trial of Hilderman was a short matter. He was defended by Judge (?) H. P. A. Smith. He had not been known as a very bad man; but was a weak and somewhat imbecile old fellow, reasonably honest in a strictly honest community, but easily led to hide the small treasure, keep the small secrets and do the dirty work of strong-minded, self-willed, desperate men, whether willingly or through fear the trial did not absolutely determine. The testimony of Dr. Glick, showed him to be rather cowardly and a great eater. He had known of the murder of Tbalt for some weeks, and had never divulged it. He was also cognizant of the murder near Cold Spring Ranch, and was sheltering and hiding the perpetrators. He had concealed the stolen mules too; but, in view of the disclosures made by many, after Ives was hung, and the power of the gang being broken, such disclosures did not so much damage men in the estimation of the honest mountaineer. Medical men were taken to wounded robbers to dress their wounds; they were told in what affray they were received, and the penalty of repeating the story to outsiders was sometimes told; but to others it was described by a silence more expressive than words. Other parties, too, came into possession of the knowledge of the tragedies enacted by them, from their own lips, and under circumstances rendering silence a seeming necessity. To be necessarily the repository of their dreadful secrets was no enviable position. Their espionage upon every word uttered by the unfortunate accessory was offensive, and it was not a consolatory thought that, at any moment, his life might pay the penalty of any revelation he should make; and a person placed in such a "fix" was to some extent a hostage for the reticence of all who knew the same secret.

If stronger minded men than Hilderman could pretend to be, had kept secrets at the bidding of the Road Agents, and that too in the populous places, where there were surely some to defend them—it was argued that a weak minded man, away from all neighbors, where by day and by night he could have been killed and hidden from all human eyes, with perfect impunity—had some apology for obeying their behests.

Mr. Smith's defense of Hilderman was rather creditable

to him. There was none of the braggadocio common to such occasions, and the people feeling that they had caught and executed a chief of the gang—felt kindly disposed towards the old man.

Hilderman was banished from Montana, and was allowed ten days time for the purpose of settling his affairs and leaving. When he arrived at Bannack City, Plummer told him not to go; but the old man took counsel of his fears, and comparing the agile and effeminate form of Plummer with those of the earnest mountaineers at Nevada, he concluded that he would rather bet on them than on Plummer, and being furnished by the latter with a poney and provisions, he left Montana forever.

When found guilty and recommended to mercy, he dropped on his knees, exclaiming, "My God, is it so?"

At the close of his trial, he made a statement, wherein he confirmed nearly all Long John had said of Ives.

Thus passed one of the crisis which have arisen in this new community. The result demonstrated that when the good and law abiding were banded together and all put forth their united strength, they were to strong for the lawlessness which was manifested when Ives was hung.

It has generally been supposed and believed, that Plummer was not present at the trial of Ives, or at his execution. We are bound, however, to state that Mr. Clinton, who kept a saloon in Nevada at the time, positively asserts that he was in the room when Plummer took a drink there, a few minutes before the roughs made their rush at the fall of Ives, and that he went out and headed the mob in the effort which the determination of the guard rendered unsuccessful.

Long John having turned States' evidence was set free, and we believe that he still remains in the Territory.

One thing was conclusively shown to all who witnessed the trial of Ives. If every Road Agent cost as much labor, time and money for his conviction, the efforts of the citizens would have, practically, failed altogether. Some shorter, surer, and at least equally equitable method of procedure was to be found. The necessity for this, and the trial of its efficiency when it was adopted, form the ground-work of this history.

# CHAPTER XV.

### THE FORMATION OF THE VIGILANCE COMMITTEE.

The land wants such
As dare with vigor execute the laws,
Her festered members must be lanced and tented ;
He's a bad surgeon that for pity spares
The part corrupted till the gangrene spread,
And all the body perish   he that is merciful
Unto the bad is cruel to the good.

Those who have merely read the account given in these pages of the execution of Ives, can never fully appreciate the intense popular excitement that prevailed throughout the Territory during the stormy and critical period, or the imminent peril to which the principal actors in the drama were exposed.  As an instance of the desire for murder and revenge that animated the roughs, it may be stated that Col. Sanders was quietly reading in John Creighton's store, on the night of the execution of Ives, when a desperado named Harvey Meade—the individual who planned the seizure of a Federal vessel at San Francisco—walked into the room, with his revolver stuck into the band of his pants, in front, and walking up to the Colonel, commenced abusing him and called him a ———, etc.  Col. Sanders not having been constituted with a view to the exhibition of fear, continued his reading, quietly slipping his hand out of his pocket in which lay a Derringer, and dropping it into his coat pocket, cocked his revolver as a preparative for a little shooting. Raising his eyes to the intruder, he observed, "Harvey, I should feel hurt if some men said this ; but from such a dog as you, it is not worth noticing."  A Doctor who was present laid his hand on a pick handle, and an "affair" seemed imminent; but John Creighton quietly walked up to the man and said, "You have to get out of here—quick !"  All men fond of shooting, otherwise than in self-defense, unless they take their victim at an advantage, never care to push matters to extremeties, and Meade quietly walked off—foiled. He admitted, afterwards, to Sanders, that he had intended to kill him; but he professed a recent and not unaccountable change of sentiment.

All the prominent friends of justice were dogged, threatened and watched by the roughs; but their day was passing away, and the dawn of a better state of things was even then enlivening the gloom which overspread society like a funeral pall.

Two sister towns—Virginia and Nevada—claim the honor of taking the first steps towards the formation of a Vigilance Committee. The truth is, that five men in Virginia and one in Nevada commenced simultaneously to take the initiative in the matter. Two days had not elapsed before their efforts were united, and when once a beginning had been made, the ramifications of the league of safety and order extended, in a week or two, all over the Territory, and, on the 14th day of January, 1864, the COUP DE GRACE was given to the power of the band by the execution of five of the chief villains, in Virginia City. The details of the rapid and masterly operations which occupied the few weeks immediately succeeding the execution of Ives, will appear in the following chapters.

The reasons why the organizations was so generally approved and so numerously and powerfully supported, were such as appealed to the simpathies of all men, who had anything to lose, or who thought their lives safer under the dominion of a body which, upon the whole, it must be admitted, has from the first acted with a wisdom, a justice and a vigor never surpassed on this continent, and rarely, if ever, equalled. Merchants, miners, mechanics and professional men, alike, joined in the movement, until, within an incredibly short space of time, the Road Agents and their friends were in a state of constant and well grounded fear, lest any remarks they might make confidentially to an acquaintance might be addressed to one who was a member of the much dreaded Committee.

The inhabitants of Virginia had especial cause to seek for vengeance upon the head of the blood-thirsty marauders who had, in addition to the atrocities previously recounted, planned and arranged the murder and robbery of as popular a man as ever struck the Territory—one whose praise was in all men's mouths, and who had left them, in the previous Fall, with the intention of returning to solicit their suffrages, as well as those of the people of Lewiston and Western Idaho, as their Delegate to Congress. His address, in the form of a circular, is still to be seen in the possossion of a citizen of Nevada.

Lloyd Magruder, to whom the above remarks have special reference, was a merchant of Lewiston, Idaho. He combined in his character so many good and even noble qualities, that he was one of the most generally esteemed and beloved men in the Territory, and no single act of villainy ever committed in the far West was more deeply felt, or provoked a stronger desire for retaliation upon the heads of the guilty perpetrators, than the murder and robbery of himself and party, on their journey homeward.

In the summer of 1863, this unfortunate gentleman came to Virginia, with a large pack-train, laden with merchandise, selected with great judgment for the use of miners, and on his arrival, he opened a store on Wallace street, still pointed out as his place of business by "old inhabitants."

Having disposed of his goods, from the sale of which he had realized about $14,000, he made arrangements for his return to Lewiston, by way of Elk City. This becoming known, Plummer and his band held a council in Alder Gulch, and determined on the robbery and murder of Magruder, C. Allen, Horace and Robert Chalmers, and a Mr. Phillips, from the neighborhood of Marysville. During the debate, it was proposed that Steve Marshland should go on the expedition, along with Jem Romaine, Doc Howard, Billy Page and a man called indifferently Bob or Bill Lowry. The programme included the murder of the five victims, and Marshland said he did not wish to go, as he could make money without murder. He was, he said, "On the rob, but not on the kill." Cyrus Skinner, laughed at his notion, and observed that "Dead men tell no tales." It was accordingly decided that the four miscreants above named should join the party and kill them all at some convenient place on the road. Accordingly they offered their services to Magruder, who gave them a free passage and a fat mule each to ride, telling them that they could turn their lean horses along with the band.

Charley Allen, it seems had strong misgivings about the character of the ruffians, and told Magruder that the men would not harm him, (Allen,) as they were under obligations to him; but they would, likely enough try to rob Magruder. His caution was ineffectual, and Mr. McK Denneé, we believe, fixed up for the trip the gold belonging to Magruder.

It is a melancholy fact that information of the intention of the murderers had reached the ears of more than one citizen; but such was the terror of the Road Agents that they dared not tell any of the party.

Having reached the mountain beyond Clearwater River, on their homeward journey, the stock was let out to graze on the slope, and Magruder, in company with Bill Lowry, went up to watch it. Seizing his opportunity, the ruffian murdered Magruder, and his confederates assassinated the four remaining in camp, while asleep. Romain said to Phillips, when shooting him down, "You ———, I told you not to come." The villains having possessed themselves of the treasure, rolled up the bodies, baggage and arms, and threw them over a precipice. They then went on to Lewiston, avoiding Elk City on their route, where the first intimation of foul play was given by the sight of Magruder's mule, saddle, leggings, etc., in the possession of the robbers. Hill Beechey, the Deputy Marshal at Lewiston, and owner of the Luna House, noticed the cantinas filled with gold, and suspected something wrong, when they left by the coach for San Francisco. A man named Goodrich recognized Page, when he came to ranch the animals with him.

The murderers were closely muffled and tried to avoid notice. Beechey followed them right through to California, and there arrested them on the charge of murdering and robbing Magruder and his party. He found that they had changed their names at many places. Every possible obstacle was interposed that the forms of law allowed; but the gallant man fought through it all, and brought them back, on requisition of the Governor of Idaho, to Lewiston. Page turned State's evidence, and the men, who were closely guarded by Beechy all the time, in his own house, were convicted after a fair trial, and hanged. Romaine, who had been a barber, and afterwards a bar-keeper, was a desperate villain. At the gallows, he said that there was a note in his pocket, which he did not wish to be read until he was dead. On opening it, it was found to contain a most beastly and insolent defiance of the citizens of Lewiston. Before he was swung off, he bade them "Launch their ——— old boat," for it was "only a mud-scow, any way."

A reconnoisance of the ground, in Spring, discovered a few bones, some buttons from Magruder's coat, some fire-arms, etc. The coyotes had been too busy to leave much.

Page, at the last advices, was still living at the Luna House. Even a short walk from home produces, it is said, a feeling of tightness about the throat, only to be relieved by going back in a hurry. He was not one of the original plotters, but not being troubled with too much sense, he was frightened into being a tool.

The perpetration of this horrible outrage excited immense indignation, and helped effectually to pave the way for the advent of the Vigilantes. Reviewing the long and bloody lists of crimes against person and property, which last included several wholesale attempts at plunder of the stores in Virginia and Bannack, it was felt that the question was narrowed down to "Kill or be killed." "Self preservation is the first law of nature," and the mountaineers took the right side. We have to thank them for the peace and order which exist to-day in what are, by the concurrent testimony of all travellers, the best regulated new mining camps in the West.

The record of every villain who comes to Montana arrives with him, or before him; but no notice is taken of his previous conduct. If, however, he tries his hand at his trade in this region, he is sure of the reward of his crimes, and that on short notice; at least such is the popular belief.

## CHAPTER XVI.

### THE DEER LODGE SCOUT.

The sleuth hound is upon the trail.
Nor speed nor force shall aught avail.

Almost instantly after the commencement of the organization of the Vigilance Committee, it was determined that
the pursuit of the miscreants—the comrades of Ives—should
be commenced and maintained with a relentless earnestness,
which should know no abatement until the last blood-stained
marauder had paid the penalty of his crimes by death on
the gallows ; or had escaped the retribution in store for him
by successful flight to other countries. Foremost on the
list stood Aleck Carter, the accomplice, at any rate, in the
murder of Tbalt.

Twenty-four men were mustered, whose equipments con-
sisted of arms, ammunition, and the most modest provision
for the wants of the inner man that could possibly be conceived sufficient. The volunteers formed a motley group;
but there were men enough among them of unquestioned
courage, whom no difficulty could deter and no danger
affright. They carried, generally, a pair of revolvers, a
rifle or shot-gun, blankets and some ROPE. Spirits were for-
bidden to be used.

The leader of the party was one of those cool, undaunted
and hardy men, whose career has been marked by honesty
of purpose and fearlessness concerning the consequences of
any just or lawful action, and to whom society owes a large
debt for perils and hardships voluntarily undergone for the
salvation of the lives and property of the people of this Territory, and for the punishment of wrong doers.

On the 23d of December, 1863, the party, on horse and
mule-back, went by way of the Stinkingwater, on to the Big
Hole, and over the Divide in the main range. The weather
was very cold, and there was a large quantity of snow upon

the ground. Fires could not be lighted when wanted at
night, for fear of attracting attention. The men leaving
their horses under a guard, lay down in their blankets on the
snow—the wisest of them IN it. As the riders had been
taken up from work, without time for the needful prepara-
tion in the clothing department, they were but ill prepared
to face the stormy and chilling blast, which swept over the
hills and valleys crossed by them on this arduous journey.
Few know the hardships they encountered. The smiles of
an approving conscience are about all, in the shape of a reward, that is likely to be received by any of them for their
brilliant services.

On Deer Lodge Creek, the foremost horsemen met Red,
(Erastus Yager ;) but, being unacquainted with him, all the
troop allowed him to pass the different sections of the command as they successively encountered him on the road.
Red, who was now acting as letter carrier of the band, was
a light and wiry built man, about five feet five inches high,
with red hair and red whiskers. On inquiry, he told the
officers that he had ascertained that Aleck Carter, Whiskey
Bill (Graves,) Bill Bunton, and others of the gang were
lying at Cottonwood, drunk; that they had attended a ball
given there, and that they had been kicked out of it. A defiance accompanied this account, couched in the following
euphonious and elegant strain : "The Stinkingwater ——
may come; we're good for thirty of them." This most in-
genious fable was concocted to put the scouts off their guard
and to gain time for the fugitives. The same night the last
of the party had crossed the Divide, and camped on Deer
Lodge Creek—seventeen miles above Cottonwood, at John
Smith's Ranch.

At this place the men lay over till three o'clock in the
afternoon, and then saddling up, rode into Cottonwood to
take their prey by surprise. Arriving there, they put up
their horses, took their supper, and discovered, both by
actual search and the information of chosen parties, that the
birds had flown, no one knew whither; though a camp fire
far away among the hills was distinctly visible, and evoked
from some of the old mountaineers a hearty malediction, for

their experienced eyes had quickly marked the blaze, and they knew that it meant—escape.

On inquiry, it was found that a message had arrived from Virginia, warning the robbers to "Get up and dust, and lie low for black ducks." A letter was found afterwards delivered to Tom Reilly and he showed it to the Vigilantes. It was written by Brown, and Red carried it over, travelling with such rapidity as to kill two horses.

Vexed and dispirited, the men started on their return by way of Beaverhead Rock. Here they camped in the willows, without shelter or fire, except such as could be made with the green twigs. On Saturday, it turned cold and snowed heavily, getting worse and worse, until on Sunday the cold became fearful, and the sufferings of the party were intense. Some of the stock stampeded to the canyon, out of the way of the storm. The rest were tied fast in the willows. It was no small job to hunt up the runaways.

At the Station near the camp, the party met two friends, who told them that Red was at Rattlesnake, and volunteers were called for to go in pursuit of him. A small party of picked men started, and followed up this rapid horseman, enduring on their march great hardships from the inclemency of the weather. The open air restaurant of the main body was not furnished with any great variety in the line of provisions. Sometimes the meal was bread and bacon—minus the bacon; and sometimes bacon and bread—minus the bread. Some choice spirits did venture, occasionally, on a song or a jest; but these jocular demonstrations were soon checked by the freezing of the beard and moustaches. The disconsolate troopers slapped their arms to keep themselves warm; but it was a melancholy and empty embrace, giving about as much warmth and comfort as the dream begotten memory of one loved and lost.

In the meantime the little party of volunteers wended their toilsome way through the deep snow, and riding till midnight, journeyed as far as Stone's Ranch. Here they obtained remounts from the stock of Oliver & Co., and then resumed their cheerless progress towards Rattlesnake, at which place they arrived, after a ride of twenty miles. One of the party afterwards confidentially observed that "It was cold enough to freeze the tail of a brass monkey," which observation had at least the merit of being highly metaphorical and forcibly descriptive.

The ranch was surrounded and one of the party entering, discovered Buck Stinson, Ned Ray, and a prisoner, whom, as Deputy Sheriffs (?), they had arrested. Stinson, who had a strong antipathy towards the gentleman who entered first, appeared, revolver in hand; but finding that the "drop" was falling the wrong way, restrained his bellicose propensities, and, eventually, not being able to fathom the whole purpose of his unwelcome visitor, who amused him with a fictitious charge of horse stealing against Red, set free his prisoner, on his promise to go and surrender himself up, and, much moved in spirit, made his horse do all he knew about galloping, on his road to Bannack City.

The party, who knew where to look for their man, rode straight for a wakiup a few hundred yards up the creek, and surrounded it instantly, their guns bearing on it. One of them dismounted, and throwing open the flap, entered with the amicable remark, "It's a mighty cold night; won't you let a fellow warm himself?" Seeing Red, he further remarked, "You're the man I'm seeking; come along with me."

The captive seemed perfectly unconcerned; he was as iron-nerved a man as ever leveled a shot-gun at a coach. He was told that he was wanted to go to Virginia; but he asked no questions. From his arrest till the moment of his execution, he seemed possessed with the idea that it was his fate to be taken then and there, and that his doom was irrevocably sealed. They stayed all night at the ranch, Red going to bed with his boots on, "all standing," as the sailors say.

The next morning they got up their horses, Red—unarmed, of course—riding his own. One trooper rode beside him all the time; the remainder were strung out on the road, like beads. While loping along, the mule of the leader stumbled and rolled over, making two or three complete somersaults before he fetched up; but the snow was so deep that no great harm was done, and a merry laugh enlivend the spirits of the party. The escort safely brought their prisoner to Dempsey's Ranch, where they overtook and rejoined the main body that had camped there for two days, awaiting their coming. The demeanor of the captive was cheerful, and he was quite a pleasant companion. He asked no questions relative to his arrest, and rode from Rattlesnake to Dempsey's as if on a pleasure excursion, behaving in a most courteous and gentlemanly manner all the time, and this, be it remembered, with the conviction that his hours were numbered, and that the blood of his victims was about to be avenged. After reporting the capture of Yager, the party took supper and went to bed.

There was in the house, at this time, the secretary—Brown—who had written the letter warning his comrades to fly from Cottonwood, and which missive Red had carried only too speedily. He acted as bar-keeper and man of all work at the ranch. This individual was the very opposite of Yager, in all respects. He was cowardly and had never worked on the road, but had always done his best to assist the gang, as an outsider, with information calculated to ensure the stoppage of treasure laden victims. He was in the habit of committing minor felonies and of appearing as a straw witness, when needed.

After breakfast, the two men were confronted. Brown—who had evidently suspected danger, ever since the arrival of the Vigilantes—was greatly terrified. Red was as cool and collected as a veteran on parade. Previously to the two robbers being confronted, the captain took Red into a private room, and told him that he was suspected of being in league with a band of Road Agents and murderers. He denied the charge altogether. The captain then asked him why—if he was innocent—should he take such pains to inform the gang that the Vigilantes were after them? He said that he came along to Bob's, on his way to Deer Lodge, and that Brown asked him to carry a letter along to Aleck Carter and some friends, and that having said he would do so, he did it. The two men were called up to the bar, and there Red again admitted the carrying of the letter which Brown had written. Brown having told his examiners that he had seen one of their number before, and knew him, was asked what sort of a man was the one he referred to. He replied that he took him to be a half-breed. The Vigilanter, who had come in, heard the description, and ejaculating, "You ———, you call de Dutchmans half-breeds, you do, do you ?" made at him with his fists; but his comrades almost choking with laughter, held him off the horrified Brown, whose fear of instantaneous immolation at the hands of the fiery Dutchlander had blanched his cheek to a turnip color.

The captain then told Brown that he must consider himself under arrest, and remain there. He was taken out to Dempsey's house and kept there till the examination and trial of Red was concluded. Being then brought in and questioned, he testified that Red came to Dempsey's and said that he was going to see the boys, and asked if Brown had anything to tell them, offering to carry the letter. He said that Red was Ives' cousin, (this was untrue;) that he wrote the letter advising them to leave, for that the Vigilantes were after them.

At Smith's Ranch it had been found, on comparing notes, that the statements of Red to the successive portions of the command that he had met while crossing the Divide, were not consistent, and, as frequently happens, the attempt at deception had served only to bring out the truth. Red was incontrovertibly proven to be one of the gang. The confession of each man conclusively established the guilt of the other.

A guard was placed over the two men and the remainder of the Vigilantes went out on the bridge and took a vote upon the question as to whether the men should be executed or liberated. The captain said, "All those in favor of hanging those two men step to the right side of the road, and those who are for letting them go, stand on the left." Before taking the vote he had observed to them, "Now, boys, you have heard all about this matter, and I want you to vote according to your consciences. If you think they ought to suffer punishment, say so. If you think they ought to go free vote for it." The question having been put, the entire command stepped over to the right side, and the doom of the robbers was sealed.

One of the party, who had been particularly lip-courageous now began to weaken, and discovered that he should lose $2,000 if he did not go home at once. Persuasion only paled

his lips, and he started off. The click! click! click! of four
guns, however, so far directed his fears into an even more
personal channel, that he concluded to stay.

The culprits were informed that they should be taken to
Virginia, and were given in charge to a trustworthy and
gallant man, with a detachment of seven, selected from the
whole troop. This escort reached Lorraine's in two hours.
The rest of the men arrived at sun down. The prisoners
were given up, and the leader of the little party, who had
not slept for four or five nights, lay down to snatch a brief,
but welcome repose. About 10 P. M., he was awakened, and
the significant, "We want you," announced "business."

The tone and manner of the summons at once dispelled
even his profound and sorely needed slumber. He rose without further parley and went from the parlor to the bar-room
where Red and Brown were lying in a corner, asleep. Red
got up at the sound of his footsteps, and said, "You have
treated me like a gentlemen, and I know I am going to die
—I am going to be hanged." "Indeed," said his quondom
custodian, "that's pretty rough." In spite of a sense of duty,
he felt what he said deeply. "It is pretty rough," continued
Yager, "but I merited this, years ago. What I want to say
is that I know all about the gang, and there are men in it
that deserve this more than I do; but I should die happy if
I could see them hanged, or know that it would be done. I
don't say this to get off. I don't want to get off." He was
told that it would be better if he should give all the information in his possession, if only for the sake of his kind.
Times had been very hard, and "you know, Red," said the
Vigilanter, "that men have been shot down in broad day
light—not for money, or even for hatred, but for LUCK, and
it must be put a stop to."

To this he assented, and the captain being called, all that
had passed was stated to him. He said that the prisoner
had better begin at once, and his words should be taken
down. Red began by informing them that Plummer was
chief of the band; Bill Bunton second in command and stool
pigeon; Sam Bunton, roadster, (sent away for being a drunk-
ard;) Cyrus Skinner, roadster, fence and spy. At Virginia
City, George Ives, Steven Marshland, Dutch John (Wag-

ner,) Aleck Carter, Whiskey Bill, (Graves,) were roadsters; Geo. Shears was a roadster and horse-thief; Johnny Cooper and Buck Stinson were also roadsters; Ned Ray was council-room keeper at Bannack City; Mexican Frank and Bob Zachary were also roadsters; Frank Parish was roadster and horse-thief; Boon Helm and Club-Foot George were roadsters; Haze Lyons and Bill Hunter were roadsters and telegraph men; George Lowry, Billy Page, Doc Howard, Jem Romaine, Billy Terwilliger and Gad Moore were roadsters. The pass-word was "Innocent." They wore a necktie fastened with a "sailor's knot," and shaved down to moustache and chin whiskers. He admitted that he was one of the gang; but denied—as they invariably did—that he was a murderer. He also stated that Brown—his fellow captive—acted in the capacity before mentioned.

He spoke of Bill Bunton with a fierce animosity quite unlike his usual suave and courteous manner. To him, he said, he owed his present miserable position. He it was that first seduced him to commit crime, at Lewiston. He gave the particulars of the robberies of the coaches and of many other crimes, naming the perpetrators. As these details have been already supplied or will appear in the course of the narrative, they are omitted, in order to avoid a useless repetition.

After serious reflection, it had been decided that the two culprits should be executed forthwith, and the dread preparations were immediately made for carrying out the resolution.

The trial of George Ives had demonstrated most unquestionably that no amount of certified guilt was sufficient to enlist popular sympathy exclusively on the side of justice, or to render the just man other than a mark for vengeance. The majority of men sympathize, in spite of the voice of reason, with the murderers instead of the victims; a course of conduct which appears to us inexplicable, though we know it to be common. Every fibre of our frame vibrates with anger and disgust when we meet a ruffian, a murderer or a marauder. Mawkish sentimentalism we abhor. The thought of murdered victims, dishonored females, plundered wayfarers, burning houses, and the rest of the sad evidences of vil-

lainy, completely excludes mercy from our view. Honor,
truth and the sacrifice of self to considerations of justice and
the good of mankind—these claim, we had almost said our
adoration; but for the low, brutal, cruel, lazy, ignorant, insolent, sensual and blasphemous miscreants that infest the
frontiers, we entertain but one sentiment—aversion—deep,
strong, and unchangeable. For such cases, the rope is the
only prescription that avails as a remedy. But, though such
feelings must be excited in the minds of good citizens, when
brought face to face with such monsters as Stinson, Helm,
Gallagher, Ives, Skinner, or Graves, the calm courage and
penitent conduct of Erastus Yager have the opposite effect,
and the loss of the goodly vessel thus wrecked forever, must
inspire sorrow, though it may not and ought not to disarm
justice.

Brief were the preparations needed. A lantarn and some
stools were brought from the house, and the party, crossing
the creek behind Lorraine's Ranch, made for the trees that
still bear the marks of the axe which trimmed off the superfluous branches. On the road to the gallows, Red was cool,
calm and collected. Brown sobbed and cried for mercy, and
prayed God to take care of his wife and family in Minnesota. He was married to a squaw. Red, overhearing him,
said, sadly but firmly, "Brown, if you had thought of this
three years ago, you would not be here now, or give these
boys this trouble."

After arriving at the fatal trees, they were pinioned and
stepped on to the stools, which had been placed one on the
other to form a drop. Brown and the man who was adjus-
ting the rope, tottered and fell into the snow; but recovering himself quickly, the Vigilanter said quietly, "Brown we
must do better than that."

Brown's last words were, "God Almighty save my soul."
The frail platform flew from under him, and his life passed
away almost with the twang of the rope.

Red saw his comrade drop; but no sign of trepidation
was visible. His voice was as calm and quite as if he had
been conversing with old friends. He said he knew that
he should be followed and hanged when he met the party
on the Divide. He wished that they would chain him and

carry him along to where the rest were, that he might see them punished. Just before he was launched into eternity, he asked to shake hands with them all, which having done, he begged of the man who had escorted him to Lorraine's, that he would follow and punish the rest. The answer was given in these words, "Red we will do it, if there's any such thing in the book." The pledge was kept.

His last words were, "Good bye, boys; God bless you. You are on a good undertaking." The frail footing on which he stood gave way, and this dauntless and yet guilty criminal died without a struggle. It was pitiful to see one whom nature intended for a hero, dying—and that justly— like a dog.

A lable was pinioned to his back bearing the legend:

"RED! ROAD AGENT AND MESSENGER."

The inscription on the paper fastened on to Brown's clothes was:

"BROWN! CORRESPONDING SECRETARY."

The fatal trees still smile as they don the green livery of Spring, or wave joyfully in the Summer breeze; but when the chill blast of winter moans over the snow-clad prairie, the wind sighing and creaking through the swaying boughs seems, to the excited listener, to be still laden with the sighs and sounds of that fatal night. FIAT JUSTITIA RUAT CÆLUM.

The bodies were left suspended, and remained so for some days before they were buried. The ministers of justice expected a battle on their arrival at Nevada; but they found the Vigilantes organized in full force, and each man, as he uncocked his gun and dismounted, heaved a deep sigh of relief. THE CRISIS WAS PAST.

---

## CHAPTER XVII.

### DUTCH JOHN (WAGNER.)

"Give me a horse! Bind up my wounds!"—RICHARD III.

The tidings of Ives' execution and the deep and awe-strik-

ing news of the organization of the Vigilantes in the camps
on Alder Gulch, flew like wildfire, exciting wherever they
were received, the most dread apprehension in the minds of
those whose consciences told them that their capture and
their doom were convertible terms.

Among these men was Dutch John (Wagner.) His share
in the robbery of the train, and his wound from the pistol of
Lank Forbes, pressed upon his memory. By a physical reminder, he was prevented from forgetting, even in his sleep,
that danger lurked in every valley, and waited his coming
on every path and track by which he now trusted to escape
from the scene of his crimes. Plummer advised him to
leave the Territory at once, but he offered him no means of
locomotion. This, however, was of small consequence to
Wagner. He knew how to obtain a remount. Taking his
saddle on his back, he started for the Ranch of Barret &
Shineberger, on Horse Prairie where he knew there was a
splendid gray horse—the finest in the country. The possession was the trouble—the title was quite immaterial. A
friend seeing him start from Bannack with the saddle, sent
word to the owners of the gallant gray, who searched for him
without delay, taking care to avoid the willows for fear of
a shot. One of them, after climbing a hill, discovered the
robber sitting among the underwood. The place was surrounded and the capture was made secure.

Short shrift was he allowed. His story was disbelieved,
and his captors went for his personal outfit, if not for his
purse. They lectured him in the severest terms on the de-
pravity which alone rendered horse stealing possible, and
then started him off down the road, minus his saddle and
pistol, but plus an old mule and blanket.

With these locomotive treasures, Dutch John left Horse
Prairie, and took the Salt Lake road. He was accompanied
by an Indian of the Bannack tribe, armed with bow, quiver
and knife. Ben. Peabody was the first who espied them,
He was going to Salt Lake City with a cayuse pack-train,
for goods, and saw the Road Agent and his aboriginal companion at Dry Creek Canyon Ranch, since used by Oliver
& Co., as a station on the road to the metropolis of the
Latter Day Saints.

About two miles below this place, he met Neil Howie, who was coming from the same City of Waters, along with three wagons laden with groceries and flour. A long consultation was the consequence, and a promise was given that the aid of the train men would be given to secure the fugitive from justice. The same pledge was obtained from Neil's own party, and from the owner of a big train further down.

Shortly after, Dutch John and the Indian hove in sight; but this did not mend matters, for the parties "weakened" at once, and left Neil cursing their timidity, but determined that he should not escape. Wagner rode up and asked for some tobacco. He was told that they had none to spare, but that there was a big train (Vivion's) down below, and that he might get some there. During the conversation he looked suspicious and uneasy; but at last went on, parting amicably from them, and attended by his copper colored satellite, whose stolid features betrayed no sign of emotion. Neil felt "bad" but determined that his man should not escape thus easily, he mounted his pony and galloped after him, resolved to seek for help at the big train. He soon came up with the pair, and Neil fancied that Wagner gave some directions to the Indian, for he put his hand to his quiver, as if to see that all was right for action. Dutch John held his rifle ready and looked very suspiciously at Neil. The Indian kept behind, prepared for business.

After the usual salutations of the road, Neil told John that he wanted to borrow a shoeing hammer to prepare his stock for crossing the Divide, and thereupon he noticed a sudden, joyful expansion in the eyes of Dutch John, and, with a friendly salute they parted company.

It was ticklish work for Neil to ride with his back to Wagner, right under the muzzle of his rifle, but the brave fellow went along as if he suspected nothing, and never drew rein till he came to the train. The owner—who had often lectured, in strong language, on the proper way to deal with (ABSENT) Road Agents—backed square down, notwithstanding all the arguments of Neil, some of which were of a nature to bring out any concealed courage that his friend possessed. Wagner rode up, and glancing quickly and sharply at the two conversing, asked for tobacco, and received for reply—not the coveted weed—but an inquiry as to whether he had any money; which not being the case, he was informed that there was none for him. Neil immediately told the trader to let the man have what he wanted, on his credit. Wagner appeared deeply grateful for this act of kindness, and having received the article, set forward on his journey. Neil made one more solemn appeal not to "let a murderer and Road Agent escape;" but the train-owner said nothing.

In an instant he determined to arrest the robber at all risks, single handed. He called out, "Hallo, Cap; hold on a minute." Wagner wheeled his horse half round, and Neil fixing his eyes upon him, walked straight towards him, with empty hands. His trusty revolver hung at his belt, however, and those who have seen the machine-like regularity and instantaneous motion with which Howie draws and cocks a revolver, as well as the rapidity and accuracy of his shooting, well know that few men, if any, have odds against him in an encounter with fire-arms. Still not one man in a thousand would, at a range of thirty yards, walk up to a renowned desperado, sitting quietly with a loaded rifle in his hand, and well knowing the errand of his pursuer. Yet this gallant fellow never faltered. At twenty yards their eyes met, and the gleam of anger, hate and desperation that shot from those of Dutch John, spoke volumes. He also slewed round his rifle, with the barrel in his left hand, and his right on the small of the stock. Howie looked him straight down, and, as Wagner made the motion with his rifle, his hand mechanically sought his belt. No further demonstration being made, he continued his progress, which he had never checked, till be arrived within a few steps of the Dutchman, and there red perplexity, hesitation, anger and despair in his fiery glances. Those resolved and unwavering grey eyes seemed to fascinate Wagner. Five paces separated them, and the twitchery of Wagner's muscles showed that it was touch and go, sink or swim. Four!—three!—two!—one! Fire flashes from John's eyes. He is awake at last; but it is too late. Neil has passed the butt of his rifle, and in tones quiet but carrying authority with them, he broke the silence with the order, "Give me your gun and

get off your mule." A start and a shudder ran through
Wagner's frame, like an electric shock. He complied, however, and expressed his willingness to go with Neil, both
then and several times afterwards, adding that he need fear
nothing from him.

Let it not be imagined that this man was any ordinary
felon, or one easy to capture. He stood upwards of six feet
high; was well and most powerfully built, being immensely
strong, active, and both coolly and ferociously brave. His
swarthy visage, determined looking jaw and high cheek-
bones were topped off with a pair of dark eyes, whose deadly glare few could face without shrinking. Added to this,
he knew his fate if he were caught. He traveled with a rifle
in his hand, a heart of stone, a will of iron, and the frame of
a Hercules. It might also be said, with a rope round his
neck. For cool daring and self-reliant courage, the single
handed capture of Dutch John, by Neil Howie, has always
appeared to our judgment as the most remarkable action of
this campaign against crime. Had he met him and taken
him alone, it would have been a most heroic venture of life
for the public good; but to see scores of able-bodied and
well armed men refusing even to assist in the deed, and then
—single handed—to perform the service from which they
shrank from bodily fear of the consequences, was an action
at once noble and self-denying in the highest sense. Physical courage we share with the brutes; moral courage is the
stature of manhood.

The prisoner being brought to the camp-fire, was told of the
nature the of charge against him, and informed that if he were
the man, a bullet wound would be found on his shoulder. On
removing his shirt, the fatal mark was there. He attempted
to account for it by saying, that when sleeping in camp his
clothes caught fire, and his pistol went off accidentally; but
neither did the direction of the wound justify such an assumption, nor was the caused alleged received as other than
proof of attempted deceit, and, consequently, of guilt. The
pistol could not have been discharged by the fire, without the
wearer being fatally burned, long before the explosion took
place, as was proved by actual experiment at the fire, by
putting a cap on a stick, and holding it right in the blaze.

The ocular demonstration of the prisoner's guilt afforded by the discovery of the bullet wound, was conclusive. Neil left him in charge, at the big train, and rode back to see who would help him to escort the prisoner to Bannack. Volunteering was out of fashion just then, and there was no draft. Neil started back and brought his prisoner to Dry Creek, where there were fifty or sixty men; but still no one seemed to care to have anything to do with it. The fear of the roughs was so strong that every one seemed to consider it an almost certain sacrifice of life to be caught with one of their number in charge.

One of Neil Howie's friends came to him and told him that he knew just the very man he wanted, and that he was camped with a train near at hand. This was good news, for he had made up his mind to go with his prisoner alone. John Fetherstun at once volunteered to accompany him, Road Agents, horse thieves and roughs in general to the contrary notwithstanding. The two brave men here formed that strong personal attachment that has ever since united them in a community of sentiment, hardship, danger and mutual devotion.

The prisoner, who continually protested his innocence of any crime, and his resolution to give them no trouble, seemed quite resigned, and rode with them unfettered and unrestrained, to all appearance. He was frequently fifty yards ahead of them; but they were better mounted than he was, and carried both pistols and shot-guns, while he was unarmed. His amiable manners won upon them, and they could not but feel a sort of attachment to him—villain and murderer though they knew him to be. The following incidents, however, put a finale to this dangerous sympathy, and brought them back to stern reality.

The weather being intensely cold, the party halted every ten or fifteen miles, lit a fire, and thawed out. On one of these occasions, Fetherstun, who usually held the horses while Neil raised a blaze, in order to make things more comfortable, stepped back about ten paces and set down the guns. He had no sooner returned than Wagner "made a break" for them, and but for the rapid pursuit of Howie and Fetherstun—whose line of march cut him off from the coveted artillery—it is likely that this chapter would never have been written, and that the two friends would have met a bloody death at the hands of Dutch John.

One night, as they were sleeping in the open air, at Red Rock, fatigue so overcame the watcher that he snored, in token of having transferred the duties of his position to

Watchful stars that sentinel the skies.

This suited Wagner exactly. Thinking that the man off guard was surely wrapt in slumber, he raised up and took a survey of the position, his dark eyes flashing with a stern joy. As he made the first decisive movement towards the accomplishment of his object, Neil, who sleeps with an eye open at such times, but who, on this particular occasion, had both his visual organs on duty—suddenly looked up. The light faded from Wagner's eyes, and uttering some trite remark about the cold, he lay down again. After a lapse of about an hour or two, he thought that, at last, all was right, and again, but even, more demonstratively, he rose. Neil sat up, and said quietly, "John, if you do that again, I'll kill you." A glance of despair deepened the gloom on his swarthy brow, and, with profuse and incoherent apologies, he again lay down to rest.

On another occasion, they saw the smoke of a camp-fire, in close proximity to the road, and Wagner, who noticed it even sooner than his guards, at once thought that it must be the expected rescuers. He sang and whistled loudly, as long as they were within hearing, and then became sad, silent and downcast.

"Fortune favors the brave," and they arrived without interruption, at Horse Prairie. Neil Howie rode on to Bannack to reconnoitre—promising to be back, if there was any danger, in an hour or so. After waiting for two hours, Fetherstun resumed his journey and brought in his man, whom he took to his hotel. Neil met Plummer and told him of the capture of Wagner. The Sheriff (? ) demanded the prisoner; but Neil refused to give him up. He soon found out that he would be backed by the "powers behind the throne." There were no Vigilantes organized in Bannack at that time; but four of the Committee, good men and true, were, even then, in the saddle, on their road from

Virginia, with full powers to act in the matter. Neil knew very well that a guard under the orders of Plummer, and composed of Buck Stinson, Ned Ray and their fellows, would not be likely to shoot at a prisoner escaping. Dueth John proposed to Fetherstun that they should take a walk, which they did. Fetherstun did not know Bannack; but they sauntered down to Durand's saloon. After a few minutes had elapsed, Neil came in, and told Fetherstun to keep a close wacth on Wagner, stating that he would be back in a few minutes. The two sat down and played a couple of games at "seven-up." Buck Stinson and Ned Ray came in and shook hands with the prisoner. Four or five more also walked up, and one of them went through that ceremony very warmly, looking very sharply at Fetherstun. After taking a drink, he wheeled round, and, saying that he was on a drunk, stepped out of doors. This raised Fetherstun's suspicions, which were apparently confirmed when he came in after a few minutes, with a party of nine. The whole crowd numbered fifteen. Fetherstun made sure that they were Road Agents; for one of them stepped up to John and said, "You are my prisoner." John looked at his quondam jailor, and laughed. Fetherstun understood him to mean :"You had me once, and now I have you." He stepped into the corner and drew his revolver, fully expecting death, but determined to put as much daylight through them as the size of his lead would allow. He permitted them to take away the prisoner, seeing that resistance was absurd, and went off to his hotel, where he found four or five men, and being told, in answer to his question, that Neil had not been there, he said, "Gentlemen, I don't know whom I am addressing; but if you're the right kind of men, I want you to follow me; I am afraid the Road Agents have killed Neil Howie; for he left me half an hour ago, to be back in five minutes." They all jumped up, and Fetherstun saw that they were the genuine article. He was taking his shot-gun, when a man put his head in at the door and told him not to be uneasy. The rest seemed satisfied. He asked if he could go too, and was answered "no." He said he would go, anyhow, and started down street, gun in hand. He could not see the man, but walking on, he came to a cabin and descried Dutch John, surrounded by a group of some twenty men. He knocked, but was refused admittance. The party did not know him. It was a mutual mistake. Each thought the other belonged to the class "Road Agent." Fetherstun said Wagner was his prisoner, and that he must have him. They said it was all right; they only wanted to question him. The same mistake occurred with regard to Neil Howie, whom Fetherstun found shortly after, being aided by one of the new captors. He was as hot as calf love at the news, but, like it, he soon cooled, when he saw things in the right light.

The men at once gave up the prisoner to Neil and Fetherstun, who marched him back to the hotel, and, afterwards, to a cabin. Seven or eight parties gathered and questioned him as to all that he knew, exhorting him to confess. He promised to do so, over and over again; but he was merely trying to deceive them and to gain time. The leader in the movement took up a book, observing that he had heard enough and would not be fooled any more. The remainder went on with their interrogations; but at last ceased in despair of eliciting anything like truth, from John.

The literary gentleman closed the book, and approaching Wagner, told him that he was notoriously a highwayman and a murderer, and that he must be hanged; but that if he had any wish as to the precise time for his execution he might as well name it, as it would be granted if at all reasonable. John walked up and down for a while, and then burst into tears, and, lamenting his hard lot, agreed to make his confession, evidently hoping that it might be held to be of sufficient importance to induce them to spare his life. He then gave a long statement, corroborating Red's confession in all important particulars; but he avoided inculpating himself to the last moment, when he confessed his share in the robbery of the train by himself and Steve Marshland. This ended the examination for the night.

It was at this time that the Vigilance Committee was formed in Bannack. A public meeting had been held in Peabody's to discuss the question, and the contemplated organization was evidently looked upon with favor. The most energetic citizen, however, rather threw cold water on the proposition. Seeing Ned Ray and Stinson there present, he wisely thought that that was no place for making such a movement, and held himself in reserve for an opportunity to make an effort, at a fitting time and place, which offered itself in the evening.

At midnight he had lain down to rest, when he was awakened from sleep by a summons to get up, for that men had come from Virginia to see him. He put on his clothes hastily, and found that four trustworthy individuals had arrived, bearing a communication from the Vigilantes of Virginia, which, on inspection, evidently took for granted the fact of their organization, and also assumed that they would be subordinate to the central authority. This latter question was put to the small number of the faithful, and, by a little management, was carried with considerable unanimity of feeling. It was rather a nice point; for the letter contained an order for the execution of Plummer, Stinson and Ray—the first as captain, and the others as members of the Road Agent Band. Four men had comprised those first enrolled as Vigilantes at Bannack.

It was resolved to spend the following day in enlisting members, though no great progress was made after all.

Towards night, the people, generally, became aware that Wagner was a prisoner and a Road Agent. No one would let him into his house. Neil Howie and Fetherstun took him to an empty cabin on Yankee Flat.

---

# CHAPTER XVIII.

### THE ARREST AND EXECUTION OF HENRY PLUMMER, THE ROAD AGENT CHIEF, BUCK STINSON AND NED RAY.

United there that trio died,
By deeds of crime and blood allied.

At dusk, three horses were brought into town, belonging severally and respectively to the three marauders so often mentioned, Plummer, Stinson and Ray. It was truly conjectured that they had determined to leave the country, and it was at once settled that they should be arrested that night. Parties were detailed for the work. Those entrusted with the duty, performed it admirably. Plummer was undressing when taken at his house. His pistol (a self-cocking weapon) was broken and useless. Had he been armed, resistance would have been futile; for he was seized the moment the door was opened in answer to the knocking from without. Stinson was arrested at Toland's, where he was spending the evening. He would willingly have done a little firing, but his captors were too quick for him. Ray was lying on a gaming table, when seized. The three details marched their men to a given point, en route to the gallows. Here a halt was made. The leader of the Vigilantes and some others, who wished to save all unnecessary hard feeling, were sitting in a cabin, designing not to speak to Plummer, with whom they were so well acquainted. A halt was made, however, and, at the door, appeared Plummer. The light was extinguished; when the party moved on, but soon halted. The crisis had come. Seeing that the circumstances were such as admitted of neither vacillation nor delay, the citizen leader, summoning his friends, went up to the party and gave the military command, "Company! forward—march!" This was at once obeyed. A rope taken from a noted functionary's bed had been mislaid and could not be found. A nigger boy was sent off for some of that highly necessary, but unpleasant remedy for crime, and the bearer made such good time that some hundreds of feet of hempen neck-tie were on the ground before the arrival of the party at the gallows. On the road, Plummer heard the voice and recognized the person of the leader. He came to him and begged for his life; but was told, "It is useless for you to beg for your life; that affair is settled and cannot be altered. You are to be hanged. You cannot feel harder about it than I do; but I cannot help it, if I would." Ned Ray, clothed with curses as with a garment, actually tried fighting, but found that he was in the wrong company for such demonstrations; and Buck Stinson made the air ring with the blasphemous and filthy expletives which he used in addressing his captors. Plummer exhausted every argument and plea that his imagination could suggest, in order to induce his captors to spare his life. He begged to be chained own in the meanest cabin; offered to leave the country forever; wanted a jury trial; implored time to settle his affairs; asked to see his sister-in-law, and, falling on his knees, with tears and sighs declared to God that he was too wicked to die. He confessed his numerous murders and crimes, and seemed almost frantic at the prospect of death.

The first rope being thrown over the cross-beam, and the noose being rove, the order was given to "Bring up Ned Ray." This desperado was run up with curses on his lips. Being loosely pinioned, he got his fingers between the rope and his neck, and thus prolonged his misery.

Buck Stinson saw his comrade robber swinging in the death agony, and blubbered out, "There goes poor Ed Ray." Scant mercy had he shown to his numerous victims. By a sudden twist of his head at the moment of his elevation, the knot slipped under his chin, and he was some minutes dying.

The order to "Bring up Plummer" was then passed and repeated; but no one stirred. The leader went over to this PERFECT GENTLEMAN, as his friends called him, and was met by a request to "Give a man time to pray." Well knowing that Plummer relied for a rescue upon other than Divine aid, he said briefly and decidedly, "Certainly; but let him say his prayers up here." Finding all efforts to avoid death were useless, Plummer rose and said no more prayers. Standing under the gallows which he had erected for the execution of Horan, this second Haman slipped off his necktie and threw it over his shoulder to a young friend who had boarded at his house, and who believed him innocent of crime, saying as he tossed it to him, "Here is something to remember me by." In the extremity of his grief, the young man threw himself weeping and wailing, upon the ground. Plummer requested that the men would give him a good drop, which was done, as far as circumstances permitted, by hoisting him up as high as possible, in their arms, and letting him fall suddenly. He died quickly and without much strugle.

It was necessary to seize Ned Ray's hand and by a violent effort to draw his fingers from between the noose and his neck before he died. Probably he was the last to expire, of the guilty trio.

The news of a man's being hanged flies faster than any other intelligence, in a Western country, and several had gathered round the gallows on that fatal Sabbath evening —many of them friends of the Road Agents. The spectators were allowed to come up to a certain point, and were then halted by the guard, who refused permission either to depart or to approach nearer than the "dead line," on pain of their being instantly shot.

The weather was intensely cold; but the party stood for a long time round the bodies of the suspended malefactors, determined that rescue should be impossible.

Loud groans and cries uttered in the vicinity, attracted their attention, and a small squad started in the direction from which the sound proceeded. The detachment soon met Madam Hall, a noted courtezan—the mistress of Ned Ray—who was "Making night hideous" with her doleful wailings. Being at once stopped, she began inquiring for her paramour, and was thus informed of his fate, "Well if you must know, he is hung." A volcanic eruption of oaths and abuse was her reply to this information; but the men were on "short time," and escorted her towards her dwelling without superfluous display of courtesy. Having arrived at the brow of a short descent, at the foot of which stood her cabin, STERN necessity compelled a rapid and final progress in that direction.

Soon after, the party formed and returned to town, leaving the corpses stiffening in the icy blast. The bodies were eventually cut down by the friends of the Road Agents and buried. The "Reign of Terror," in Bannack, was over.

## CHAPTER XIX.

THE EXECUTION OF "THE GREASER" (JOE PIZANTHIA,) AND
DUTCH JOHN, (WAGNER.)

Hope withering fled, and mercy sighed, farewell.—CAMPBELL.

A marked change in the tone of public sentiment was the
consequence of the hanging of the blood-stained criminals
whose deserved fate is recorded in the preceeding chapters.
Men breathed freely; for Plummer and Stinson especially
were dreaded by almost every one. The latter was of the
type of that brutal desperado whose formula of introduction
to a Western bar-room is so well known in the Mountains:
"Whoop! I'm from Pike County, Missouri; I'm ten feet
high; my abode is where lewd women and licentious men
mingle; my parlor is the Rocky Mountains. I smell like a
wolf. I drink water out of a brook, like a horse. Look out
you ———, I'm going to turn loose," etc. A fit mate for
such a God-forgotten outlaw was Stinson, and he, with the
oily and snake-like demon, Plummer, the wily, red-handed,
and politely merciless chief, and the murderer and robber,
Ray, were no more. The Vigilantes organized rapidly.
Public opinion sustained them.

On Monday morning, it was determined to arrest "the
Greaser," Joe Pizanthia, and to see precisely how his record
stood in the Territory. Outside of it, it was known that
he was a desperado, a murderer and a robber; but that
was not the business of the Vigilantes. A party started for
his cabin, which was built in a side-hill. The interior looked
darker than usual, from the bright glare of the surrounding
snow. The summons to come forth being disregarded,
Smith Ball and George Copley entered, contrary to the advice
of their comrades, and instantly received the fire of their
concealed foe. Copley was shot through the breast. Smith
Ball received a bullet in the hip. They both staggered out,
each ejaculating, "I'm shot." Copley was led off by two

friends, and died of his wound. Smith Ball recovered himself, and was able to empty his six-shooter into the body of the assassin, when the latter was dragged forth.

The popular excitement rose nearly to madness. Copley was a much esteemed citizen, and Smith Ball had many friends. It was the instant resolution of all present that the vengeance on the Greaser should be summary and complete.

A party whose military experience was still fresh in their memory, made a rush at the double-quick, for a mountain howitzer, which lay dismounted, where it had been left by the train to which it was attached. Without waiting to place it on the carriage, it was brought by willing hands, to within five rods of the windowless side of the cabin, and some old artillerists, placing it on a box, loaded it with shell, and laid it for the building. By one of those omissions so common during times of excitement, the fuse was left uncut, and, being torn out in its passage through the logs, the missile never exploded, but left a clean breach through the wall, making the chips fly. A second shell was put into the gun, and this time, the fuse was cut, but the range was so short that the explosion took place after it had traversed the house.

Thinking that Pizanthia might have taken refuge in the chimney, the howitzer was pointed for it, and sent a solid shot through it. Meanwhile the military judgment of the leader had been shown by the posting of some riflemen opposite the shot-hole, with instructions to maintain so rapid a fire upon it, that the beleaguered inmate should not be able to use it as a crenelle through which to fire upon the assailants. No response being given to the cannon and small-arms, the attacking party began to think of storming the dwelling.

The leader called for volunteers to follow him. Nevada cast in her lot first, and men from the crowd joined. The half dozen stormers moved steadily, under cover, to the edge of the last building, and then dashed at the house, across the open space. The door had fallen from the effects of the fusilade; but, peeping in, they could see nothing, until a sharp eye noticed the Greaser's boots protruding. Two lifted the door, while Smith Ball drew his revolver and stood ready. The remainder seized the boots.

On lifting the door, Pizanthia was found lying flat, and badly hurt. His revolver was beside him. He was quickly dragged out, Smith Ball paying him for the wound he had received by emptying his revolver into him.

A clothes line was taken down and fastened round his neck; the leader climbed a pole, and the rest holding up the body, he wound the rope round the top of the stick of timber, making a jam hitch. While aloft, fastening all securely, the crowd blazed away upon the murderer swinging beneath his feet. At his request—"Say, boys! stop shooting a minute"—the firing ceased, and he came down "by the run. Over one hundred shots were discharged at the swaying corpse.

A friend—one of the four BANNACK ORIGINALS—touched the leader's arm, and said, "Come and see my bon-fire." Walking down to the cabin, he found that it had been razed to the ground by the maddened people, and was then in a bright glow of flame. A proposition to burn the Mexican was received with a shout of exultation. The body was hauled down and thrown upon the pile, upon which it was burned to ashes so completely that not a trace of a bone could be seen when the fire burned out.

In the morning some women of ill-fame actually panned out the ashes, to see whether the desperado had any gold in his purse. We are glad to say that they were not rewarded for their labors by striking any auriferous deposit.

The popular vengeance had been only partially satisfied, so far as Pizanthia was concerned; and it would be well if those who preach against the old Vigilance Committee would reflect upon the great difference which existed between the prompt and really necessary severity which they exercised and the wild and ungovernable passion which goads the masses of all countries, when roused to deeds of vengeance of a type so fearful, that humanity recoils at the recital. Over and over again, we have heard a man declaring that it was "A ——— shame," to hang some one that he wished to see punished. "———, he ought to be burnt; I would pack brush three miles up a mountain myself." "He ought to be fried in his own grease," etc., and it must not be supposed that such expressions were mere idle bravado.

The men said just what they meant. In cases where criminals convicted of grand larceny have been whipped, it has never yet happened that the punishment has satisfied the crowd. The truth is, that the Vigilance Committee simply punished with death, men unfit to live in any community, and that death was, usually, almost instantaneous, and only momentarily painful. With the exceptions recorded (Stinson and Ray) the drop and the death of the victim seemed simultaneous. In a majority of cases, a few almost imperceptible muscular contortions, not continuing over a few seconds, were all that the keenest observer could detect; whereas, had their punishment been left to outsiders, the penalty would have been cruel and disgusting in the highest degree. What would be thought of the burning of Wagner and panning out his ashes, BY ORDER OF THE VIGILANTES. In every case where men have confessed their crimes to the Vigilantes of Montana, they dreaded the vengeance of their comrades far more than their execution at the hands of the Committee, and clung to them as if they considered them friends.

A remarkable instance of this kind was apparent in the conduct of John Wagner. While in custody at the cabin, on Yankee Flat, the sound of footsteps and suppressed voices was heard, in the night. Fetherstun jumped up, determined to defend himself and his prisoner to the last. Having prepared his arms, he cast a look over his shoulder to see what Dutch John was doing. The Road Agent stood with a double-barrelled gun in his hand, evidently watching for a chance to do battle on behalf of his captor. Fetherstun glanced approvingly at him, and said, "That's right, John, give them ————." John smiled grimly and nodded, the muzzle of his piece following the direction of the sound, and his dark eyes glaring like those of a roused lion. Had he wished, he could have shot Fetherstun in the back, without either difficulty or danger. Probably the assailants heard the ticking of the locks of the pieces, in the still night, and therefore determined not to risk such an attack, which savages of all kinds especially dislike.

The evening after the death of Pizanthia, the newly organized Committee met, and, after some preliminary discussion, a vote was taken as to the fate of Dutch John. The result was that his execution was unanimously adjudged, as the only penalty meeting the merits of the case. He had been a murderer and a highway robber, for years.

One of the number present at the meeting was deputed to convey the intelligence to Wagner; and, accordingly, he went down to his place of confinement and read to him his sentence of death, informing him that he would be hanged in an hour from that time. Wagner was much shocked by the news. He raised himself to his feet and walked with agitated and tremulous steps across the floor, once or twice. He begged hard for life, praying them to cut off his arms and legs, and then to let him go. He said, "You know I could do nothing then." He was informed that his request could not be complied with, and that he must prepare to die.

Finding death to be inevitable, Wagner summoned his fortitude to his aid and showed no more signs of weakness. It was a matter of regret that he could not be saved for his courage, and (outside of his villainous trade) his good behaviour won upon his captors and judges to an extent that they were unwilling to admit, even to themselves. Amiability and bravery could not be taken as excuses for murder and robbery, and so Dutch John had to meet a felon's death and the judgment to come, with but short space for repentence.

He said that he wished to send a letter to his mother, in New York, and inquired whether there was not a Dutchman in the house, who could write in his native language. A man being procured qualified as desired, he communicated his wishes to him and his amanuensis wrote as directed. Wagner's fingers were rolled up in rags and he could not handle the pen without inconvenience and pain. He had not recovered from the frost-bites which had moved the pity of X. Beidler when he met John before his capture, below Red Rock. The epistle being finished, it was read aloud by the scribe; but it did not please Wagner. He pointed out several inaccuracies in the method of carrying out his instructions, both as regarded the manner and the matter of the communication; and at last, unrolling the rags from his fingers, he sat down and wrote the missive himself.

He told his mother that he was condemned to die, and

had but a few minutes to live; that when coming over from the other side, to deal in horses; he had been met by bad men, who had forced him to adopt the line of life that had placed him in his present miserable position; that the crime for which he was sentenced to die was assisting in robbing a wagon, in which affair he had been wounded and taken prisoner, and that his companion had been killed. (This latter assertion he probably believed.) He admitted the justice of his sentence.

The letter, being concluded, was handed to the Vigilantes for transmission to his mother. He then quietly replaced the bandages on his wounded fingers. The style of the composition showed that he was neither terrified nor even disturbed at the thought of the fast approaching and disgraceful end of his guilty life. The statements were positively untrue, in many particulars, and he seemed to write only as a matter of routine duty; though we may hope that his affection for his mother was, at least, genuine.

He was marched from the place of his confinement to an unfinished building, where the bodies of Stinson and Plummer were laid out—the one on the floor and the other on a work bench. Ray's corpse had been handed over to his mistress, at her special request. The doomed man gazed without shrinking on the remains of the malefactors, and asked leave to pray. This was of course, granted, and he knelt down. His lips moved rapidly; but he uttered no word audibly. On rising to his feet, he continued, apparently to pray, looking round, however, upon the assembled Vigilantes all the time. A rope being thrown over a crossbeam, a barrel was placed ready for him to stand upon. While the final preparations were making, the prisoner asked how long it would take him to die, as he had never seen a man hanged. He was told that it would be only a short time. The noose was adjusted; a rope was tied round the head of the barrel and the party took hold. At the word, "All ready," the barrel was instantly jerked from beneath his feet, and he swung in the death agony. His struggles were very powerful, for a short time; so iron a frame could not quit its hold on life as easily as a less muscular organization. After hanging till frozen stiff, the body was cut down and buried decently.

---

# CHAPTER XX.

THE CAPTURE AND EXECUTION OF BOONE HELM, JACK GALLA-
GHER, FRANK PARISH, HAZE LYONS AND CLUB-
FOOT GEORGE (LANE.)

"'Tis joy to see the engineer hoist
With his own petard."—SHAKSPEARE.

The effect of the executions noticed in the foregoing chapters, was both marked and beneficial. There was much to be done, however, to insure anything like lasting peace to the community. Ives, Yager, Brown, Plummer, Stinson, Ray, Pizanthia and Wagner were dead; but the five villains whose names head this chapter, together with Bunton, Zachary, Marshland, Shears, Cooper, Carter, Graves, Hunter and others were still at large, and were supported by many others equally guilty, though less daring and formidable as individuals.

Threats of vengeance had been made, constantly, against the Vigilantes, and a plot to rob several stores in Virginia had nearly matured, when it was discovered and prevented. Every man who had taken part in the pursuit of the criminals whose fate has been recorded, was marked for slaughter by the desperadoes, and nothing remained but to carry out the good work so auspiciously begun, by a vigorous and unhesitating severity, which should know no relaxation until the last blood-stained miscreant that could be captured had met a felon's doom.

On the evening of the 13th of January, 1864, the Executive Committee, in solemn conclave assembled, determined on hanging six of them forthwith. One of the doomed men—Bill Hunter—suspecting danger, managed to crawl away, along a drain-ditch, through the line of pickets that surrounded the town, and made his escape. He was badly frozen by exposure to the cold, and before his capture, was discovered by J. A. Slade, while lying concealed under a bed at a ranch, and told that the Vigilantes were after him, which information caused him to move his quarters to Gallatin valley, where he was caught and executed soon after, as will appear in the course of this narrative.

While the Committee were deliberating in secret, a small party of the men who were at that moment receiving sentence of death, were gathered in an upper room at a gambling house, and engaged in betting at faro. Jack Gallagher suddenly remarked, "While we are here betting, those Vigilante sons of ——— are passing sentence on us." This is considered to be the most remarkable and most truthful saying of his whole life; but he might be excused telling the truth once, as it was entirely accidental.

Express messengers were sent to warn the men of the neighboring towns, in the gulch, and the summons was instantly obeyed.

Morning came—the last on earth that the five desperadoes should ever behold. The first rays of light showed the pickets of the Vigilantes stationed on every eminence and point of vantage round the city. The news flew like lightning through the town. Many a guilty heart quaked with just fear, and many an assassin's lip turned pale and quivered with irrepressible terror. The detachments of Vigilantes, with compressed lips and echoing footfall, marched in from Nevada, Junction, Summit, Pine Grove, Highland and Fairweather, and halted in a body in Main street. Parties were immediately detailed for the capture of the Road Agents, and all succeeded in their mission, except the one which went after Bill Hunter, who had escaped.

Frank Parish was brought in first. He was arrested without trouble, in a store, and seemed not to expect death. He took the executive officer one side, and asked, "What am I arrested for?" He was told, "For being a Road Agent and thief, and accessory to the murders and robberies on the road." At first he pleaded innocent; but at last he confessed his complicity with the gang, and admitted being one of the party that robbed the coach between Bannack and Virginia, and that he was guilty of stealing horses and

stock for them.   He used to butcher stolen cattle, and attend
to the commissariat business.  He gave some directions
about articles of clothing belonging to him, and the settlement of some debts.   Until his confession, it was not known
that he had any share in the robbery of the coach.

Club-Foot George (George Lane) was arrested at Dance
& Stuart's.   He was living there, and working at odd times.
He was perfectly cool and collected, and inquired the reason
of his arrest, as Parish had done previously.   On receiving
the same answer, he appeared surprised, and said, "If you
hang me you will hang an innocent man."   He was told
that the proof was positive, and that if he had any prepara-
tion to make he must do it at once, as his sentence was death.
He appeared penitent and sat down for some time, covering
his face with his hands.   He then asked for a minister, and
one being immediately sent for, he talked and prayed with
him till the procession to the gallows was formed.   In his
pocket-book was found an extract from a western news-
paper, stating that George Lane, the notorious horse-thief,
was Sheriff of Montana.   Lane was a man of iron nerve; he
seemed to think no more of the hanging than a man would of
eating his breakfast.

Boone Helm was brought in next.   He had been arrested
in front of the Virginia Hotel.   Two or three were detailed
for his capture of whom he would entertain no suspicion,
and they played their part, apparently, so carelessly and
well, that he was seized without being able to make any
effort at resistance.   A man at each arm, and one behind,
with a cocked revolver, brought him to the rendezvous.   He
lamented greatly that he "had no show" when taken, as he
said, "They would have had a gay old time taking me, if
I had known what they were after."   His right hand was
in a sling.   He quietly sat down on a bench, and on being
made acquainted with his doom, he declared his entire innocence.   He said, "I am as innocent as the babe unborn; I
never killed any one, or robbed or defrauded any man; I am
willing to swear it on the Bible."   Anxious to see if he was
really so abandoned a villain as to swear this, the book was
handed to him, and he, with the utmost solemnity, repeated
an oath to that effect, invoking most terrific penalties on his

soul, in case he was swearing falsely. He kissed the book most impressively. He then addressed a gentlman, and asked him to go into a private room. Thinking that Boone wanted him to pray with him, he proposed to send for a clergyman; but Boone said, "You'll do." On reaching the inner room, the prisoner said, "Is there no way of getting out of this?" Being told that there was not, and that he must die, he said, "Well, then, I'll tell you, I did kill a man named Shoot, in Missouri, and I got away to the West; and I killed another chap in California. When I was in Oregon I got into jail, and dug my way out with tools that my squaw gave me." Being asked if he would not tell what he knew about the gang, he said, "Ask Jack Gallagher; he knows more than I do." Jack, who was behind a partition, heard him, and burst out into a volley of execrations, saying that it was just such cowardly sons of ——— and traitors that had brought him into that scrape.

Helm was the most hardened, cool and deliberate scoundrel of the whole band, and murder was a mere pastime to him. He killed Mr. Shoot, in Missouri, (as will be afterwards narrated,) and testimony of the most conclusive character, showed that his hands were steeped in blood, both in Idaho and since his coming to the Territory. Finding that all his asseverations and pleas availed him nothing, he said, I have dared death in all its forms, and I do not fear to die." He called repeatedly for whiskey, and had to be reprimanded several times for his unseemly conduct.

The capture of Lyons, though unattended with danger, was affected only by great shrewdness. He had been boarding at the Arbor Resturant, near the "Shades." The party went in. The owner said he was not there, but that they might search if they liked. The search was made, and was ineffectual. He had left in the morning. During the search for Lyons, Jack Gallagher was found, in a gambling room, rolled up in bedding, with his shot-gun and revolver beside him. He was secured too quickly to use his weapons, if, indeed he had had the courage; but his heart failed him, for he knew that his time was come. He was then taken to the place of rendezvous.

In the meantime the other party went after Haze Lyons,

and found that he had crossed the hill, beyond the point overhanging Virginia, and, after making a circuit of three miles through the mountains, he had come back to within a quarter of a mile of the point, from which he started to a miner's cabin, on the west side of the gulch, above town. At the double-quick, the pursuers started, the moment they received the information. The leader threw open the door, and bringing down his revolver to a present, said, "Throw up your hands." Lyons had a piece of hot slapjack on his fork; but dropped it instantly, and obeyed the order. He was told to step out. This he did at once. He was in his shirt-sleeves, and asked for his coat which was given to him. He was so nervous that he could hardly get his arms into it. A rigid search for weapons was made; but he had just before taken off his belt and revolver, laying them on the bed. He said that that was the first meal he had sat down to with any appetite, for six weeks. Being told to finish his dinner, he thanked the captain, but said he could eat no more. He then inquired what was going to be done with him, and whether they would hang him. The captain said, "I am not here to promise you anything; prepare for the worst." He said, "My friends advised me to leave here, two or three days ago." The captain asked why he did not go. He replied that he had "done nothing, and did not want to go." (He was one of the murderers of Dillingham, in June, '63, and was sentenced to death, but spared, as before related.) The real reason for his stay, was his attachment for a woman in town, whose gold watch he wore when he died on the scaffold. He was asked if he had heard of the execution of Plummer, Buck Stinson and Ned Ray. He replied that he had; but that he did not believe it. He was informed that it was true in the following words, "You may bet your sweet life on it." He then inquired, "Did they fight?" and was informed that they did not; for that they had not any opportunity. By this time they had arrived at the rendezvous, and Lyons found himself confronted by some familiar faces.

Jack Gallagher came in swearing, and appeared to be inclined to pretend that the affair was a joke, asking, "What the ―――― is it all about?" and saying, "This is a pretty break ain't it?" Being informed of his sentence, he appeared much affected, and sat down, crying; after which he jumped up, cursing in the most ferocious manner, and demanded who had informed of him. He was told that it was "Red, who was hung at Stinkingwater." He cursed him with every oath he could think of. He said to himself. "My God! must I die in this way?" His general conduct and profanity were awful; and he was frequently rebuked by the chief of the executive.

Haze Lyons was last fetched in, and acquainted with his sentence. He, of course, pleaded innocent, in the strongest terms; but he had confessed to having murdered Dillingham, to a captain of one of the squads of the guard, in the presence of several witnesses; and he was a known Road Agent. He gave some directions for letters to be written, and begged to see his mistress; but warned by the experiment of the previous year, his request was denied.

The chief dispatched an officer, with fifteen men, who went at the double-quick to Highland District, where two suspicious looking characters had gone, with blankets on their backs, the evening before, and making the "surround" of the cabin, the usual greeting of "throw up your hands," enforced by a presented revolver, was instantly obeyed, and they were marched down after being disarmed. The evidence not being conclusive, they were released though their guilt was morally certain. The Vigilantes rigidly abstained, in all cases, from inflicting the penalty due to crime, without entirely satisfactory evidence of guilt.

After all was arranged for hanging them, the prisoners were ordered to stand in a row, facing the guard, and were informed that they were about to be marched to the place of execution. Being asked if they had any requests to prefer, as that would be their last opportunity, they said they had none to make. They were then asked if they had anything to communicate, either of their own deeds or their comrade Road Agents; but they all refused to make any confession. The guard were ordered to pinion their prisoners. Jack Gallagher swore he would never be hung in public; and drawing his knife he clapped the blade to his neck, saying that he would cut his throat first. The executive

officer instantly cocked his pistol, and told him that if he
made another movement, he would shoot him, and ordered
the guard to disarm him. One of them seized his wrist and
took the knife, after which he was pinioned, cursing horribly
all the time. Boon Helm was encouraging Jack, telling him
not to "make a ——— fool of himself," as there was no use
in being afraid to die.

The chief called upon men that could be depended upon,
to take charge of the prisoners to the place of execution.
The plan adopted was to march the criminals, previously
pinioned, each between two Vigilantes, who grasped an arm
of the prisoner with one hand, and held in the other a "Navy"
—ready for instant use. When Haze Lyons heard the order
above mentioned, he called out, "X, I want you to come and
stay with me till I die," which reasonable request was at
once complied with.

The criminals were marched into the center of a hollow
square, which was flanked by four ranks of Vigilantes, and
a column in front and rear, armed with shot guns and rifles
carried at a half present, ready to fire at a moments warning, completed the array. The pistol men were dispersed
through the crowd to attend to the general deportment of
outsiders, or, as a good man observed, to take the roughs
"out of the wet."

At the word "march!" the party started forward, and
halted, with military precision, in front of the Virginia
Hotel. The halt was made while the ropes were preparing
at the unfinished building, now Clayton & Hale's Drug
Store, at the corner of Wallace and Van Buren streets. The
logs were up to the square, but there was no roof. The
main beam for the support of the roof, which runs across the
center of the building, was used as a gallows, the rope being
thrown over it, and then taken to the rear and fastened
round some of the bottom logs. Five boxes were placed
immediately under the beam, as substitutes for drops.

The prisoners were, during this time, in front of the Virginia Hotel. Club-Foot George called a citizen to him, and
asked him to speak as to his character; but this, the gentleman declined saying, "Your dealings with me have been
right; but what you have done outside of that I do not

know." Club-Foot then asked him to pray with him, which he did, kneeling down and offering up a fervent petition to the throne of grace on his behalf. George and Jack Gallagher knelt. Haze Lyons requested that his hat should be taken off, which was done. Boone Helm was cracking jokes all the time. Frank Parish seemed greatly affected at the near prospect of death. Boone Helm, after the prayer was over, called to Jack Gallagher, "Jack, give me that coat; you never gave me anything." "D—d sight of use you'd have for it," replied Jack. The two worthies kept addressing short and pithy remarks to their friends around, such as "Hallo, Jack, they've got me this time;" "Bill, old boy, they've got me, sure," etc.

Jack called to a man, standing at the windows of the Virginia Hotel, "Say! I'm going to Heaven! I'll be there in time to open the gate for you, old fellow." Jack wore a very handsome United States cavalry officer's overcoat, trimmed with Montana beaver.

Haze begged of his captor that his mistress might see him, but his prayer was refused. He repeated his request a second time, with the like result. A friend offered to fetch the woman; but was ordered off; and on Haze begging for the third time, to see her, he received this answer: "Haze! emphatically! by G—d, bringing women to the place of execution played out in '63." This settled the matter. The Vigilantes had not forgotten the scene after the trial of Dillingham's murderers.

The guard marched at the word to the place of execution; opened ranks, and the prisoners stepped up on the boxes. Club-Foot George was at the east side of the house; next to him was Haze Lyons; then Jack Gallagher and Boone Helm. The box next to the west end of the house was occupied by Frank Parish. The hats of the prisoners were ordered to be removed. Club-Foot, who was somewhat slightly pinioned, reached up to his California hat, and dashed it angrily on the ground. The rest were taken off by the guards.

The nooses were adjusted by five men, and—all being ready—Jack Gallagher, as a last request, asked that he might have something to drink, which, after some demur, was acceded to. Club-Foot George looked round, and, seeing an old friend clinging to the logs of the building, said, "Good-bye, old fellow—I'm gone;" and, hearing the order, "Men, do your duty"—without waiting for his box to be knocked away—he jumped off, and died in a short time.

Haze stood next; but was left to the last. He was talking all the time, telling the people that he had a kind mother, and that he had been well brought up; that he did not expect that it would have come to that; but that bad company had brought him to it.

Jack Gallagher, while standing on the box, cried all the time, using the most profane and dreadful language. He said, "I hope that forked lightning will strike every strangling ———— of you." The box flying from under his feet, brought his ribaldry and profanity to a close, which nothing but breaking his neck would ever have done.

Boone Helm, looking coolly at his quivering form, said, "Kick away, old fellow; I'll be in Hell with you in a minute." He probably told the truth, for once in his life. He then shouted, "Every man for his principles—hurrah for Jeff Davis! Let her rip!" The sound of his words was echoed by the twang of the rope.

Frank Parish requested to have a handkerchief tied over his face. His own black neck-tie, fastened in the Road Agents knot, was taken from his throat and dropped over his face like a veil. He seemed serious and quiet, but refused to confess anything more; and was launched into eternity. A bystander asked the guard who adjusted the rope, "Did you not feel for the poor man as you put the rope round his neck?" The Vigilanter, whose friend had been slaughtered by the Road Agents, regarded his interrogator with a stern look, and answered slowly, "Yes! I felt for his left ear!"

Haze Lyons seemed to expect a second deliverance from death, up to the last moment; looking right and left at the swaying bodies of the desperadoes, his countenance evidently indicating a hope of reprieve. Finding entreaty useless, he sent word to his mistress that she should get her gold watch, which he wore, and requested that his dying regards might be conveyed to her. He expressed a hope that she would see that his body was taken down, and that it was not left to hang to long. Also he charged her to see him decently buried. He died, apparently without pain. The bodies, after hanging for about two hours, were cut down, and carried to the street, in front of the house, where their friends found them, and took them away for burial. They sleep on Cemetery Hill, awaiting, not the justice of man, but the judgment of the last Day.

The man who dug the graves intended for Stinson and Lyons—after their sentence of death, for the murder of Dillingham—received no pay, and the two murderers actually committed an offense revolting to all notions of decency, in those very graves, in derision of their judges, and in contempt for their power. The sexton "pro tem" was in the crowd in front of the gallows where Lyons paid the penalty of his crimes, and said to him, "I dug your grave once for nothing; this time I'll be paid, you bet." He received his money.

As Jack Gallagher has not been specially referred to, the following short account of a transaction in which he was engaged, in Virginia City, is here presented :

Near the end of 1863, Jack Gallagher, who had hitherto occupied the position in Montana, of a promising desperado —raised himself to the rank of a "big medicine man," among the Road Agents, by shooting a blacksmith, named Jack Temple, as fine a man as could be found among the trade. He did not kill him; but his good intentions were credited to him, and he was thenceforth respected as a proved brave. Temple had been shoeing oxen, and came up to Coleman & Lœb's saloon, to indulge in a "Thomas and Jeremiah," with some friends. Jack Gallagher was there. A couple of dogs began to fight, and Temple gave one of them a kick, saying to the dog. "Here, I don't want you to fight here." Jack said there was not a —— there that should kick that dog, and he was able to whip any man in the room. Temple, who, though not quarrelsome, was as brave as a lion, went up to him and said, "I'm not going to fight in here; but if you want a fight so bad, come into the street, and I'll give you a 'lay out;' I'll fight you a square fight." He immediately went to the door. Jack Gallagher, seeing him so nicely planted for a shot, in a narrow door-way, whipped out his pistol, and fired twice at him. The first ball broke his wrist. "You must do better than that," said Temple, "I can whip you yet." The words were hardly out of his mouth when the second ball pierced his neck, and he fell. Gallagher would have finished him where he lay, but his friends interfered. The unfortunate man said: "Boys carry me somewhere; I don't want to die, like a dog, in the street." He remained, slowly recovering, but suffering considerably, for several weeks, and at the execution of Gallagher, he was walking round town, with his arm in a sling, greatly grieved at the sudden end of his antagonist. "I wish," said he, "you had let him run till I got well; I would have settled that job myself."

Bill Hunter and Gallagher robbed a Mormon of a large amount of greenbacks, which he had been foolish enough to display, in a saloon, in Virginia. They followed him down the road, on his way to Salt Lake City, and, it is presumed they murdered him. The money was recognized by several while the thieves were spending it in town. The Mormon was never heard of more. All the robbers whose death has been recorded wore the "Cordon knot" of the band, and nearly all, if not every one of them, shaved to the Road Agent pattern.

These executions were a fatal blow to the power of the band, and, henceforth, the RIGHT was the stronger side. The men of Nevada deserve the thanks of the people of the Territory for their activity, brave conduct and indomitable resolution. Without their aid, the Virginians could never have faced the roughs, or conquered them in their headquarters —their own town. The men of Summit, especially, and "up the Gulch," generally, were always on hand, looking business, and doing it. Night fell on Virginia; but sleep forsook many an eye; while criminals of all kinds fled for their lives, from the fatal City of the Vigilantes.

# CHAPTER XXI.

THE DEER LODGE AND HELL GATE SCOUT—CAPTURE AND
EXECUTION OF STEPHEN MARSHLAND, BILL BUNTON,
CYRUS SKINNER, ALECK CARTER, JOHNNY COOPER,
GEROGE SHEARS, ROBERT ZACHARY AND
WILLIAM GRAVES, (WHISKEY BILL.)

"He dies and makes no sign;
So bad a death argues a monstrous life."—SHAK.

The operations of the Vigilantes were, at this time, especially, planned with a judgment, and executed with a vigor that never has been surpassed by any body, deliberative or executive. On the 15th of January, 1864, a party of twenty-one men left Nevada, under the command of a citizen whose name and actions remind us of lightning. He was prompt, brave, irresistible, (so wisely did he lay his plans,) and struck where least expected.

The squadron rode to Big Hole, the first day, and, while on the road, detached a patrole to Clarke's Ranch, in pursuit of Steve Marshland, who was wounded in the breast, when attacking Forbes' train. His feet had been badly frozen, and flight was impossible. Leaving the horses behind, one of the party (No. 84) went in to arrest him, after knocking four times without answer, and discovered him in company with a dog, the two being the sole tenants of the Ranch.

When the Vigilanter entered, he found all quite dark; but taking a wisp of dried grass, he groped his way to the fire-place, and kindled a light with a match. The blaze revealed Steve Marshland in bed. "Hands up, if you please," was the salute of his captor; and a pointed suggestion from one of Col. Colt's pacification agents, caused an instant compliance with this demand. Seeing that he was sick, he was asked what was the matter, and replied that he had the chills. This novel "winter sickness" not being accepted as a sufficient excuse, a further interrogatory elicited the fact that he had frozen his feet. "No. 84" removed two double-barrelled shot-guns, a yager and another rifle, from beside the bed, and asked him where he froze them. He said he was prospecting at the head of Rattlesnake. "Did you raise the 'color?'" said his interrogator. "No," replied Marshland, "I could not get to the bed-rock, for water." The party commenced cooking supper, and invited him to eat with them. He took a cup of coffee, and was quite merry. After supper, he was informed by the leader of the nature of the charge against him; viz: the robbery of Forbes' train. He denied having any wound, and slapped his breast, saying that it was "as sound as a dollar." Being asked if he had any objection to being examined, he said he had not; but the moment his shirt was lifted, the fatal mark of guilt was visible, in the shape of a recent bullet wound.

The prisoner was told that the evidence was complete, and that he must die. He then confessed, begging them to spare his life. He had matches and tobacco in every pocket of his clothes. A pole was stuck into the ground, and leaned over the corral; a box was placed for him to stand on, and, all being ready, he once more begged them to save him, saying "have mercy on me for my youth." He died almost instantly.

His feet being frozen and partially mortified, the scent attracted the wolves, and the party had to watch both him and the horses. He was buried close by. The patrole then started to overtake the main body, and coming up with them about four miles above Evans' Ranch, they reported the execution of Marshland. They had been absent only one night, leaving the command in the morning, and rejoining them the next day.

Up to this time, the scouting party had met no one, but marched in double-file, at the rate of from sixty to seventy miles per day. They kept double watch over the horses when camped, and lit no fires, being fearful of attracting notice, and of thus defeating the object of their journey. The men were divided into four messes, with a cook to each, and every party carried its own "grub," (the universal mountain word for "food.") Each man had a revolver, and some sported two. A shot-gun or a rifle was also part of the equipment. The captain rode foremost. A spy was dispatched to reconnoitre the town, and to meet the party at Cottonwood Creek. He performed his part satisfactorily. When within about seventeen miles of Cottonwood, at Smith's Ranch, on Deer Lodge Creek, a halt was made about four p. m. After dark, they started, and with perfect quiet and caution, rode to within a short distance of the town. They found that the robbers were gone; but, surrounding Bill Bunton's saloon and dwelling house, they proceeded to business. Bill was in his house, but he refused to open the door. The three men detailed for his arrest said they wanted to see him. For a long time he refused. At last, he told a man named Yank, and a young boy, who was stopping with him, to open the door. The men made him light a candle, before they would enter. This being done, Bunton's captors rushed in, and told him that he was their prisoner. He asked them for what, and was told to come along, and that he would find out.

A Vigilanter of small stature, but of great courage fastened upon him. He found, however, that he had caught a Tartar, so another man "piled on," (Montanice,) and soon, his arms were fast tied behind him. A guard was detailed to escort him down to Pete Martin's house, the rest being sent for to assist in taking Tex out of the saloon.

A similar scene occurred here, when the robber came out. He was instantly siezed, pinioned, and taken down to keep company with his friend, Bill Bunton.

Pete Martin was frightened out of a years' growth, when the Vigilanters surrounded his house. He was playing cards with some friends, and for a long time refused to come out; but finding that, as he said, "he wasn't charged with nothing," he ascertained what was wanted, and then returned to finish his game. As the exigencies of the times had rendered a little hanging necessary in that neighborhood, he felt small concern about the fate of Bunton and Tex, who were of a dangerous religion.

The party slept and breakfasted at the house. In the morning, a stranger who was conversing with Bunton, to whom he was unknown, informed the Vigilantes that the culprit had said that "he would 'get' one of the ——— yet." On being searched, a Derringer was found in his vest pocket. As he had been carefully overhauled the night before, it was evident that some sympathizer had furnished him with the weapon. He refused to confess anything, even his complicity in the robbery of the coach, where he played "pigeon." Red had testified that he shared the money. He also denied killing Jack Thomas' cattle; but Red had confessed that he himself was the butcher, and that he had been hired by Bunton, who called him a coward, when he spoke about the skins lying round the house, as being likely to be identified.

There being no possible doubt of his criminality, the vote on his case was taken with the uplifted hand, and resulted in a unanimous verdict of guilty.

The captain then told him that he was to be hanged, and that if he had any business to attend to, he had better get some one to do it. He gave his gold watch to his partner, Cooke, and his other property to pay his debts. He had won his interest in the saloon some fourteen days before, by gambling it from its owner.

Tex was taken to another house, and was separately tried. After a patient investigation, the robber was cleared—the evidence not being sufficient to convict him. Had the Vigilantes held him in custody, for a time, Tex would have experienced a difficulty in his breathing, that would have proved quickly fatal; for testimony in abundance was afterward obtained, proving conclusively that he was a highwayman and common thief. He made all sail for Kootenai, and there boasted that he would shoot any Vigilanter he could set eyes on.

About two hundred and fity feet to the left-front of Pete Martin's house, at the gate of Louis Demorest's corral, there were two upright posts, and a cross-beam, which looked quite natural, and appeared as if they had been made for Bunton.

The prisoner was taken out, and put up on a board supported by two boxes. He was very particular about the exact situation of the knot, and asked if he could not jump off, himself. Being told that he could, if he wished, he said that he didn't care for hanging, any more than he did for taking a drink of water; but he should like to have his neck broken.

He seemed quite satisfied when his request was granted. He continued to deny his guilt to the very last moment of his life, repeating the pass-word of the gang "I am innocent." Two men were stationed at the board—one at each end—and, all being ready, he was asked if he had anything to say, or any request to make. He said, "No; all I want is a mountain three hundred feet high, to jump off" He said he would give the time—"one," "two," "three." At the word "ready," the men stationed at the plank prepared to pull it from under him, if he should fail to jump; but he gave the signal, as he promised, and adding, "here goes it," he leaped into the embrace of death. The cessation of muscular contraction was almost instantaneous, and his death was accompanied by scarcely a perceptible struggle.

The corral keepers' wife insisted, in terms more energetic than polite, that her husband should get the poles cut down. With this request he was forced to comply, as soon as the corpse of the Road Agent was removed for burial.

The parties knew that the robbers were to be found at Hell Gate, which was so named, because it was the road which the Indians took when on the war-path, and intent on scalping and other pleasant little amusements, in the line of ravishing, plundering, fire-raising, etc., for the exhibition of which genteel proclivities, the Eastern folks recommend a national donation of blankets and supplies, to keep the thing up. As independent and well educated robbers, however sedulously reared to the business, from childhood, it must be admitted that, in case anything is lacking, they at once proceed to supply the deficiency from the pilgrims' trains, and from settlers homesteads. If the Indians were left to the Vigilantes of Montana, they would contract to change their habits, at small cost; but an agency is too fat a thing for pet employees, and, consequently a treaty is entered into, the only substantial adjunct of which is the quantity of presents which the Indians believe they have frightened out of the white men. Probably, in a century or so, they will see that our view is correct.

On their road from Cottonwood to Hell Gate, the troop was accompanied by Jemmy Allen, towards whose Ranch they were directing their steps. The weather was anything

but pleasant for travelling, the quantity of snow making it
laborious work for the Vigilantes, and the cold was very hard
to endure, without shelter.    At the crossing of Deer Lodge
Creek, the ice gave way, and broke through with the party.
It was pitch dark at the time, and much difficulty was experienced in getting out both men and horses.    One cavalier
was nearly drowned; but a lariet being put round the horses'
neck, it was safely dragged out.    The rider scrambled to the
bank, somehow or other—memory furnishes the result only,
not the detail—and jumping on to the "animal," he rode, on
a keen run, to the Ranch, which was some four or five miles
ahead.

The remainder of the cavalcade travelled on more leisurely, arriving there about 11 p. m., and having recruited a
little, they wrapped themselves in blankets and slumber
without delay.

Next morning, in company with Charley Eaton, who was
acquainted with the country and with the folks around Hell
Gate, they started for that locality, and after riding fifteen
or sixteen miles through snow, varying in depth from two
to three feet, they camped for the night.    The horses being
used to foraging, pawed for their food.

The next morning the party crossed the bridge, and rode
to the workmen's quarters, on the Mullan Wagon Road,
where, calling a halt, they stopped all night.    Accidents
will happen in the best regulated families, and in a winter
scout in the wilds of Montana, casualties must be expected
as a matter of course.    The best mountaineer is the man
who most quickly and effectually repairs damages, or finds a
substitute for the missing article.    While driving the ponies
into camp, one of them put his foot into a hole and broke
his leg.    As there was no chance to attend to him, he was
at once shot.    Another cayuse, by a similar accident, strip-
ped all the skin off his hind legs, from the hough down.    He
was turned loose to await the return of the expedition.

At daylight, the troop were in their saddles, and pushing
as rapidly as possible for the village.    On arriving within
six miles of the place, the command halted on the bank of a
small creek, till after dark, to avoid being seen on the road.
As soon as night threw her mantle over the scene, they con-

tinued their journey, till within two hundred yards of Hell Gate, and there, dismounting, they tied their horses.

Their scout had gone ahead to reconnoitre, and, returning to the rendezvous, he informed the captain of the exact position of affairs. Coming through the town on a tight run, they mistook the houses; but, discovering their error, they soon returned, and surrounding Skinner's saloon, the owner, who was standing at the door, was ordered to throw up his hands. His woman (Nelly) did not appear to be pleased at the command, and observed that they must have learned that from the Bannack stage folks.

Skinner was taken and bound immediately. Some of the men went for Alick Carter, who was in Miller's, the next house. Dan Harding opened the door, and seeing Carter, said, "Alick, is that you?" to which the Road Agent promptly replied "yes." The men leveled their pieces at him, and the leader, going over to the lounge on which he was lying, rather drunk, took his pistol from him and bound him, before he was thoroughly aroused. When he came to himself, he said, "this is tight papers, ain't it, boys?" He then asked for a smoke, which being given to him, he inquired for the news. On hearing of the hanging of the blood-stained miscreants whose doom has been recorded in these pages, he said, "all right; not an innocent man hung yet."

He was marched down, under guard, to Higgins' store, where he and Skinner were tried, the examination lasting about three hours. Skinner's woman came down, bent on interference in his behalf. The lady was sent home with a guard, who found Johnny Cooper lying wounded in the house. He had been shot in three places, by Carter, whom he had accused of stealing his pistol. He was, of course, instantly secured.

Some of the guard happening to remark that Johnny seemed to be suffering "pretty bad," the lady expressed a conviction, with much force and directness, that "by ———, there were two outside suffering a ——— sight worse;" (meaning Skinner and Alick Carter.)

Cooper was one of the lieutenants of the gang. He was a splendid horseman, and a man named President, who was present at his apprehension, knew him well on the "other side." He had murdered a man, and being arrested, was on his way to the court, when he suddenly broke from his captors, leaped with a bound on to a horse standing ready, and was off like a bird. Though at least one hundred shots were sent after him, he escaped uninjured, and got clear away.

While Alick Carter was on trial, he confessed that the two mules of which Nicholas Tbalt was in charge, when shot by Ives, were at Irwin's Ranch, at Big Hole, and that he, Irwin and Ives had brought them there. It will be remembered that, besides robbing the coach, Alick was accessory both before and after the fact of Tbalt's murder. This was proved. That he was a principal in its perpetration is more than likely. He denied all participation in the murder, but confessed, generally speaking, much in the same style as others had done.

Skinner also refused to confess any of his crimes. "Dead men tell no tales" was his verdict, when planning the murder of Magruder, and he it was, who ingratiated himself into the favor of Page, Romaine and others, and prompted them to the deed, so that Mugruder thought his murderers were his friends, and went on his last journey without suspicion. . He said he could have saved him, if he had liked; but he added that he "would have seen him in —— first." He wouldn't leave himself open to the vengeance of the band. He was a hardened, merciless and brutal fiend.

The same night a detachment of eight men went in pursuit of Bob Zachary, and coming up to Barney O'Keefe's, that gentleman appeared in the uniform of a Georgia major, minus the spurs and shirt collar, and plus a flannel blouse. He mistook the party for Road Agents, and appeared to think his time had come. He ejaculated, with visible horror, "Don't shoot, gentlemen; I'm Barney O'Keefe." It is useless to say that no harm was done to the "Baron," as he is called. There are worse men living in all countries than Barney, who is a good soul in his own way, and hospitable in his nature. Finding that Bob Zachary was inside, one of the party entered, and, as he sat up in bed, threw himself upon him, and pushed him backwards. He had a pistol and a knife. He was taken to Hell Gate shortly after his capture. The fate of his friends was made known to him, and vouched for by a repetition of the signs, grips, pass-words, etc. On seeing this, he turned pale; but he never made any confession of guilt. He was the one of the stage robbers who actually took the money from Southmayde. Like all the rest, he repeated the pass-word of the gang, "I am innocent."

On the road back the guard had wormed out of Barney that a stranger was stopping at Van Dorn's, in the Bitter Root valley. "No. 84," who was leading the party who captured Shears, asked, "Does Van live here?" "Yes," said the man himself. "Is George Shears in your house?" asked 84. "Yes," said Van. "Where is he?" "In the next room." "Any objection to our going in?" The man replied by opening the door of the room, on which George became visible, knife in hand. He gave himself up quietly, and seemed so utterly indifferent to death, that he perfectly astonished his captors. Taking a walk with 84, he pointed out to him the stolen horses in the corral, and confessed his guilt, as a man would speak of the weather. He said, "I knew I should have to go up, some time; but I thought I could run another season." When informed of his doom, he appeared perfectly satisfied. On being taken into the barn, where a rope was thrown over a beam, he was asked to walk up a ladder, to save trouble about procuring a drop. He at once complied, addressing his captors in the following unique phraseology: "Gentlemen, I am not used to this business, never having been hung before. Shall I jump off or slide off?" Being told to jump off, he said "all right; good-bye," and leaped into the air, with as much sang froid as if bathing.

The drop was long and the rope tender. It slowly untwisted, and Shears hung, finally, by a single strand. George's parting question was, for a long time, a by-word among the Vigilantes.

A company of three, headed by the "old man," started off to Fort Owen, in the Bitter Root Valley, in pursuit of Whiskey Bill, (Bill Graves, the coach robber.) This worthy was armed and on the look out for his captors; but, it seems, he had become partially snow-blind by long gazing. At all

events, he did not see the party with sufficient distinctness
to ascertain who they were, until the "old man" jumped
from his horses and covered him with his revolver.  He gave
up, though he had repeatedly sworn that he would shoot
any ——— Vigilanter who would come his way.  His guilt
was notorious throughout all the country, and his capture
was merely a preliminary to his execution.  The men took
him away from the Fort, in deference to the prejudices of
the Indians, who would have felt no desire to live near where
a man had been hanged.  Graves made no confession.  He
was what is called in the mountains a "bull-head," and was
a sulky, dangerous savage.  Being tied up to a limb, the
difficulty was to make a "drop;" but the ingenuity of the
leader was equal to the emergency.  One of the men mounted his horse; Graves was lifted up behind him, and, all
being ready, "Good-bye, Bill," said the front horseman, driving his huge rowels into the horse's flanks, as he spoke.
The animal made a plunging bound of twelve feet, and Bill
Graves swept from his seat by the fatal noose and lariet,
swung lifeless.  His neck was broken by the shock.

The different parties rendezvoused at Hell Gate, and a
company of eight men were dispatched to the Pen de'Oreille
reserve, to get Johnny Cooper's horses, six or seven in number.  They were poor in condition and were nearly all sold
to pay the debts which the Road Agent had incurred in the
country round about the village.  The remainder were
brought to Nevada.  It seems that Alick Carter and Cooper
were about to start for Kootenai, on the previous day, and
that their journey was prevented only by their quarrel about
the pistol, which Cooper charged Alick with stealing, and
which resulted in the wounding of Cooper, the delay of their
journey, and, in fact, in their execution.  A pack animal,
laden with their baggage and provisions, carried $130 worth
of goods.  These were taken for the use of the expedition;
but on a representation made by Higgins that he had supplied them to Carter to get rid of him, but that he had received nothing for them, they were paid for, on the spot by
the Vigilantes.

There had been a reign of terror in Hell Gate.  The robbers did as they pleased took what they chose.  A Colt's

revolver was the instrument ever ready to enforce the transfer. Brown, a Frenchman, living in the neighborhood, stated to the Vigilantes, that he was glad to see them, for that the robbers used to ride his stock whenever they pleased, and that they always retained possession of such steeds as they especially fancied.

Cooper had determined to marry his daughter, a pretty half-breed girl, and then, after getting all that he could lay hands on, he intended to turn the old man adrift. He used to go to his intended father-in-law, and inform him that he wanted another of those pretty pocket pieces, ($20 gold pieces,) and he always obtained what he asked; for death would have been the instant penalty of refusal. Other parties had supplied Cooper and Carter with money, pistols and whatever else they asked, for the same potent and unanswerable reasons. Any demand for payment was met by a threat to shoot the creditor.

At the conclusion of the trials of Carter and Skinner, a vote was taken by stepping to the opposite sides of the room; but the verdict of guilty, and a judgment of death to the culprits, were unanimously rendered.

Cooper was tried separately, and interrogated by Mr. President concerning his conduct on the "other side." He denied the whole thing; but this gentleman's testimony, the confession of Red, and the witness of the inhabitants rendered a conviction and sentence of death inevitable.

Carter and Skinner were taken to Higgins' corral and executed by torchlight, shortly after midnight. Two poles were planted, leaning over the corral fence; to these the ropes were tied, and store-boxes served for "drops."

On the road to the gallows, Cyrus Skinner broke suddenly from the guard, and ran off, shouting, "shoot! shoot!" His captors were too old hands to be thus baffled. They instantly secured him. He again tried the trick, when on the box; but he was quickly put up and held there till the rope was adjusted. This being finished, he was informed that he could jump whenever he pleased. Alick seemed ashamed of Skinner's attempt to escape, which the latter explained by saying that he "was not born to be hanged"—a trifling error.

While on the stand, one of the men asked Carter to confess his share in the murder of the Dutchman; but he burst
forth with a volley of oaths, saying, "If I had my hands free,
you ———, I'd make you take that back." As Skinner was
talking by his side, Alick was ordered to keep quiet. "Well
then, let's have a smoke," said he. His request being granted, he became more pacific in demeanor. The criminals
faces being covered with handkerchiefs, they were launched
into eternity, with the pass-word of the gang on their lips, "I
am innocent." Both died easily and at once. The people
had, of their own accord, made all the preparations for their
burial.

Immediately after the execution, the parties were detailed
and dispatched after Zachary, Graves and Shears. The
death of the last two has been recorded.

The squad that arrested Zachary returned between seven
and eight o'clock, that morning. He was at once tried,
found guilty, and sentenced to death. By his direction, a
letter was written to his mother, in which he warned his
brothers and sisters to avoid drinking whiskey, card playing
and bad company, which, he said, had brought him to the
gallows. Zachary once laid in wait for Pete Daly, and
snapped two caps at him; but, fortunately, the weapon
would not go off.

Being brought to the same spot as that on which Skinner
and Carter were hanged, he commenced praying to God to
forgive the Vigilantes for what they were doing, for it was
a pretty good way to clear the country of Road Agents. He
died at once, without any apparent fear or pain.

Johnny Cooper was hauled down on a sleigh, by hand, owing
to his leg being wounded, and was placed on the same box
that Skinner had stood upon. He asked for his pipe, saying
he wanted a good smoke, and he enjoyed it very much. A
letter had been written to his parents, in York State. Cooper
dodged the noose for a time, but being told to keep his head
straight, he submitted. He died without a struggle.

During the trial of the men, the people had made Cooper's
coffin, and dug his grave, Zachary was buried by the Vigilantes. The other malefactor, the citizens knew better, and
hated worse.

Skinner left all his property to Higgins, the store-keeper, from whom he had received all his stock, on credit. Alick had nothing but his horse, his accoutrements and his appointments.

Their dread mission of retribution being accomplished, the captain ordered everything to be made ready for their long homeward march, and in due time they arrived at Cottonwood, where they found that X had settled everything relating to Bunton's affairs. At Big Hole, they made search for Irwin; but he had fled, and has never been taken. Tired and worn, the command reached Nevada, and received the congratulations and thanks of all good men. Like Joshua's army, though they had been rewarded with success, yet often in that journey over their cold and trackless waste, the setting sun had seen them
"Faint, yet pursuing."

---

# CHAPTER XXII.

### CAPTURE AND EXECUTION OF BILL HUNTER.

"Round he throws his baleful eyes,
That witness naught but huge destruction and dismay."
—MILTON.

At the time of the execution of Boone Helm and his four confederates in crime, Bill Hunter, as before narrated, managed to escape his pursuers and, for a time, to baffle the vengeance of the Vigilantes, by hiding among the rocks and brush by day, and then seeking food at night among the scattered settlements in the vicinity of the Gallatin river.

At the time of Barney Hughes' stampede, the country in the neighborhood became alive with men, and his whereabouts was discovered. Information was received at Virginia that he was living as described about twenty miles above the mouth of the Gallatin. A severe snow storm had driven him to seek refuge in a cabin, near the place of his concealment, and here he was overtaken and captured.

A party of four resolute men volunteered for the work, and left Virginia City with a good prospect of fine weather for the trip before them.  Crossing the Divide between the Stinkingwater and the Madison, they forded the last named river with some difficulty, the huge cakes of floating ice striking the horses' flanks and threatening to carry them down.  Their camping ground was the frozen earth on its banks; and having built a fire, they laid down to sleep with no shelter but their blankets.  Though the weather was intensely cold, the spirits of the party never flagged, and they derived not a little amusement from occurrences which, under other circumstances, would have been regarded as anything but amusing incidents of travel.

One of the Vigilantes, determined on securing a good share of heat, lay with his head on the top of a hillock that sloped towards the fire, and, as a natural consequence, gradually slid down, till he woke with his feet in the hot embers. His position was changed with marvellous rapidity, amid the laughter of his comrades.

Another of the party had a pair of mammoth socks, into which he thrust his feet loosely.  As the sleeper began to feel the cold, he kept pushing his feet into the socks, until he pushed himself out of bed, and woke half frozen.  He glanced, with a comic expression, at the cause of his misfortunes, and taking a good warm at the fire, in a more legitimate fashion, he crept back to bed.

Early in the morning, the men rose from their slumbers; renewed their fire, and while some cooked, others hunted up the stock.  Soon all was prepared, and dispatched with a mountaineers' appetite; the horses were saddled and they departed on their mission.  The weather had changed very much for the worse.  At about ten o'clock a fierce snow storm, driven by a furious wind, blew right in their faces; but as the tempest was a most useful auxiliary towards the success of their enterprise, they pushed on, hour after hour, and, at 2 P. M., reached the Milk Ranch, about twenty miles from the place where they expected to find their game. Here they stayed for supper, and engaged a guide who knew the country well, and was acquainted with the locality of the robbers' city of refuge.  Being warmed and refreshed, they started at a rapid pace, which was continued until, at midnight, they drew bridle near a lone cabin, into which they felt certain that the severity of the storm had driven the object of their journey.

Having halted and unsaddled, they rapped loudly at the door. When it was opened, the gentleman who presented himself, took a view of the party, which, with the guide and a gentleman who had joined them, numbered six individuals. "Good evening," was the salutation of the travellers. Sleep, suspicion, and an uneven temper, probably, jointly provoked the response, "Don't know whether it is or not." However, at their request, he soon had a fire blazing on the hearth, which the party thoroughly enjoyed, after their long ride. Before allowing themselves to be thus, even temporarily, luxurious, they had carefully inspected the premises and, as the lawyers say, all the appendages and appurtenances therunto belonging; when, having found that the only practicable method of egress was by the door, a couple of them lay down in such a manner, when they retired to rest, that any one trying to escape must inevitably wake them. Six shot-guns constituted half a dozen weighty arguments against forcible attempts at departure, and the several minor and corroborative persuasions of a revolving class completed a clear case of "stand off," under all circumstances.

A sentry was placed to see that nobody adopted the plan of "evaporation" patented by Santa Claus, that is to say, by ascent of the chimney. His duty, also was, to keep up a bright fire, and the room being tenanted to its utmost capacity, all promised an uninterrupted night's slumber.

A very cursory inspection of the interior of the premises had satisfied the Vigilantes that the occupants of the cabin were three in number. Of these, two were visible; but one remained covered up in bed, and never stirred till the time of their departure in the morning. The curiosity of the inmates being roused by the sudden advent of the travellers, questions as to their names, residences, occupation and intentions were freely propounded, and were answered with a view to "business" exclusively. Before turning over to sleep, the party conversationally descanted on mining, stampeding, prospecting, runs, panning-out, and all the technical magazine of mining phrases was ransacked with a view to throwing their hosts off the trial. In this they succeeded. All was quiet during the night, and until a late hour in the morning. Every one of the friends of justice had exchanged private signals by Vigilante telegraph and were satisfied that all was right.

Nothing was said about the real object of their visit, until the horses were saddled for the apparent purpose of continuing the journey. Two only went out at a time, and the mute eloquence of the shot-guns in the corner was as effective in the morning as it had been at midnight.

When all was ready, one of the party asked who was the unknown sleeper that, at that late hour, had never waked or uncovered his face. The host said that he did not know; but upon being asked, "when did he come here?" he informed them that he had come at the beginning of the great snow storm, and had been there two days.

The man was requested to describe his person and appearance. He complied at once, and in so doing, he gave a perfect picture of Bill Hunter.

With arms prepared for instant service, the Vigilantes approached the bed, and the leader called out, "Bill Hunter!" The occupant of the bed hastily drew the covering from his face, and wildly asked who was there. His eyes were greeted with the sight of six well armed men, whose determined countenances and stern looks told him only too truly the nature of their errand. Had he been in doubt, however, this matter would soon have been settled; for the six shot-guns leveled at his head were answer enough to palsy the arm of grim despair himself. On being asked if he had any arms, he said, "Yes, I have a revolver;" and accordingly, he handed it from beneath the bed-clothes, where he had held it, lying on his breast, ready cocked for use. The old Vigilanter who made the inquiries, not being very soft or easily caught at a disadvantage, took the precaution when approaching him, to lay his hand on his breast, so that, had he been willing, he could have done nothing; for his weapon was mastered while his hand was covered. He was, of course, informed that he was a prisoner, upon hearing which he at once asked to be taken to Virginia City. One of the men gave him to understand that he would be taken there. He further inquired whether there was any conveyance for him, and was told that there was a horse for him to ride.

He rose from his bed, ready dressed for the occasion except his overcoat and hat, and mounted the horse prepared for him; but upon preparing to take the rein, his motion was politely negatived, and the bridle was handed to a horseman who held it as a leading bridle. He looked suspiciously round, and appeared much perturbed when he saw a foot-man following, for he at once guessed that it was his horse that he was riding, and the incident seemed to be regarded by him in the light of an omen foreboding a short journey for him. His conscience told him that what was likely to be the end of his arrest. The real reason why an evasive answer had been given to the prisoner, when he expressed a wish to be taken to Virginia City, was that his captors were anxious to leave the place without exciting suspicion of any intention to execute Bill Hunter, in the neighborhood.

The escort proceeded on their way homewards, for about two miles, and halted at the foot of a tree which seemed as if it had been fashioned by nature for a gallows. A horizontal limb at a convenient height was there for the rope, and on the trunk was a spur like a belaying pin, on which to fasten the end. Scraping away about a foot of snow, they camped, lit a fire and prepared their breakfast. An onlooker would never have conjectured for a moment, that anything of a serious nature was likely to occur, and even Hunter seemed to have forgotton his fears, laughing and chatting gaily with the rest.

After breakfast, a consultation was held as to what should be done with the Road Agent, and after hearing what was offered by the members of the scouting party, individually, the leader put the matter to vote. It was decided by the majority that the prisoner should not go to Virginia; but that he should be executed then and there. The man who had given Hunter to understand that he would be taken to Virginia, voted for the carrying out of this part of the programme; but he was overruled.

The earnest manner of the Vigilantes, and his own sense of guilt, overpowered Hunter; he turned deadly pale, and faintingly asked for water. He knew, without being told that there was no hope for him. A brief history of his crimes was related to him by one of the men, and the necessity of the enforcement of the penalty was pointed out to him. All was too true for denial. He merely requested that his friends should know nothing of the manner of his death, and stated that he had no property; but he hoped they would give him a decent burial. He was told that every reasonable request would be granted; but that the ground was to hard for them to attempt his interment without proper implements. They promised that his friends should be made acquainted with his execution, and that they would see to that. Soon after, he shook hands with each of the company, and said that he did not blame them for what they were about to do.

His arms were pinioned at the elbows; the fatal noose was placed round his neck, and the end of the rope being thrown over the limb, the men took hold and with a quick, strong pull, ran him up off his feet. He died almost without a struggle; but, strange to say, he reached as if for his pistol, and went through the pantomime of cocking and discharging his revolver six time. This is no effort of fancy. Every one present saw it, and was equally convinced of the fact. It was a singular instance of "the ruling passion, strong in death."

The place of the execution was a lone tree, in full view of the travellers on the trail, about twenty miles above the mouth of the Gallatin. The corpse of the malefactor was left hanging from the limb, and the little knot of horsemen was soon but a speck in the distance. The purpose of the Barney Hughes stampede had been accomplished. So secretly had everything been manged that one of their four who started from Virginia did not know either the real destination of the party, or the errand of the other three. He was found to be sound on the Road Agent question; and, instead of being dismissed he rode on as one of the party.

It seemed as if fate had decreed the death of Bill Hunter. He was a man of dauntless courage, and would have faced a hundred men to the last, being a perfect desperado when roused, though ordinarily peaceful in demeanor. At his capture he was as weak as a child, and had scarcely strength to ask for what he wanted.

The only remarkable circumstance attending the return journey was the inconvenience and pain caused by the reflection of the sun's rays from the snow. It produced temporary blindness, and was only relieved by blacking their faces. Riding late at night, one of the horsemen dismounted, with a view of easing his steed, which was tired with the long march, and walked some distance by his side. On getting again into the saddle, he accidentally discharged his gun, which was slung muzzle down, by his side. The charge passed down the leg of his boot, between the counter and the lining, lodging an ounce ball and six buckshot, in the heel. All started at the sudden flash and report. The man himself believed that his foot was shot to pieces, and they spurred forward at hot speed, for the next Ranch, where an examination revealed the above state of facts, much to the consolation of the excited mind of the owner of the boot. He was wounded only in spirit, and reached home safely.

One of the Vigilantes "bagged" a relic. He had promised to bring back a token of having seen Bill Hunter, either dead or alive, and, accordingly, while talking to him at the fire, he managed to detach a button from his coat, which he fetched home as he had promised.

Some days after, men who were hauling wood discovered the body, and determined to give it burial. It was necessary to get the corpse over a snow drift ; so they tied a rope to the heels and essayed to drag it up; but finding that this was the wrong way of the grain, as they said, they replaced the noose round the neck, and thus having pulled him over, they finally consigned to mother earth THE LAST OF HENRY PLUMMER'S BAND.

Bill Hunter was, we have said the last of the old Road Agent band that met death at the hands of the Committee. He was executed on the 3d of February, 1864. There was now no openly organized force of robbers in the Territory, and the future acts of the Committee were confined to taking measures for the maintenance of the public tranquility and the punishment of those guilty of murder, robbery and other high crimes and misdemeanors against the welfare of the inhabitants of Montana.

On looking back at the dreadful state of society which necessitated the organization of the Vigilantes, and on reading these pages, many will learn for the first time the deep debt of gratitude which they owe to that just and equitable body of self-denying and gallant men. It was a dreadful and a disgusting duty that devolved upon them; but it was a duty, and they did it. Far less worthy actions have been rewarded by the thanks of Congress, and medals glitter on many a bosom, whose owner won them, lying flat behind a hillock, out of range of the enemy's fire. The Vigilantes, for the sake of their country encountered popular dislike, the envenomed hatred of the bad, and the cold toleration of some of the unwise good. Their lives they held in their hands. "All's well that ends well." Montana is saved, and they saved it, earning the blessings of future generations, whether they receive them or not. Our next chapter will record the execution of the renowned Capt. J. A. Slade, of whom more good and evil stories have been told than would make a biography for the seven champions of Christendom, and concerning whose life and character there have been more contradictory opinions expressed, than have been uttered for or against any other individual that has figured in the annals of the Rocky Mountains.

## CHAPTER XXIII.

### THE ARREST AND EXECUTION OF CAPTAIN J. A. SLADE WITH A SHORT ACCOUNT OF HIS PREVIOUS CAREER.

> Some write him hero, some a very knave ;
> Curses and tears are mingled at his grave.—ANON.

J. A. Slade, or, as he was often called, Captain Slade, was raised in Clinton County, Ill., and was a member of a highly respectable family. He bore a good character for several years in that place. The acts which have given so wide a celebrity to his name, were performed especially on the Overland Line, of which he was, for years, an official. Reference to these matters will be made in a subsequent part of this chapter.

Captain J. A. Slade came to Virginia City in the Spring of 1863. He was a man gifted with the power of making money, and, when free from the influence of alcoholic stimulants, which seemed to reverse his nature, and to change a kind hearted and intelligent gentleman into a reckless demon, no man in the Territory had a greater faculty of attracting the favorable notice of even strangers, and in spite of the wild lawlessness which characterized his frequent spells of intoxication, he had many, very many friends whom no commission of crime itself could detach from his personal companionship. · Another, and less desirable class of friends were attracted by his very recklessness. There are probably a thousand individuals in the West possessing a correct knowledge of the leading incidents of a career that terminated at the gallows, who still speak of Slade as a perfect gentleman, and who not only lament his death, but talk in the highest terms of his character, and pronounce his execution a murder. One way of accounting for the diversity of opinion regarding Slade is sufficiently obvious. Those who saw him in his natural state only, would pronounce him to be a kind husband, a most hospitable host and a courteous gentleman. On the contrary, those who met him when maddened with liquor and surrounded by a gang of armed roughs, would pronounce him a fiend incarnate.

During the summer of 1863, he went to Milk river as a freighter. For this business he was eminently qualified, and he made a great deal of money. Unfortunately his habit of profuse expenditure was uncontrollable, and at the time of his execution he was deeply in debt almost everywhere.

After the execution of the five men, on the 14th of January, the Vigilantes considered that their work was nearly ended. They had freed the country from highwaymen and murderers to a great extent, and they determined that, in the absence of the regular civil authority, they would establish a People's Court, where all offenders should be tried by

Judge and Jury. This was the nearest approach to social order that the circumstances permitted, and, though strict legal authority was wanting, yet the people were firmly determined to maintain its efficiency, and to enforce its decrees. It may here be mentioned that the overt act which was the last round on the fatal ladder leading to the scaffold on which Slade perished, was the tearing in pieces and stamping upon a writ of this court, followed by the arrest of the Judge, Alex. Davis by authority of a presented Derringer, and with his own hands.

J. A. Slade was himself, we have been informed, a Vigilanter; he openly boasted of it, and said he knew all that they knew. He was never accused, or even suspected of either murder or robbery, committed in this Territory, (the latter crimes were never laid to his charge, in any place;) but that he had killed several men in other localities, was notorious, and his bad reputation in this respect was a most powerful argument in determining his fate, when he was finally arrested for the offense above mentioned. On returning from Milk River he became more and more addicted to drinking; until at last, it was a common feat for him and his friends to "take the town." He and a couple of his dependants might often be seen on one horse, galloping through the streets, shouting and yelling, firing revolvers, etc. On many occasions he would ride his horse into stores; break up bars; toss the scales out of doors, and use most insulting language to parties present. Just previous to the day of his arrest, he had given a fearful beating to one of his followers; but such was his influence over them that the man wept bitterly at the gallows, and begged for his life with all his power. It had become quite common, when Slade was on a spree, for the shop-keepers and citizens to close the stores and put out all the lights; being fearful of some outrage at his hands. One store in Nevada he never ventured to enter—that of the Lott brothers—as they had taken care to let him know that any attempt of the kind would be followed by his sudden death, and, though he often rode down there, threatening to break in and raise ———, yet he never attempted to carry his threat into execution. For his wanton destruction of goods and furniture, he was always ready to pay, when sober if he had money; but there were not a few who regarded payment as small satisfaction for the outrage, and these men were his personal enemies.

From time to time, Slade received warnings from men that he well knew would not deceive him, of the certain end of his conduct. There was not a moment, for weeks previous to his arrest, in which the public did not expect to hear of some bloody outrage. The dread of his very name, and the presence of the armed band of hangers-on, who followed him alone prevented a resistance, which must certainly have ended in the instant murder or mutilation of the opposing party.

Slade was frequently arrested by order of the court whose organization we have described, and had treated it with respect by paying one or two fines, and promising to pay the rest when he had money; but in the transaction that occurred at this crisis, he forgot even this caution, and goaded by passion and the hatred of restraint, he sprang into the embrace of death.

Slade had been drunk and "cutting up" all night. He and his companions had made the town a perfect hell. In the morning, J. M. Fox, the Sheriff, met him, arrested him, took him into court, and commenced reading a warrant that he had for his arrest, by way of arraignment. He became uncontrollably furious, and seizing the writ, he tore it up, threw it on the ground and stamped upon it. The clicking of the locks of his companions revolvers was instantly heard and a crisis was expected. The Sheriff did not attempt his capture; but being at least as prudent as he was valiant, he succumbed, leaving Slade the master of the situation and the conqueror and ruler of the courts, law and law-makers. This was a declaration of war, and was so accepted. The Vigilance Committee now felt that the question of social order and the preponderance of the law abiding citizens had then and there to be decided. They knew the character of Slade, and they were well aware that they must submit to his rule without murmur, or else that he must be dealt with in such fashion as would prevent his being able to wreak his vengeance on the Committee, who could never have hoped to live in the Territory secure from outrage or death, and who could never leave it without encountering his friends, whom his victory would have emboldened and stimulated to a pitch that would have rendered them reckless of consequences. The day previous, he had ridden into Dorris' store, and on being requested to leave, he drew his revolver and threatened to kill the gentleman who spoke to him.  Another saloon he had led his horse into, and buying a bottle of wine, he tried to make the animal drink it.  This was not considered an uncommon performance, as he had often entered saloons, and commenced firing at the lamps, causing a wild stampede.

A leading member of the committee met Slade, and informed him in the quiet earnest manner of one who feels the importance of what he is saying : "Slade, get your horse at once, and go home, or there will be ——— to pay."  Slade started and took a long look with his dark and piercing eyes, at the gentleman—"what do you mean ?" said he. "You have no right to ask me what I mean," was the quiet reply, "get your horse at once, and remember what I tell you."  After a short pause he promised to do so, and actually got into the saddle ; but, being still intoxicated, he began calling aloud to one after another of his friends, and, at last seemed to have forgotten the warning he had received and became again uproarious, shouting the name of a well known prostitute in company with those of two men whom he considered heads of the Committee, as a sort of challenge ; perhaps, however as a simple act of bravado.  It seems probable that the intimation of personal danger he had received had not been forgotten entirely ; though fatally for him, he took a foolish way of showing his remembrance of it.  He sought out Alexander Davis, the Judge of the Court, and drawing a cocked Derringer, he presented it at his head, and told him that he should hold him as a hostage for his own safety.  As the Judge stood perfectly quiet, and offered no resistance to his captor, no further outrage followed on this score.  Previous to this, on account of the critical state of affairs, the Committee had met, and at last resolved to arrest him.  His execution had not been agreed upon, and, at that time, would have been negatived, most assuredly.  A messenger rode down to Nevada to inform the leading men of what was on hand, as it was desirable to show that there was a feeling of unanimity on the subject, all along the gulch.

The miners turned out almost en masse, leaving their work and forming in solid column, about six hundred strong, armed to the teeth, they marched up to Virginia. The leader of the body well knew the temper of his men, on the subject. He spurred on ahead of them, and hastily calling a meeting of the Executive, he told them plainly that the miners meant " business, " and that, if they came up, they would not stand in the street to be shot down by Slade's friends; but that they would take him and hang him. The meeting was small, as the Virginia men were loath to act at all. This momentous announcement of the feeling of the Lower Town was made to a cluster of men, who were deliberating behind a wagon, at the rear of a store on Main street, where the Ohlinghouse stone building now stands.

The Committee were most unwilling to proceed to extremities. All the duty they had ever performed seemed as nothing to the task before them; but they had to decide, and that quickly. It was finally agreed that if the whole body of the miners were of the opinion that he should be hanged, that the Committee left it in their hands to deal with him. Off, at hot speed, rode the leader of the Nevada men to join his command.

Slade had found out what was intendend, and the news sobered him instantly. He went into P. S. Pfout's store, where Davis was, and apologized for his conduct, saying that he would take it all back.

The head of the column now wheeled into Wallace street and marched up at quick time. Halting in front of the store, the executive officer of the Committee stepped forward and arrested Slade, who was at once informed of his doom, and inquiry was made as to whether he had any business to settle. Several parties spoke to him on the subject; but to all such inquiries he turned a deaf ear, being entirely absorbed in the terrifying reflections on his own awful position. He never ceased his entreaties for life, and to see his dear wife. The unfortunate lady referred to, between whom and Slade there existed a warm affection, was at this time living at their

Ranch on the Madison. She was possessed of considerable personal attractions; tall, well-formed, of graceful carriage, pleasing manners, and was, withal, an accomplished horsewoman.

A messenger from Slade rode at full speed to inform her of her husband's arrest. In an instant she was in the saddle, and with all the energy that love and despair could lend to an ardent temperament and a strong physique, she urged her fleet charger over the twelve miles of rough and rocky ground that intervened between her and the object of her passionate devotion.

Meanwhile a party of volunteers had made the necessary preparations for the execution, in the valley traversed by the branch. Beneath the site of Pfouts and Russell's stone building there was a corral, the gate-posts of which were strong and high. Across the top was laid a beam, to which the rope was fastened, and a dry-goods box served for the platform. To this place Slade was marched, surrounded by a guard, composing the best armed and most numerous force that has ever appeared in Montana Territory.

The doomed man had so exhausted himself by tears, prayers and lamentations, that he had scarcely strength left to stand under the fatal beam. He repeatedly exclaimed, "my God! my God! must I die? Oh, my dear wife!"

On the return of the fatigue party, they encountered some friends of Slade, staunch and reliable citizens and members of the Committee, but who were personally attached to the condemned. On hearing of his sentence, one of them, a stout-hearted man, pulled out his handkerchief and walked away, weeping like a child. Slade still begged to see his wife, most piteously, and it seemed hard to deny his request; but the bloody consequences that were sure to follow the inevitable attempt at a rescue, that her presence and entreaties would have certainly incited, forbade the granting of his request. Several gentlemen were sent for to see him, in his last moments, one of whom, (Judge Davis) made a short address to the people; but in such low tones as to be inaudible, save to a few in his immediate vicinity. One of his friends, after exhausting his powers of entreaty, threw off his coat and declared that the prisoner could not be hanged until he himself was killed. A hundred guns were instantly leveled at him; whereupon he turned and fled; but, being brought back, he was compelled to resume his coat, and to give a promise of future peaceable demeanor.

Scarcely a leading man in Virginia could be found, though numbers of the citizens joined the ranks of the guard when the arrest was made. All lamented the stern necessity which dictated the execution.

Everything being ready, the command was given, " Men, do your duty," and the box being instantly slipped from beneath his feet, he died almost instantaneously.

The body was cut down and carried to the Virginia Hotel, where, in a darkened room, it was scarcely laid out, when the unfortunate and bereaved companion of the deceased arrived, at headlong speed, to find that all was over, and that she was a widow. Her grief and heart-piercing cries were terrible evidences of the depth of her attachment for her lost husband, and a considerable period elapsed before she could regain the command of her excited feelings.

J. A. Slade was, during his connection with the Overland Stage Company, frequently involved in quarrels which terminated fatally for his antagonists. The first and most memorable of these was his encounter with Jules, a station-keeper at Julesburg, on the Platte River. Between the inhabitants, the emigrants and the stage people, there was a constant feud, arising from quarrels about missing stock, alleged to have been stolen by the settlers, which constantly resulted in personal difficulties such as beating, shooting, stabbing, etc., and it was from this cause that Slade became involved in a transaction which has become inseparably associated with his name, and which has given a coloring and tone to all descriptions of him, from the date of the occurrence to the present day.

There have been so many versions of the affair, all of them differing more or less in important particulars, that it has seemed imposssible to get at the exact truth; but the following account may be relied on as substantially correct.

From over-landers and dwellers on the road, we learn that Jules was himself a lawless and tyrannical man, taking such liberties with the coach stock and carrying matters with so high a hand that the company determined on giving the agency of the division to J. A. Slade. In a business point of view, they were correct in their selection. The coach went through at all hazards. It is not to be supposed that Jules would submit to the authority of a new comer, or, indeed, of any man that he could intimidate; and a very limited intercourse was sufficient to increase the mutual dislike of the parties, so far as to occasion an open rupture and bloodshed. Slade, it is said, had employed a man discharged by Jules, which irritated the latter considerably; but the overt act that brought matters to a crisis was the recovery by Slade of a team "sequestrated" by Jules. Some state that there had been a previous altercation between the two; but, whether this be true or not, it appears certain that on the arrival of the coach, with Slade as a passenger, Jules determined to arrest the team, then and there; and that, finding Slade was equally determined on putting them through, a few expletives were exchanged, and Jules fired his gun, loaded with buck-shot, at Slade, who was unarmed at the time, wounding him severely. At his death, Slade carried several of these shot in his body. Slade went down the road, till he recovered of his wound. Jules left the place, and in his travels never failed to let everybody know that he would kill Slade, who, on his part, was not backward in reciprocating such promises. At last, Slade got well; and, shortly after, was informed that his enemy had been " corralled by the boys," whereupon he went to the place designated, and, tying him fast, shot him to death by degrees. He also cut off his ears, and carried them in his vest pocket for a long time.

One man declares that Slade went up to the ranch where he had heard that Jules was and, "getting the drop on him," that is to say, covering him with his pistol before he was ready to defend himself, he said, " Jules, I am going to kill you;" to which the other replied, "Well, I suppose I am gone up; you've got me now;" and that Slade immediately opened fire and killed him with his revolver.

The first story is the one almost universally believed in the West, and the act is considered entirely justifiable by the wild Indian fighters of the frontier. Had he simply killed Jules, he would have been justified by the accepted western law of retaliation. The prolonged agony and mutilation of his enemey, however, admit of no excuse.

While on the road, Slade ruled supreme. He would ride down to a station, get into a quarrel, turn the house out of windows, and maltreat the occupants most cruelly. The unfortunates had no means of redress, and were compelled to recuperate as best they could. On one of these occasions, it is said, he killed the father of the fine little half-breed boy, Jemmy, whom he adopted, and who lived with his widow after his execution. He was a gentle, well-behaved child, remarkable for his beautiful, soft black eyes, and for his polite address.

Sometimes Slade acted as a lyncher. On one occasion, some emigrants had their stock either lost or stolen, and told Slade, who happened to visit their camp. He rode, with a single companion, to a ranch, the owners of which he suspected, and opening the door, commenced firing at them, killing three and wounding the fourth.

As for minor quarrels and shootings, it is absolutely certain that a minute history of Slade's life would be one long record of such practices. He was feared a great deal more, generally, than the Almighty, from Kearney, West. There was, it seems, something in his bold recklessness, lavish generosity, and firm attachment to his friends, whose quarrel he would back, everywhere and at any time, that endeared him to the wild denizens of the prairie, and this personal attachment it is that has cast a veil over his faults, so dark that his friends could never see his real character, or believe their idol to be a blood-stained desperado.

Stories of his hanging men, and of innumerable assaults, shootings, stabbings and beatings, in which he was a principal actor, form part of the legends of the stage line; nevertheless, such is the veneration still cherished for him by many of the old stagers, that any insult offered to his memory would be fearfully and quickly avenged. Whatever he did to others, he was their friend, they say; and so they will say and feel till the tomb closes over the last of his old friends and comrades of the Overland.

It should be stated that Slade was, at the time of his

coming West, a fugitive from justice in Illinois, where he killed a man with whom he had been quarreling. Finding his antagonist to be more than his match, he ran away from him, and, in his flight, picking up a stone, he threw it with such deadly aim and violence that it penetrated the skull of his pursuer, over the eye, and killed him. Johnson, the Sheriff, who pursued him for nearly four hundred miles, was in Virginia City not long since, as we have been informed by persons who knew him well.

Such was Captain J. A. Slade, the idol of his followers, the terror of his enemies and of all that were not within the charmed circle of his dependents. In him, generosity and destructiveness, brutal lawlessness and courteous kindness, firm friendship and volcanic outbreaks of fury, were so mingled that he seems like one born out of date. He should have lived in feudal times, and have been the comrade of the Front de Bœufs, de Lacys, and Bois Guilberts, of days almost forgotten. In modern times, he stands nearly alone.

The execution of Slade had a most wonderful effect upon society. Henceforth, all knew that no one man could domineer or rule over the community. Reason and civilization then drove brute force from Montana.

One of his principal friends wisely absconded, and so escaped sharing his fate, which would have been a thing almost certain had he remained.

It has often been asked why Slade's friends were permitted to go scot free, seeing that they accompanied him in all his "raids," and both shared and defended his wild and lawless exploits. The answer is very simple. The Vigilantes deplored the sad, but imperative necessity for the making of one example. That, they knew, would be sufficient. They were right in their judgment, and immovable in their purpose. Could it but be made known how many lives were at their mercy, society would wonder at the moderation that ruled in their counsels. Necessity was the arbiter of these men's fate. When the stern Goddess spoke not, the doom was unpronounced, and the criminal remained at large. They acted for the public good, and when examples were made, it was because the safety of the community demanded a warning to the lawless and the desperate, that might neither be despised nor soon forgotten.

The execution of the Road Agents of Plummer's gang was the result of the popular verdict and judgment against robbers and murderers. The death of Slade was the protest of society on behalf of social order and the rights of man.

---

## CHAPTER XXIV.

### THE EXECUTION OF JAMES BRADY, FOR SHOOTING MURPHY, AT NEVADA.

"Murder most foul and most unnatural.—SHAKSPEARE.

Early in the summer of 1864, the Committee were called upon to visit the stern retribution due to those who wantonly and maliciously attempt to assassinate a fellow-creature, upon James Brady, a resident of the Lower-Town, more generally known as Nevada City. The case was clear, so far as the moral guilt of the accused was concerned, as will fully appear from the subjoined account of the transaction; but there are not a few who measure the extent of guilt by its consequences, and refuse to examine the act itself, on its own merits. Now, we have always held that a man who fires at another, deliberately and with malice prepense, inflicting upon him a wound of any kind, is as much a murderer as if the shot had proved instantly fatal. The other judgment of the case depends upon the relative goodness or badness of ammunition, the efficiency of the weapon, and the expertness of the marksman. Hence, to hit the mark is murder; but to aim at it, and make rather a wide shot, is manslaughter only. If a ball glances on a man's ribs, it is manslaughter; if it goes between them, it is murder. This line of argument may satisfy some people; and that it does do so, we know; at the same time, it is not a doctrine that we can endorse, being fully convinced of its utter want of foundation, in right reason or common sense. Murphy, the victim of Brady's shot, was believed to be dying; the physicians declared he could not live many hours, and for this crime Brady was executed. Some kind-hearted, but weak-headed individuals think that the murderer ought to have been spared, because Murphy had a strong constitution, and contrary to all expectations, recovered; but what the state of a man's health has to do with the crime of the villain who shoots him, will to us, forever remain an enigma as difficult as the unraveling of the Gordian knot. The proper course, in such cases, seems to be, not the untying of the knot aforesaid, but the casting on of another, in the shape of a Road Agent's neck-tie.

At about 11 p. m., the stillness of the summers night that had closed in upon the citizens of Nevada, was broken by two pistol shots fired in rapid succession. The executive officer of the Committee heard the reports, as he was retiring to bed; but the sounds were too familiar to a mountaineer to attract any special attention, and he laid down at once, to sleep. In a few moments, however, he was startled from his quick coming slumber by the sudden entrance of a friend who told him to get up, for there was a man shot. Hastily dressing himself, he found that an individual named Jem Kelly was a prisoner on the charge of being an accomplice in the deed. Who had fired the shots was not known, the man having run off with all speed, before he could be arrested. A guard of two Vigilantes was left in charge of Kelly and the officer went quickly to Brady's saloon, where he first heard, from bystanders, that they thought Brady himself was the criminal, but that he had escaped. The wounded man confirmed this statement, and an examination of the premises showed a bullet-hole in the window through which the assassin had fired. The second shot had been fired from the door-step.

A detail of twelve men were ordered to search the town, for Brady, while the captain and three others started for Virginia City, with the intention of capturing him if he could be found there, or on the road thither. On arriving at Central City, they ascertained from a citizen whom they met on the street, that a man dressed in black clothes, and otherwise answering the description of the fugitive, had passed through, and that he was apparently intoxicated.

They went on to Virginia, and on arriving there, just about midnight, they found that the only house in which a light appeared was the Beaverhead saloon, at the corner of Idaho and Jackson streets, now John How & Co.'s store.

One of the party knew Brady personally, and on entering he at once recognized him in the act of drinking with another man at the bar. The captain stepped up and asked, "Is your name Brady?" "Yes," said he. "Then you are my prisoner," answered the captain. On his inquiring what was the charge against him, he was told that he was arrested for the murder of Murphy. The prisoner immediately started off on a loud harangue, but was stopped by the captain, who told him to keep quiet, and added, "You will have a fair trial in the morning."

Brady was taken down to Nevada by his captors, and confronted with his victim, who was lying in his own house. "Murphy," said the captain, "is this the man that shot you?" The wounded man fixed his gaze on the prisoner, and replied faintly, "It is." The guard then took Brady and marched him down town, to the house where Kelly was confined. The two men were given into the custody of a strong and well armed party, for the night. The death of Murphy was hourly expected by the attendeant surgeons, and all around him.

In the morning, Brady, was taken before the Committee, who sat in the Adelphi Hall, whither they had been convened for that purpose. About fifty members were present and the charge against the prisoner was thoroughly investigated. The trial commenced about 11 A. M.

Meanwhile, Kelly had confessed that he had kept bar for Brady, on that day, and that he knew that there was an old quarrel, and consequently ill-feeling existed between Brady and Murphy. The commencement of this feud dated back as far as the preceding summer. This much of his testimony was correct and truthful, and was corroborated by other witnesses. He then went on to swear that he had nothing to do with the murder himself; that the first thing he knew about the affray was the firing of a shot through the window, followed by the discharge of another into the door-step, and before he could see who it was that had done the deed, the man had run away.

Brady, at first, pretended that he had shot the wrong man by mistake; but he admitted, at his trial that he had really aimed and fired the (supposed) fatal shot. He said that had he been sober, he would not have committed the rash act, and he added, that after shooting, he went next door to his cabin, and sat there for about five minutes; that he then became uneasy, and started for Virginia, flinging his pistol away into the gulch, on his road up. The pistol was found and produced at the trial.

The evidence produced was so entirely conclusive as to admit of no doubt. The offense was deliberate and cold-blooded murder, so far as the prisoner was concerned, and he believed the same till the moment of his execution. Sentence of death by hanging was pronounced.

With regard to Kelly, the evidence adduced at the trial had led to some new developments concerning his share in the transaction. It was positively sworn that he had handed the pistol to Brady, across the bar; and that the understanding was that he was to take the assassin's place, inside the saloon, leaving him free to act on the outside; that, on receiving the pistol, Brady went out with it under his coat, and going into his cabin, he remained there for a few minutes, and then, walking to the window he fired, with deliberate aim, through the window, without previous words, or warning of his intention.

Kelly was sentenced to receive fifty lashes on the bare back, which punishment he duly received, after the execution.

The prisoner (Brady,) sent for W. Y. Pemberton, now practising law at Helena, and requested him to settle his worldly affairs, in legal form. Accordingly, that gentleman drew his will, and the necessary deeds for the disposal of his property, after which he said that he must have a letter written to his daughter. He commenced to dictate it, but the language of the epistle reminded him so forcibly of his own wretched condition, that he was unable to proceed, and covering his face with his hands, he ran to his bed, exclaiming, " Oh! my God! finish it yourself." The writer furnishes the following note of the letter:

"MY DEAR DAUGHTER: You will never see me again. In an evil hour, being under the control and influence of whiskey, I tried to take the life of my fellow-man. I tried to shoot him through a window. He will in all probability die—and that, at my hands. I cannot say that I should not suffer the penalty affixed to the violation of law. I have been arrested, tried and sentenced to be hanged by the Vigilance Committee. In one short hour I will have gone to eternity. It is an awful thought; but it is my own fault. By the love I feel for you, in this, my dying hour, I entreat you to be a good girl. Walk in the ways of the Lord. Keep Heaven, God and the interest of your soul, before your eyes. I commend and commit you to the keeping of God. Pray for my soul. Farewell, forever.

Your father,         JAMES BRADY."

At four o'clock P. M., he was marched from his place of confinement to the gallows, escorted by a guard of two hundred men, fully armed. At least five thousand persons were present at the execution. The gallows was about half a mile east of Nevada, and to save time and expense, a butchers hoist was used for the purpose, a box and plank being rigged for a drop. When the rope had been adjusted, and the fatal preparations were all completed, he was asked if he wished to say anything to the people. He addressed the crowd, telling them that it was the first action of the kind that he had done; that he was intoxicated and insane; that he hoped his execution would be a warning to others, and that God would have mercy on his soul. The trap fell, and James Brady ceased to exist. After hanging for half an hour, the corpse was cut down and given to the friends of the deceased for burial.

Jem Kelly was present at the execution of his friend, and when all was over, he was marched by the guard, down to an unfinished house in Nevada. Here a halt was called, and the necessary arrangements for the whipping were quickly made. Being asked to take off his shirt, he said, "———— the shirt, leave it on;" but on being told that it would be spoiled, he removed it. The culprit's hands were now tied together, and made fast to a beam overhead; after which five men inflicted the punishment, each giving ten lashes with a raw-hide. Kelly showed no fortitude whatever, roaring and screaming at every lash of the hide. At the termination of the flogging, he remarked, "Boys, if I hadn't been so fat, I should have died sure." Nevada was no home for this low-minded villain, who left with all speed; and resuming the career most congenial to a man as fond as he was, of gold without labor, and horses without purchase, he came to the same end as his companion, Brady; but there was this difference between them—Kelly was a thief and murderer by trade; Brady was an honest man, and had never before ventured into the path of crime. Many felt sorry for his fate; but the old miners who heard of Kelly's execution, shrugged their shoulders and muttered, "Served him right; he ought to have gone up long ago; I don't believe in whipping and banishing; if a fellow ain't fit to live here, he ain't fit to live nowhere by thunder—that's so, you bet your life," etc., etc., which terse and technical series of interjectional syllogisms contain more good practical common sense than many a calf-bound folio, embodying the result of the labors of many a charter-granting, plunder-seeking body, humorously styled a "Legislature," west of "the River."

---

## CHAPTER XXV.

THE SNAKE RIVER SCOUT—CAPTURE AND EXECUTION OF JEM
KELLY.

"The pitcher that went often to the well was broken at last."

IRISH PROVERB.

In the month of July, 1864, the coach going from Virginia to Salt Lake was robbed, and a large booty in gold dust was the reward of the Road Agents. This was no sooner reported to the Committee, than prompt measures were taken to pursue the perpetrators of the crime.

A party of twenty-one of the old veterans who had hunted down Plummer's band, left Nevada, on Sunday, the 28th day of August, and camped at .William's Ranch for the night. On Monday, the party rode all day, never halting from breakfast time till evening. The rain fell in torrents, rendering cooking impossible; so a hard bite was all that was available, and each man coiled himself up in his blanket with his saddle for a pillow, and growled himself to sleep as best he could. Four guards came into camp with the stock, at daylight; whereupon the troop saddled up, without taking breakfast, every one of the "crowd" being at the same time wet, "dry," hungry and saucy. One of the boys had managed to bring along a bottle of (contraband) whiskey, as he said, in case of snake-bites; but, under the circumstances, as far as can be ascertained, no one refused a mouthful of the aqua vitæ. They had forgotten the "weights and measures" of their school days, and at that camp, it was found that there was no scruples to a dram. As one of the party observed, it was "big medicine, you bet." A ride in the wet of fifteen miles, brought them to Joe Patte's and breakfast, which latter being despatched, and the former having received their adieux, the "boot and saddle" once more sounded, and they proceeded on their journey, changing horses at the Canyon Station, and finally halting on the banks of Medicine Lodge Creek, in the midst of a heavy rain, storm, without shelter.

In the morning everybody felt wet, of course, and unamiable, probably; but as "business is business" when Montana Vigilantes are afoot, nothing objectionable to morality was offered, except an odd oath, caused by a stiff-legged cayuse or a refractory buckle, which, it is charitably hoped, the rain washed from the record. The probabilities favor the supposition, if the angel made the entry in his book on the banks of that creek. If not, provided he was a good angel, he took no notes till after breakfast and dinner, at Camos Creek, had somewhat soothed and mollified the water-soaked, but irrepressible rangers.

Saddling up once more, the party loped along a little more cheerfully, reaching Snake river at ten P. M., where they, "their wearied limbs to rest," lay down—in a haystack.

After breakfast, they turned their horses heads down stream, and camped in the sage brush, without water, and

with poor feed for stock.   The Vigilantes were supperless.
On Friday, they borrowed the necessary "batterie de cuis-
ine" from the Overland station, and cooked their breakfast
after which they rode to Meek and Gibson's Ferry, where
they camped, and turned out the stock in Fort Hall bottom.

A suspicious character having entered the camp, two of
the boys tracked him to his own "lodging on the cold
ground;" finding however, that there were no evidence of
anything wrong about his halting place, they returned.

At the Ferry, the Vigilantes met an old friend—a brother
of the early days of '63-4.   He was freighting poultry and
hogs to Virginia, from Salt Lake City.   Glad to see his old
comrades on their righteous errand, he presented them with
a thirty pound pig.   A family of Morrisites living in a cabin
at the Ferry cooked it for them, and it was consumed with
immense zest.   Here they learned that Jem Kelly had boarded in the house, and on being asked to pay, he had threatened to whip the old man.   He said that he had a partner
coming from Salt Lake, and that when he arrived he should
have a plenty of money.   He also intimated to one of the
men living there that his partner was one of the men who
robbed Hughes, when a passenger in the coach.   Kelly also
said that there was a big camp of emigrants, with a lot of
mules, near there, on their way to Oregon.   He proposed
that they should stampede the stock, and that if the men
offered a large enough reward, they should return them; but
if not, they would drive them off and sell them.   The man
refused to have any hand in the matter, and was traveling
towards the Butte, to buy some lame cattle from the emigrants, when Kelly who started with him, fell behind, and
drawing a pistol, presented it at him.   The man turned at
once, and Kelly, who saw something that scared him in the
expression of the man's eye, had not nerve to shoot, though
he wanted his money.   He therefore turned it off as a joke.

The man failed to purchase the cattle and returned.
Kelly, who had parted from him, came in some time during
the next day, bringing with him a horse, saddle and bridle.
The emigrants had this horse to drive loose stock, and as is
usual with animals so trained, he followed the wagons, picking up his own living.   One day he lagged behind, and they

went back for him. It is supposed Kelly watched them from behind the crest of a hill, and catching the horse rode of with him.

A party of ten men, with a captain, were sent to scout on the Portneuf Creek, and were mounted on the best animals. They went to Junction Station, Fort Hall, where the Overland boys shod the horses for them. From that place they rode to Portneuf. The squad made a night march, and camped at 11 P. M., without feed for man or beast, during a hurricane of wind. Oliver's coach went by, and when the driver spied the horses, he thought of robbers, and the passengers looked mightily scared. They drove by on a keen run, much to the amusement of the boys, who saddled up at two o'clock A. M. The men had no bedding and no "grub." The culinary furniture was a tin cup in each man's belt, and a good set of teeth. They started at two o'clock A. M., because the stock was so hungry and restless. They kept a bright lookout for Kelly.

At day-break they saw a camp-fire. They rode up thinking of good times, but found only a lot of Shoshone Indians, who had little but choke-cherries to eat. The chief shortly after came up to the captain, and offered him a broiled trout, which he ate and then fell asleep, while the others were regailing themselves on choke-cherries, supplied by little naked pappooses. An old squaw seeing the leader asleep, when the sun rose, built a willow wigwam over him, and when he woke, he seemed considerably exercised at the sight of his house, which seemed like Jonah's gourd. This was too much for both the boys and the Indians, and they laughed heartily.

The detachment saddled up and went on to Portneuf, where they ordered breakfast at 11 P. M., at Oliver's station. Here they learned that a party of California prospectors, ten in number, all dressed in buckskin, had caught Kelly, in a haystack. He had another horse by this time, (he had sold one at the Ferry.) The party went back for two and a half miles, on Sunday morning. The captain was ahead, scouting, with one of the boys, and found the dead body of a man floating in the creek. There was a shot wound through the back of the head. The corpse was wrapped in a grey blanket, with a four strand lariet round the neck and shoulders, as though the body had been dragged and sunk. There were two camp fires near, which seemed to be ten or fifteen days old. They were situated in a thicket of willows. There was a large boulder at the bottom of the eddy, where there was no current, and the men thought that the body had been tied to it, but that it had broken loose and floated. The Vigilantes went back, got a pick and shovel, and buried him. The body was dreadfully decomposed, and it was both difficult and disgusting to raise it; however, they consulted, and slipping willows under it, they reached over, and joining the tops, lifted out altogether, and laid the putrefied remains in their willow grave. Willows were placed below and around them, and having covered them with earth and stone, they, getting a tail-board from a pilgrim's wagon, wrote an inscription, stating his finding by the Vigilantes, and the date of his burial. The men then jumped into the saddle, and rode until after night, coming up with a freight train for Virginia, camped on the road. The captain told his story, whereupon the wagon-boss order them a good warm drink and a hearty supper, sending his herder to look after the stock. The command slept soundly till day-light, and then rode twenty-five miles to the Ferry, to breakfast. They found the main body still camped there, and they were glad to see the California buckskin-rangers, and Jem Kelly in custody.

A trial was called, and the evidence being heard, Kelly was unanimously condemed to death. While pinioned, he asked for his pipe, and got a smoke, which he seemed to enjoy very much. A knot was tied and greased, and when all was working right, the party marched down to a Balm of Gillead tree, and in presence of the prisoner rigged a scaffold by cutting a notch into the tree, and putting one end of a plank from a pilgrim-wagon, into the notch, and supporting the other on a forked stick. The captain asked Kelly if he had anything to say. He answered that if he had never drank any whiskey he would have been a better man. He said it was hard to hang him, after whipping him. While he was on the trap, a couple of Shoshone warriors came up, and looked on with evident amazement. When the plank was knocked from under him, the Indians gave a loud "Ugh!" and started at full speed for their camp. After he had hung some fifteen minutes, the buckskin party came up, and having made some inquiries, they helped to burry him, in a willow coffin. The Vigilantes then returned home without any further incident of travel worth recording.

## CHAPTER XXVI.

ARREST AND EXECUTION OF JOHN DOLAN, ALIAS JOHN COYLE, ALIAS "HARD HAT," FOR ROBBING JAMES BRADY OF $700 IN GOLD.

As the stout fox, on thieving errand caught,
Silent he dies, nor hopes nor cares for aught.—ANONYMOUS.

Late in the month of August, 1864, a man named James Brady, of Nevada, was robbed of $700 in gold by John Dolan, alias John Coyle, alias "Hard Hat," who had been living with him, and took the money from his trousers' pocket. For some time, the real thief remained unsuspected. He cunningly offered to assist in the search, and treated Brady out of the money; but suspicion being aroused by his sudden disappearance, pursuit was made in the direction of Utah. John McGrath followed him to Salt Lake City, and there found that he had changed his name to John Coyle, and that he had gone on to Springville, whither his pursuer followed and arrested him. Dolan stipulated that he should be preserved from the Vigilantes, on the road home, which was agreed to, and McGrath and his prisoner arrived at Nevada on the 16th of September. In the meantime, letters had been received from parties ignorant of this transaction, informing the Committee that Dolan was a pal of Jem Kelly, who was hanged at Snake river; and evidence of his complicity with the Road Agents was also satisfactorily adduced. He was the spy who "planted" the robbery of Hughes in the Salt Lake coach. It is nearly certain that the reason he fled to Utah was that he might receive his share of the plunder.

After a patient and lengthened trial, his guilt being perfectly clear, he was condemned to be executed by a unanimous vote of the Committee. Three hundred dollars of the lost money was recovered, and, though Dolan at first denied his guilt, yet the production of peculiar nuggets being irresistible evidence, he at last confessed the crime and offered to make up the balance, if he should be let go. This could not be acceded to, and, therefore, the Committee made good the amount lost by their refusal, to Brady.

It was on Saturday evening, September 17th, that the execution of Dolan took place, and a scene more fraught with warning to the desperate never was enacted before the gaze of assembled thousands.

About sun-down, strong parties of Vigilantes from Highland, Pine Grove and Virginia, joined the armed force already on the ground belonging to Nevada and Junction. The prisoner was confined in the ball-room, next door to the Jackson House, and here he was pinioned before being brought out. The companies from Virginia, armed to the teeth, formed in two parallel lines, enclosing an avenue reaching from the door through which the prisoner must make his exit on his way to the scaffold. The silence and the sternly compressed lips of the guard showed that they felt the solemnity of the occasion, and that they were prepared to repulse, with instant and deadly action, any attempt at the rescue threatened by the prisoner's companions in crime and sympathizers. All being ready, a small posse of trustworthy men were detailed as a close guard in front, rear and on both flanks of the prisoner. The signal being given, the commander of the guard gave the word, " Company ! draw revolvers !" A moment more and the weapons, ready for instant use, were held at the Vigilantes' "ready," that is to say, in front of the body, the right hand level with the center of the breast, muzzle up, thumb on the cock, and the fore finger extended along-side the trigger-guard. " Right face ! Forward, march !" followed in quick succession, and, immediately the procession was fairly in motion, the files of the guard were doubled. In close order they marched through a dense crowd, to the gallows, a butchers hoist standing in the plain, at the foot of the hills, about half a mile north-east of Nevada, where a fatigue party and guard had made the necessary preparations for the execution. The multitude must have considerably exceeded six thousand in number, every available spot of ground being densely packed with spectators. The face of the hill was alive with a throng of eager and excited people. The column of Vigilantes marched steadily and in perfect silence through the gathering masses, right up to the gallows. Here they were halted and, at a given signal, the lines first opened and then formed in a circle of about fifty yards in diameter, with an interval of about six feet between the ranks, and facing the crowd, which slowly fell back before them, till the force was in position. Renewed threats of an attempt at rescue having been made, the word was passed round the ranks, and the guard, in momentary expectation of a rush from the anti-law-and-order men, stood ready to beat them back. The prisoner, who exhibited a stolid indifference and utter unconcern, most remarkable to witness, was placed, standing, on a board supported in such a manner that a touch of a foot was all that was necessary to convert it into a drop.

The executive officer then addressed the crowd, stating that the execution of criminals such as Dolan was a matter of public necessity, in a mining country, and that the safety of the community from lawlessness and outrage was the only reason that dictated it. He raised his voice, and finished by saying, in a manner that all understood, "It has been said that you will rescue the prisoner; don't try it on, for fear of the consequences. What is to be done has been deliberately weighed and determined, and nothing shall prevent the execution of the malefactor."

Dolan being now asked if he had anything to say, he replied in a voice perfectly calm, clear and unconcerned, that he admitted having committed the crime with which he was charged; but he said that he was drunk when he did it. He added that he was well known in California and elsewhere, and had never been accused of a similar action before. He then bade them all good-bye, and requested that some of his friends would bury his body. The rope was placed round his neck; the plank was struck from beneath his feet, and the corpse swayed to and fro in the night breeze. He never made a perceptible struggle. The dull sound of the drop was followed, or rather accompanied, by the stern order to the crowd, repeated by one hundred voices, "fall back!" The glancing barrels and clicking locks of five hundred revolvers, as they came to the present, sounded their deadly warning, and the crowd, suddenly seized with a wild panic, fled, shrieking in mad terror, and rolling in heaps over one another. A wagon and team were drawn up outside the circle held by the Vigilantes, but such was the tremendous stampede, that, taking them broadside, they rolled over before the onslaught of the mob, like ninepins, and over wagon and struggling mules, poured a living torrent of people. Fortunately no great injury was done to any one, and they gradually returned to the vicinity of the scaffold. As the rush was made, the hill appeared to be moving, the simultaneous motion of the multitude giving it that appearance.

Just before the drop fell, one of the guard, who had newly arrived in the country, being pressed on by a tall, swarthy-looking reprobate, ordered him back, dropping his revolver level with his breast at the same instant. The villain quickly thrust his hand into his bosom, and the butt of a pistol was instantly visible within his grasp. "I say, you, sir!" observed the guard, "just move your arm a couple of inches or so, will you? I want to hit that big white button on your coat." "H—l!" ejaculated the worthy, retiring with the rapidity of chain lightning, among the crowd.

The people were then addressed by a gentleman of Nevada, who forcibly showed to them the necessity of such examples as the present. He reminded them that nothing but severe and summary punishment would be of any avail to prevent crime, in a place where life and gold were so much exposed. The prisoner had declared that he was drunk; but he had offered to return the money, though only in case he would be pardoned. This offer, a due regard for the safety of the community forbade their accepting.

Dolan having been pronounced dead by several physicians, the body was given into the care of his friends; the

Vigilantes marched off by companies, and the crowd dispersed. There was a solemnity and decorum about the proceedings of the Vigilantes that all admired.

Before leaving the ground, a subscription was opened on behalf of the man whose money had been stolen, and the whole sum missing ($400) was paid to him by the Committee. This was an act of scrupulous honesty; probably never before paralleled in any citizens' court in the world.

---

## CHAPTER XXVII.

### CAPTURE AND EXECUTION OF R. C. RAWLEY.

"Justice is blind; but she has a long memory and a strong arm."
PROVERB.

Since the execution of Plummer, Ray, Stinson, Pizanthia and Wagner, there had been no execution in Bannack. The example had been sufficient, and, though it could not be said that there was no crime in Bannack, yet the change from the wild lawlessness of the roughs, and the reign of terror caused by the presence of Plummer and his satellites, was most encouraging. Scores of men silently and quickly left Bannack for other regions. The dread of the "Vigilantes" was strongly impressed on every person, and though it is not easy to suppose that the nature of the desperadoes can be materially changed, yet it is tolerably certain, to those who have witnessed the effect of what the heralds would call "a noose pendant from a beam proper,"—that men of the worst morals and most unquestioned bravery—men whom nothing else could daunt—still maintain a quietness of demeanor that, under any other circumstances than the fear of retribution by the halter, would surely be foreign to their very nature.

Among those who dreaded the arrival of the day of vengeance was a man passing by the assumed name of R. C. Rawley. He was no common loafer, originally; but was under another name and with a fairer character, a merchant

in a large Western city, from which, owing to what precise
discreditable cause we are uninformed, authentically he emigrated to Colorado, and there gradually sank down to the
character and standard of a "bummer." It was evident to
all who knew him that he was a man of education and of
some refinement; occasionally remarks made in his sober
moments 'attested this, but a long course of brutal dissipa-
tion had rendered his acquirements worthless, and had so
debased his morals, that he associated only with the thieves
and marauders whose guilty career terminated as these pages
have shown, upon the gallows. Robbed of all self-respect,
and even ambition, R. C. Rawley, on his arrival in this
country, attached himself as a hanger-on to the Road Agents
and was the constant tool and companion of Stinson, Forbes
Lyons and their associates. He sometimes seemed to become
ashamed of his conduct, and worked for short periods, honestly earning his living; but such spells of good conduct
were only occasional. He returned, uniformly, to his old
habits, "like the sow that is washed to her wallowing in the
mire." ˉRawley was a good looking man, and, but for his
habit of intoxication, he must have been handsome.

In the winter of 1863-4, Rawley, though not closely identified with the band, yet bore a suspicious character, owing
to his connection and association with them. He was seldom, indeed, on the road; but he acted as an inside spy. As
soon as the first blow was struck at the Road Agents, he
became nervous and excited in his demeanor, and warned
by the promptings of a guilty conscience, he suddenly left
Bannack, on a winters morning of such severity that nothing but the belief that detection and punishment awaited
him, could have justified a sane man in undertaking a journey of any considerable length. He was popularly supposed to have gone south or to Boise.

In an ill-starred hour, in the month of September, 1864,
unexpectedly to most people, but with the knowledge of the
Vigilantes, who had kept track of his movements, he suddenly returned to Bannack, thinking, doubtless, that all
danger was past. He came back in rags, to find all his old
friends gone, and looked like a lone chicken on a wet day.
For some time after his return he kept quiet, and went to

work for a man who lived down the canyon, in the neighborhood of New Jerusalem. Those who knew him, state that when he was sober, although he was not a first-class workman, yet he labored steadily and well; but, as may be conjectured, his frequent visits to Bannack, which always involved a spree of drunkenness, greatly impared his usefulness.

During the time when he was under the influence of strong drink, his old predilections were brought prominently forward, and he did not hesitate to utter threats of an unmistakable kind, against the members of the Committee; and also to express his sympathy and identification of interest with the men who had been hanged, stating that they were good men, and that the Committee were ——— strangling ———, etc. This kind of conduct was allowed to remain unpunished for some six weeks or two months; but as Rawley began to get bolder and to defy the Committee, it was resolved that an end should be put to such proceedings.

A meeting of the Vigilantes was called, and it was determined that his case should be thoroughly investigated. This was done, and, during the trial, evidence of the most convincing kind was adduced, of his actual complicity in the outrages perpetrated by the band; of his being a spy for them, and of his pointing out favorable opportunities for the commission of robbery. As his present line of action and speech left no doubt that he would connect himself with some new gang of thieves, and as it was more than suspected that such an organization was contemplated, it was determined to put a sudden end to all such doings, by making an example of Rawley.

A party was detailed for the work, and going down unobserved and unsuspected to New Jerusalem, they arrested him at night, and brought him up to Bannack, without the knowledge of a single soul, except his actual captors. As it was deemed necessary for the safety of society, that a sudden punishment should be meted out to him, in such a manner that the news should fall upon the ears of his associates in crime, like a thunderbolt from a clear sky, he was taken to Hangman's Gulch, and, maintaining the most dogged silence and the most imperturbable coolness, to the last moment, he was hanged on the same gallows which Plummer himself had built for the execution of his own accomplice, Horan, and on which he himself had suffered.

The first intelligence concerning his fate was obtained from the sight of his dead body, swinging in the wind on the following morning. Before his corpse was taken down for burial, a photographic artist took a picture of the scene, preserving the only optical demonstration extant of the reward of crime in Montana.

Thus died R. C. Rawley. A "passenger" or two attended his final march to the grave, and, shrouded in the rayless gloom of a night as dark as despair, thus perished, unshrieved and unknelled, the last of the tribe of spies, cut-throats and desperadoes, who, in the early days of Bannack, had wrought such horrors in the community.

The effect of the execution was magical. Not another step was taken to organize crime in Bannack, and it has remained in comparative peace and perfect security ever since.

---

# CHAPTER XXVIII.

### THE TRIAL AND DEATH OF JOHN KEENE alias BOB BLACK, THE MURDERER OF HARRY SLATER.

"Oh, my offense is rank; it smells to Heaven;
It hath the primal, eldest curse upon it."—HAMLET.

The stern, yet righteous, retribution which the Vigilantes had inflicted on the murderers and marauders in the southern and western part of the Territory, had worked its effect, and little need was there of any further examples, for a long time in the vicinity of Virginia and Bannack; but the restless spirit of enterprise which distinguishes the miners of the West, soon urged the pioneers to new discoveries, creating another centre of population, and thither, like a heron to her haunt, gathered the miners, and, of course, those harpies who live by preying upon them.

Many others who had spent a roving and ill regulated

life, poured into the new diggings, which bore the name of Last Chance Gulch, situated on the edge of the romantic valley of the Prickly Pear, where now stands the flourishing city of Helena, in the county of Edgerton, second in size and importance only to Virginia, and rapidly increasing in extent, wealth and population. This place, which was then regarded as a new theatre of operation for the desperadoes, is almost one hundred and twenty-five miles N. N. W. from the metropolis of Montana; and no sooner were the diggins struck, by a party consisting mainly, of Colorado men, than a rush was made for the new gulch, and a town arose as if by magic. As usual in such cases, the first settlers were a motley crowd, and though many good men came with them, yet the number of "hard cases" was great, and was speedily increased by refugees from justice, and adventurers not distinguished for morality, or for any undue deference for the moral precepts contained in the sixth and eighth commandments.

Among the desperadoes and refugees who went over there was Harry Slater—a professional gambler and a "rough" of reputation. At Salt Lake, he would have shot Colonel W. F. Sanders, in the back, had he not been restrained; and many an outrage had he committed. His sudden flight from Virginia alone saved his neck, a mere accident having saved him from summary execution, the night before he left for Helena, where he met his death at the hands of John Keene formerly a bar-keeper to Samuel Schwab, of the Montana Billiard Saloon, in Virginia, and originally, as will be seen from the biographical sketch appended to this chapter—from the "River," where, as " Bob Black " he figured as a first-class murderer and robber, before he came to the mining regions, and quarrelling with Slater at Salt Lake City, roused again those evil passions, the indulgence of which finally brought him to the fatal tree, in Dry Gulch, where the thieves and murderers of the northern section of the country have so often expiated their crimes by a sudden and shameful death.

Slater arrived first in Helena, and Keene, who had signalized his stay in Virginia by attempting to kill or wound Jem McCarty, the bar-keeper at Murat's Saloon, (better known as the "Court's,") with whom he had a quarrel, by throwing large pieces of rock at him, through the window, at midnight. He, however, missed his mark; the sleepers escaped, and the proprietors sustained little more damage than the price of broken windows.

Slater did not know that Keene was in town, and was sitting in the door-way of Sam Greer's saloon, with his head down, and his eyes shaded by his hat. Keene was walking along the street talking to a friend, when he spied Slater within a few feet of him, and without saying a word, or in any way attracting the notice of Slater, he drew his pistol and fired two shots, the first took effect over the outer angle of the eye, ranging downwards and producing instant death. The murderer put up his pistol and turned quickly down an alley, near the scene of the murder. Here he was arrested by C. J. D. Curtis, and " X " coming up, proposed to deliver him over to Sheriff Wood. This being done, the Sheriff put him, for want of a better place, in his own house, and kept him well guarded. As thousands of individuals will read this account who have no distinct or accurate notion of how a citizen trial, in the West, is conducted, the account taken by the special reporter of the MONTANA POST, which is minutely exact and reliable in all its details, is here presented. The report says that after the arrest of Keene and his committal to the custody of the Sheriff, strong manifestations of disgust were shown by the crowd, which soon collected in front of the temporary prison, and a committee at once formed to give the murderer a hasty trial. Sheriff Wood with what deputies he could gather around him in a few moments, sternly and resolutely refused to deliver the prisoner into the hands of the Committee, and at the same time made the most urgent and earnest appeals to those demanding the culprit; but finally, being carried by main force from his post, and overpower by superior numbers, his prisoner was taken from him.

A court-room was soon improvised in an adjacent lumber yard, the prisoner marched into it, and the trial immediately commenced, Stephen Reynolds presiding, and the Jury composed of Messrs. Judge Burchett (Foreman,) S. M. Hall, Z. French, A. F. Edwards, ——— Nichols, S. Kayser, Edward

Porter, ——— Shears, Major Hutchinson, C. C. Farmer and Ed. House.

No great formality was observed in the commencement of the impromptu trial. Dr. Palmer, Charles Greer and Samuel Greer were sworn to testify. Dr. Palmer started to give his evidence, when he was interrupted by the culprit, getting up and making a statement of the whole affair, and asserting that he acted in self-defense, as the deceased was in the act of rising with his hand on his pistol, and had threatened to take his life, and on a former occasion, in Great Salt Lake City, had put a Derringer into his mouth.

A Mr. Brobrecker then got up and made some very appropriate remarks, cautioning the men on the jury not to be too hasty, but to well and truly perform their duty; weigh the evidence well, and give a verdict such as their conscience would hereafter approve.

Sam. Greer then testified to being an eye witness of the deed. Heard the first shot, did not think anybody was hit; told Keene to "hold on," when he saw Slater fall over; did not hear any words spoken by either of the parties; did not know for certain whether the prisoner was the man who shot Slater.

Prisoner—I am the gentlemen.

Dr. Palmer said that when he made an examination of the deceased he did not find a pistol in his scabbard.

Sam. Greer—The pistol was put into my hands, and placed behind the bar by me, after the shooting took place.

Charley Greer (sworn)—I have been sick lately, and was too excited to make any close observation; was not more than three or four feet from the party killed, when the shooting occurred; thought the man was shooting at some dogs in the saloon.

Charles French (sworn) says: Came down street, stopped first door below Lyon's barber-shop, at the clothing store of Barned; saw a man coming up the street towards Greer's saloon; heard some one cry, "Don't shoot, John; you'll hurt somebody." Soon after, saw the man shoot; thought he was only firing off his pistol to scare somebody; but he saw the deceased man fall, and the other go down street and turn into an alley. Don't know the man that fired the shots.

Q.—Is this the man?

A.—Cannot tell; it is too dark. (A candle was brought) I think it is the same man; I am pretty certain it is.

Dr. Palmer again testified: The deceased was shot over the right eye; never spoke, and died in three minutes after being shot.

James Binns, (sworn)—Was on the opposite side of the street; heard the first shot fired; and saw the second one. Heard Greer say, "hold on," and saw the man fall over, and the other man go through the alley.

[Calls by the crowd for James Parker.]

James Parker, (sworn)—Keene overtook me, to-day, on the summit, coming from Blackfoot. We rode together. He inquired of me whether Slater was in town, and told me of some difficulty existing between them, originating in Salt Lake City; Slater having thrust a Derringer into his mouth, and ran him out of the city.

Prisoner here got up and said. That he had told Parker, he hoped he should not see Slater, as he did not want any difficulty with him, or some such conversation.

James Geero (Hogal) called for, (sworn)—[Here the wind extinguished our candle, and being in the open air, before we could relight it, we missed all the testimony but the last words.—REPORTER.] Know nothing about the shooting affair.

At this moment a voice in the crowd was heard crying: "John Keene, come here"—which caused the guards to close around the prisoner.

Mr. Phillips, (sworn)—Don't know anything about the affair; but saw Slater fall. Don't know who fired. Know what Jem Geero says to be true. Saw Slater sit in this position, (here Mr. P. showed the position Slater was in when shot,) saw Slater sitting in the door; did not see him have a revolver.

Prisoner asked to have some witnesses sent for; he said that the original cause of his trouble with Slater was his taking Tom Baum and Ed. Copeland's part, in a conversation about the Vigilance Committee of last year. Slater then called him a Vigilante ———, and drove him out of town; this was in Salt Lake City. Then he went to Virginia City, and from there to Blackfoot. Slater was a dangerous man; he had killed two men in Boise. He said he had gone to work at mining in Blackfoot, and came over to Helena on that day, to see a man—Harlow. "When I first saw Slater, to-day, he smacked my face with both hands and called me a ——— Irish ——— and said he would make me leave town; I went and borrowed a revolver of Walsh." He requested them to send for an Irishman called Mike, who works on the brickyard, and who heard the last conversation. He wanted Mr. Phillips to give a little more testimony.

Mr. P.—I know him to go armed and equipped; saw him draw a weapon on a former occasion; saw him make a man jump down twenty pair of stairs.

Motion of the jury to retire. Cries of "aye!" and "no! go on with the trial." A voice—"Send for Kelly, the man who was talking to Slater at the time he was shot." Cries of "Mr. Kelly! Mr. Kelly!" and "Dave St. John." Neither of these men could be found.

A motion to increase the number of the guard to forty was carried.

Prisoner again asked to have men sent for his witnesses.

Jack Edwards—I am willing to wait till morning for the continuance of the trial, but the guard must be increased; I hear mutterings in the crowd about a rescue.

A voice—It can't be done.

Prisoner—I want a fair and just trial.

Preparations were now made for a strong guard, forming a ring round the prisoner.

Objections were raised, at this juncture, to whispering being carried on between the culprit and his friends.

A report came in that the Irish brickmaker could not be found at his shanty.

A motion to guard the prisoner till morning, to give him time to procure witnesses, was lost; but being afterwards reconsidered, it was finally carried.

Judge N. J. Bond then got up, and in a short and able speech to the jury, advised them to hear more testimony before convicting the prisoner. He also proposed the hour of 8 A. M., next day, for the meeting of the jury, and the hour of 9 A. M., for bringing in their verdict. The latter proposition was agreed to, and the prisoner taken in charge by the guard.

The dense crowd slowly dispersed talking in a less blood-thirsty strain than they had done three or four hours before.

### SECOND DAY.

The morning dawned serenely upon a large concourse of people, standing before the prison and in front of the California Exchange—the place selected for a jury room.

The jury met a few minutes past 8 A. M., and Mr. Boyden was sent for, and the examination of witnesses resumed.

Mr. B., (sworn)—I have known Keene from childhood; know his parents and relatives; met Keene yesterday on the street; did not know him at first sight, until he spoke to me; told me that he was looking for a gentleman in town, who had, as an act of kindness taken up some claims for him; was walking up street with me; then stopped to shake hands with a man named Kelly, who was sitting on some logs in the street; when we left him. Keene walked faster than I did, and was a few steps ahead of me; when in front of Greer's saloon, I saw a man sitting in the door, (Greer's;) did not see Keene draw his revolver, but saw the first shot fired, and heard Keene say, "You ———, you have ruined me in Salt Lake City." This was said after the shooting. Do not think Slater saw Keene at all. Slater was sitting down; I was about five feet from both men; John Keene was about ten feet from Slater.

Q.—Was Kelly with you at that time?

A.—No; Kelly never left the place where he shook hands with Keene.

Q.—Do you know anything about his character?

A.—I have known him for about ten years; he left Saint Paul about eighteen months ago; know nothing about his course or conduct since that time; he was considered a fast young man, but good and kind-hearted; when I conversed with him yesterday, he spoke about a man that had ruined him in Salt Lake City, but he did not mention any names; I did not know anything of the particulars of his (prisoner's) former difficulties with Slater; never saw Slater and Keene together.

Michael McGregor, (sworn)—I saw Keene in the afternoon; he came to me in the flat, (a point in the lower part of the gulch;) shook hands with me, and then left for town; did not know of the difficulty between Slater and Keene; Keene never spoke to me about it.

D. St. John, (sworn)—Don't know anything about the shooting affair; was fifteen miles from here when it took place. [The witness here gave some testimony not bearing directly on the case, which was not admitted.]

This closed the examination. The jury went into secret session.

At ten minutes to ten o'clock, the jury came from their room to the place of trial, in the lumber yard, where preparations were made immediately for the reception of the prisoner.

At ten o'clock, the culprit made his appearance on the ground, under an escort of about fifty well armed men. A circle was formed by the guard and the prisoner placed in the center. His appearance was not that of a man likely to die in a few minutes. He looked bravely around the crowd, nodding here and there to his acquaintances, and calling to them by name. Captain Florman having detailed his guard, gave the word, "all ready." The foreman of the jury then opened the sealed verdict: "We, the jury, in the case of the people of Montana versus John Keene, find him guilty of murder in the first degree."

A Voice—"What shall be done?"

Several voices in the crowd—"Hang him! hang him!"

The President here rose and said he wished to hear some expression of the public sentiment or motions in the case.

Calls were made for Colonel Johnson. The Colonel addressed the assembly in an appropriate speech, which was followed by a few short and pertinent remarks from Judge Bond.

On motion of A. J. Edwards, the testimony of Messrs. Boyden and Michael McGregor was read, and thereupon Judge Lawrence rose and said he was sure Keene had all the chance for a fair trial he could have wished, and motioned to carry the jury's verdict into execution. Passed.

The prisoner here got up and said: "All I wanted was a fair and just trial; I think I have got it, and death is my doom; but I want time to settle up my business; I am not trying to get away."

He was granted an hour's time to prepare for his execution. The committee fixed the hour of execution at 11½ o'clock A. M. Keene remarked that he hadn't any money to pay expenses—and was told that it should not cost him a cent. The guard now took charge of the doomed man, and escorted him to an adjacent house, in order that he might arrange his affairs.

At 11 A. M. crowds of people could be seen ascending the hill north of Helena, and not a small number of ladies were perceptible in the throng. The place of execution was chosen with a due regard to convenience and economy—a large pine tree, with stout limbs, standing almost alone, in a shallow ravine, was selected for the gallows.

At 11 A. M., the prisoner, accompanied by the Rev. Mr. McLaughlin, arrived in a lumber wagon. A dry-goods box and two planks, to form the trap, were in the same vehicle. The unfortunate victim of his unbridled passions sat astride of one of the planks, his countenance exhibiting the utmost unconcern, and on his arrival at the tree, he said: "My honor compelled me to do what I have done." He then bade good-bye to some of his acquaintances. The wagon having been adjusted so as to bring the hind axle under the rope, a plank was laid from the dry-goods box to another plank set upon end, and the trap was ready.

At four minutes to twelve o'clock, the prisoner's arms were pinioned, and he was assisted to mount the wagon. Standing on the frail platform, he said, in a loud and distinct· voice: "What I have done, my honor compelled me to do. Slater run me from Salt Lake City to Virginia, and from there to this country. He slapped me in the face here, yesterday; and I was advised by my friends to arm myself. When Slater saw me, he said 'There is the Irish ———; he has not left town yet.' Then I commenced firing. My honor compelled me to do what I have done." Here he called for a drink of water, which was procured as speedily as it could be brought to the top of the hill. He took a long, deep draught of the water, and the rope was adjusted round his neck. A handkerchief being thrown over his face, he raised his hand to it and said: "What are you putting that there for? Take it off." Stepping to the end of the trap, he said: "What I have done to Slater, I have done willingly. He punished me severely. Honor compelled me to do what I have done. He ran me from town to town; I tried to shun him here; but he saw me—called me a ——— and smacked me in the face. I did not want any trouble with him; my honor compelled me to do what I have done. I am here, and must die; and if I was to live till to-morrow I would do the same thing again. I am ready; jerk the cart as soon as you please."

At seven minutes past twelve, the wagon started, the trap fell, and Keene was launched into eternity. He fell three and a half feet without breaking his neck. A few spasmodic struggles for three or four minutes, were all that was perceptible of his dying agonies. After hanging half an hour, the body was cut down and taken in charge by his friends.

So ended the first tragedy at Helena. The execution was conducted by Mr. J. X. Biedler, and everything went off in a quiet and orderly manner. Many familiar faces, known to Virginia men in the trying times of the winter of '64, were visible.

The effect, in Helena, of this execution was electrical. The roughs saw that the day had gone against them, and trembled for their lives. There were in town, at that time, scores of men from every known mining locality of the West, and many of them were steeped to the lips in crime. Such a decision as that now rendered by a jury of the people boded them no good. They saw that the citizens of Montana had determined that outrage should be visited with condign punishment, and that prudence dictated an immediate stampede from Helena. Walking about the streets, they occasionally approached an old comrade, and furtively glancing around, they would give expression to their feelings in the chartered form of language peculiar to mountaineers who consider that something extraordinary, unjust, cruel or hard to bear, is being enacted, "Say, Bill, this is rough, ain't it?" To which the terse reply was usually vouchsafed, "It is, by thunder; ——— rough." Cayuses began to rise rapidly in demand and price. Men went "prospecting" (?) who had never been accused of such an act before; and a very considerable improvement in the average appearance of the population soon became visible.

A constant stream of miners and others was now pouring into the Territory, from the West, and the consequence was that thinking portion of the citizens of Helena began to see that a regular organization of an independent Vigilance Committee was necessary to watch over the affairs of the young city, and to take steps for both the prevention of crime and for the punishment of criminals. There were in the town a considerable number of the old Committee; these, with few exceptions, gave the movement their sanction, and the new body was speedily and effectively organized; an executive elected, companies formed, under the leadership of old hands who had mostly seen service in the perilous times of '63-4. A sketch of their subsequent operations will appear in this work, and also an account of the terrible massacre and robbery of the passengers of the Overland coach, in the Portneuf canyon, near Snake river, I. T., together with an account of the capture and execution of Frank Williams, who drove the stage into the ambush.

As it was asserted by Keene that Slater had slapped him in the face, and otherwise insulted him in Helena, before the firing of the fatal shot, it is proper to state that such was not the case. Slater was entirely ignorant of Keene's presence in town; in fact, the other, it will be remembered, had only just previously arrived there, riding with the witness who swore he crossed the Divide in his company. It is also an entire mistake to suppose that Keene was a man of good character or blameless life. The following statement of his previous career of crime, in the East, will be read with interest by many who are under the impression that the murder of Slater was his first offense. It is taken from the Memphis "Appeal," of November 24th, 1865, and, of course, was written without any intention of being published in this work, or of furnishing any justification of the Vigilance Committee. If such had been the intention, it would have been a work of supererogation; for never was a case of murder in the first degree more fully proven. The homicide in broad day light, and the evident malice "prepense" were matters of public notoriety :

"Of the many strange circumstances born of and nurtured by the past war, a parallel to the catalogue of crime herein given has been rarely, if ever, met with.

"In this vicinity, near three years ago, the name of "Bob Black" has, on more than one occasion, struck terror to the hearts of a large number of countrymen, cotton buyers and sellers, whose business compelled them to enter or make their exit from the city by the way of the Hernando or Horn Lake roads.

"'Bob Black' came to this city about six years ago, bringing with him a good character for honesty and industry and continued to work steadily here until the outbreak of the war. At that time he desired to enter the gunboat service, and for that purpose left this city for New Orleans; and, after remaining there some time, he joined the crew of a Confederate ram, the name of which has since slipped our memory. While on his way up from New Orleans, he became enraged at some wrong, real or fancied, at the hands of the captain of the ram, and being of a very impulsive nature, seized a marling-spike, and with a blow, felled the captain to the deck. He was immediately placed in irons, and upon the arrival of the gunboat at Fort Pillow, was handed over to General Villipigue, for safe keeping. A court-martial was ordered, and while in progress, the evacuation of Fort Pillow became necessary, and the prisoner was transferred to Grenada, Mississippi. In the confusion of everything about Grenada at that time, he managed to effect his escape, and passing immediately through the Confederate lines, reached Memphis a few days after its occupation by the Federal authorities. Without any means to provide himself with food or clothing, with a mind borne down with trouble and suffering, and bereft of every hope from which the slightest consolation might be derived, the once honest man was driven to a career of desperation and crime which, if given in its details, would cause the blood-thirsty tales of the yellow-covered trash to pale for their very puerility and tameness.

"In this condition of mind and body he remained in the city

for some time, wandering about here and there; until one day, while standing at the Worsham House corner, he became involved in a quarrel with one James Dolan, a member of the Eighth Missouri Regiment, a large and powerful man, while Black was a man of medium height and stature. Words between the parties waged furious, and finally Dolan struck Black with a cane which he had with him; but quickly warding off the blow, Black wrenched the cane from his adversary and dealt him a blow, which so fractured the skull of Dolan as to cause death within a short time thereafter. Black effected his escape from the city, and with a couple of accomplices, began a system of wholesale murder and robbery on the Hernando road. The atrocity and boldness of these acts created the greatest excitement in Memphis.

"Several parties were robbed of sums varying from one to as high as ten thousand dollars, and, in one instance, a speculator was compelled to disgorge to the amount of five thousand dollars in gold. Of course, these rascals, of whom Black was the leader, often met with men who would make resistance rather than give up their money; and in this way no less than three or four fell victims to the fiendish spirit exhibited by these scoundrels. It was finally agreed upon by the military commanders of the district, on both sides, that means should be taken which would insure their capture. Accordingly a squad of Blythe's battalion, of the rebel army, were sent in pursuit, and succeeded in capturing, about ten miles out of the city, Black and his companion, a fellow young in years, named Whelan. They were placed in the guard-house in Hernando, we believe, and at a preconcerted signal attacked the guard, and mounting some horses belonging to the soldiers, made off at a rapid rate. The guard immediately started in pursuit, and coming upon Whelan, who was some distance behind Black, shot and killed him. Black again escaped, and applied himself with more vigor than ever to the plundering, stealing and robbing of everybody and everything that came within his reach. He would frequently ride into this city at night, passing through the lines at will; and, as an instance of his audacity, on one occasion rode down Adams street, and fired several shots into the station house. It was reported that he had accumulated large sums of money, and the report proved correct. As his business became either too tiresome or too dangerous, he came to the city, disguised, and took passage on a boat for the North. Since that time, and until recently, nothing has been heard from him. It seems that after leaving Memphis, he went to St. Paul, Minnesota, and embarked in the staging and saloon business, under his proper name, John Keene. His restless spirit could not stand the monotony of such a dull business (to him), and, organizing a band of some twenty men, he started for the Territories.

## CHAPTER XXIX.

CAPTURE AND EXECUTION OF JAKE SILVIE alias JACOB SEA-
CHRIEST, A ROAD AGENT AND MURDERER OF TWELVE
YEARS STANDING, AND THE SLAYER OF
TWELVE MEN.

"Whoso sheddeth man's blood, by man shall his blood be shed."
GOD'S LAW.

The crimes and punishment of many a daring desperado, have been chronicled in these pages; but among them all, none was more worthy of death than the blood-stained miscreant whose well deserved fate is recorded in this chapter. According to his own confession—made, when all hope was gone, and death was inevitable, and when nothing was to be gained by such a statement, but the disburdening of a consciense oppressed by the weight of guilt—Jacob Seachriest was a native of Pennsylvania, and had been a thief, Road Agent and murderer for twelve years; during which time he had murdered, single-handed or in company with others, twelve individuals.

In a former chapter of this history—the one detailing the arrest and execution of Jem Kelly at Snake River—it will be remembered that the body of a man, shot through the back of the head, was found in a creek by a patrol of the

Vigilantes, and buried in a willow coffin. The full particulars of the tragedy we are unable to furnish to our readers;
but Seachriest confessed that he and his comrades cast lots
to determine who should commit the bloody deed, it being
repugnant, even to their notions of manhood, to crawl up
behind an unarmed man, sitting quietly on the bank of a
creek, and to kill him for the sake of what he might chance
to possess, without exchanging a word. The "hazard of the
die" pointed out Seachriest as the assassin; and with his
pistol ready cocked, he stole upon his victim and killed him
instantly, by sending a ball through his brain. A stone was
fastened to the body, and it was sunk in a hole formed by
an eddy, in the stream, the thieves having first appropriated
every article of value about his person.

The captain was much moved by the sad spectacle, though
well accustomed to the sight of murdered victims, having
served through the war against the border ruffians, in "Blee-
ding Kansas," and having gone through a chequered career
of adventure, including five years life by the camp-fire. He
said, with much emotion, "Boys, something tells me I'll be
at the hanging of this man's murderer, within twelve months
of this day;" and so it fell out, though most unexpectedly.

Shortly after the execution of John Keene for the murder
of Slater, information was sent to the Committee, that a man
named Jake Silvie had been arrested at Diamond City—a
flourishing new mining camp in Confederate Gulch, one of
the largest and richest of the placer diggings of Montana.
The town is about fifteen miles beyond the Missouri, and
about forty miles East of Helena. The charges against the
culprit were robbery, obtaining goods under false pretenses,
and various other crimes of a kindred sort. It was also intimated that he was a man of general bad character, and
that he had confessed enough to warrant the Committee in
holding him for further examination, though the proof of his
commission of the principal offense of which he was accused
was not greater, at the time, than would amount to a strong
presumption of guilt.

The messenger brought with him copies of the confession
made by the prisoner, under oath, before the proper person
to receive an obligation. The substance of his story was

that he was an honest, hard-working miner; that he had just come into the country, by the way of Salt Lake City; that on reaching Virginia City, and while under the influence of liquor, he had fallen into bad company, and was initiated into an organized band of robbers. He gave the names of about a dozen of the members of the gang, and minutely described the signs of recognition, etc. It was evident, from his account that the ceremonies attending the entry into this villainous fraternity were simple and forcible, although not legal. The candidate was placed in the center of a circle formed of desperadoes; one or two revolvers at full cock were presented at his head, and he was then informed that his taking the obligation was to be a purely voluntary act on his part; for that he was at perfect liberty to refuse to do so; ONLY, in that case, that his brains would be blown out without any further ceremony. Though not a man of any education, Silvie could not afford to loose his brains, having only one set, and he therefore consented to proceed, and swore through a long formula, of which, he said he recollected very little, distinctly, except a pledge of secrecy and of fidelity to the band.

On receipt of the intelligence, a captain, with a squad of four or five men, was immediately dispatched to Diamond City, with orders to bring the prisoner to Helena as soon as possible. The party lost but little time in the performance of their duty, and on the followin day the chief of the Committee rode out, as previously agreed upon, in company with X (a letter of the alphabet having singular terrors for evil doers in Montana, being calculated to awaken the idea of crime committed and punishment to follow, more than all the rest of the alphabet, even if the enumeration were followed by the repetition of the ten commandments,) and meeting the guard in charge of the prisoner, they accompanied them into town. Silvie was confined in the same cabin in which John Keene past his last night on earth. A strong guard was detailed for the purpose of watching the prisoner, and the Committee being summoned, the case was investigated with all due deliberation; but the Committee were not entirely satisfied that the evidence, though complete, was all of such a reliable character as to justify a conviction;

and, therefore, they preferred to adjourn their inquiry, for the production of further testimony. This was accordingly done, and the prisoner was removed to an obscure cabin, in a more remote part of the town, where the members of the Committee would have an opportunity of free access to him and might learn from his own lips what sort of a man they had to deal with.

They were not long in arriving at a satisfactory conclusion on this point. He at first adhered to and repeated his old story and confession; but gaining a little confidence, and thinking there was not much danger to be apprehended from the action of the Committee, he at length denied every word of his former statement, made under oath; said it was all false; that he knew of no such organization as he had told of, and declared that he had been compelled to tell this for his own safety. After being cross questioned pretty thoroughly, he told the truth, stating that he had given a correct statement in the first place; only, that instead of joining the band in Virginia City, he had become acquainted with some of the leaders, on the Columbia River, on the way up from Portland, and that he had accompanied them to Virginia City, M. T., travelling thither by the way of Snake River. (It was on this trip that he committed the murder before described.) This was a fatal admission on the part of the prisoner, as it completed the chain of evidence that linked him with the desperadoes whose crimes have given an unenviable notoriety to the neighborhood of that affluent of the Columbia—the dread of storm-stayed freighters and the grave of so many victims of marauders—Snake River.

Another meeting of the Executive Committee was called during the day, and after due deliberation, the verdict was unanimous that he was a Road Agent, and that he should receive the just reward of his crimes, in the shape of the penalty attached to the commission of highway robbery and murder, by the citizens of Montana. After a long discussion, it was determined that he should be executed on the murderer's tree, in Dry Gulch, at an hour after midnight. The prison guards were doubled, and no person was allowed to hold converse with the prisoner, except by permission of the officers.

The execution at night was determined upon for many sufficient reasons. A few of them are here stated: It had been abundantly demonstrated that but for the murder of Slater having occurred in open day, and before the eyes of a crowd of witnesses, Keene would have been rescued; and the moral effect produced by a public execution, among the hardened sinners who compose a large part of the audience at such times, is infinitely less than the terror to the guilty, produced by the unannounced but inevitable vengeance which may at any moment be visited upon their own heads. Such a power is dreaded most by those who fear its exercise.

The desire to die game, so common to desperadoes, frequently robs death of half its terrors, if not of all of them, as in the case of Boon Helm, Bunton and others. Confessions are very rarely made at public executions in the mountains; though scarcely ever withheld at private ones. There are also many honest and upright men who have a great objection to be telegraphed over the west as "stranglers," yet who would cheerfully sacrifice their lives rather than by word or deed become accessory to an unjust sentence. The main question is the guilt of the prisoner. If this is ascertained without doubt, hour and place are mere matters of policy. Private executions are now fast superseding public ones, in civilized communities.

There is not now—and there never has been—one upright citizen in Montana, who has a particle of fear of being hanged by the Vigilance Committee. Concerning those whose conscience tells them that they are in danger, it is of little consequence when or where they suffer for the outrages they have committed. One private execution is a more dreaded and wholesome warning to malefactors than one hundred public ones.

If it be urged that public executions are desirable from the notoriety that is ensured to the whole circumstances, it may fairly be answered that the action of Judge, and jury, and counsel is equally desirable, and, indeed, infinitely preferable, when it is effective and impartial, to any administration of justice by Vigilance Committees; but, except in the case of renowned Road Agents and notorious criminals whose names are a by-word, before their arrest, or where the crime is a revolting outrage, witnessed by a large number, the feeling of the community in a new camp is against ANY punishment being given, and the knowledge of this fact is the desperadoes chief reliance for escape from the doom he has so often dared, and has yet escaped.

When informed of his sentence the prisoner seemed little affected by it, and evidently did not believe it, but regarded it as a ruse on the part of the Committee to obtain a confession from him. After the shades of night had settled down upon the town of Helena, a minister was invited to take a walk with an officer of the Vigilantes, and proceeded in his company to the cabin where Silvie was confined, and was informed of the object in view in requesting his attendance. He at once communicated the fact to the culprit, who feigned a good deal of repentance, received baptism at his own request, and appeared to pray with great fervor. He seemed to think that he was cheating the Almighty himself, as well as duping the Vigilantes most completely.

At length the hour appointed for the execution arrived, and the matter was arranged so that the prisoner should not know whither he was going until he came to the fatal tree. The Committee were all out of sight, except one man, who led him by the arm to the place of execution, conversing with him in the German tongue, which seemed still further to assure him that it was all a solemn farce, and that he should "come out all right;" but when he found himself standing under the very tree on which Keene was hanged and beheld the dark mass closing in on all sides, each man carrying a revolver in his hand, he began to realize his situation, and begged most piteously for his life, offering to tell anything and everything, if they would only spare him. Being informed that that was "played out," and that he must die, his manner changed, and he began his confession. He stated that he had been in the business for twelve years, and repeated the story before related, about his being engaged in the perpetration of a dozen murders, and the final atrocity committed by him on Snake River. He stated that it was thought their victim was returning from the mines, and that he had plenty of money, which on an examination of him, after his death, proved to be a mistake.

The long and black catalogue of his crimes was too much for the patience of the Vigilantes, who, though used to the confessions of ordinary criminals, were unprepared to hear from a man just baptized, such a fearful recital of disgusting enormities. They thought that it was high time that the world should be rid of such a monster, and so signified to the chief, who seemed to be of the same opinion, and at once gave the order to "proceed with the execution." Seeing that his time was come, Silvie ceased his narrative, and said to the men, "Boys, don't let me hang more than two or three days." He was told that they were in the habit of burying such fellows as him in Montana. The word "take hold," was given, and every man present "tailed on" to the rope which ran over the "limb of the law." Not even the chief was exempt, and the signal being given, he was run up all standing—the only really merciful way of hanging. A turn or two was taken with the slack of the rope, round the tree, and the end was belayed to a knot which projects from the trunk. This being completed, the motionless body was left suspended until life was supposed to be extinct, the Vigilantes gazing on it in silence.

Two men were then detailed, and stood, with an interval of about two feet between them, facing each other. Between these "testers" marched every man present, in single file, giving the pass-word of the organization in a low whisper. One man was found in the crowd who had not learned the particular "articulate sound representing an idea," which was so necessary to be known. He was scared very considerably, when singled out and brought before the chief; but, after a few words of essential preliminary precaution, he was discharged, breathing more freely, and smiling like the sun after an April shower, with the drops of perspiration still on his forehead.

The Committee gradually dispersed, not as usually is the case, with solemn countenances and thoughtful brows, but firmly and cheerfully; for each man felt that his strain on the fatal rope was a righteous duty, and a service performed to the community. Such an incarnate fiend, they knew, was totally unfit to live, and unworthy of sympathy. Neither courage, generosity, truth nor manhood, pleaded for mercy,

in his case. He lived a sordid and red-handed robber, and
he died unpitied, the death of a dog.

Very little action was necessary on the part of the Vigilance Committee, to prevent any combination of the enemies
of law and order from exerting a prejudicial influence on the
peace and good order of the capital; in fact, the organization gradually ceased to exercise its functions, and, though
in existence, its name, more than its active exertions, suf-
ficed to preserve tranquility. When Chief Justice Hosmer
arrived in the Territory, and organized the Territorial and
County Courts, he thought it his duty to refer to the Vigilantes, in his charge to the Grand Jury, and invited them to
sustain the authorities as citizens. The old guardians of
the peace of the Territory were greatly rejoiced at being
released from their onerous and responsible duties, and
most cheerfully and heartily complied with the request of
the Judiciary.

For some months no action of any kind was taken by them;
but, in the summer of 1865, news reached them of the burning
and sacking of Idaho City, and they were reliably informed
that an attempt would be made to burn Virginia, also, by
desperadoes from the West. That this was true was soon
demonstrated by ocular proof; for two attempts were made
though happily discovered and rendered abortive, to set fire
to the city. In both cases, the parties employed laid com-
bustibles in such a manner that, but for the Vigilance and
promptitude of some old Vigilantes, a most destructive con-
flagration must have occurred in the most crowded part of
the town. In one case the heap of chips and whittled wood
a foot in diameter had burnt so far only as to leave a ring of
the outer ends of the pile visible. In the other attempt a
collection of old rags were placed against the wall of an out-
building attached to the Wisconsin House, situated within
the angle formed by the junction of Idaho and Jackson
streets. Had this latter attempt succeeded, it is impossible
to conjecture the amount of damage that must have been inflicted upon the town, for frame buildings fifty feet high
were in close proximity, and had they once caught fire, the
flames might have destroyed at least half of the business
houses on Wallace, Idaho and Jackson streets.

At this time, too, it was a matter of every day remark that Virginia was full of lawless characters, and many of them thinking that the Vigilantes were officially defunct, did not hesitate to threaten the lives of prominent citizens, always including in their accusations, that they were strangling ————. This state of things could not be permitted to last; and, as the authorities admitted that they were unable to meet the emergency, the Vigilantes reorganized at once, with the consent and approbation of almost every good and order-loving citizen in the Territory.

The effect of this movement was marvellous; the roughs disappeared rapidly from the town; but a most fearful tragedy, enacted in Portneuf Canyon, Idaho, on the 13th of July roused the citizens almost to frenzy. The Overland coach from Virginia to Salt Lake City, was driven into an ambuscade by Frank Williams, and though the passengers were prepared for Road Agents, and fired simultaneously with their assailants, who were under cover and stationary, yet four of them, viz: A. S. Parker, A. J. McCausland, David Dinan and W. L. Mers were shot dead; L. F. Carpenter was slightly hurt in three places, and Charles Parks was apparently mortally wounded. The driver was untouched, and James Brown, a passenger, jumped into the bushes and got off, unhurt. Carpenter avoided death by feigning to be in the last extremity, when a villain came to shoot him a second time. The gang of murderers, of whom eight were present at the attack, secured a booty of $65,000 in gold, and escaped undetected.

A party of Vigilantes started in pursuit, but effected nothing at the time; and it was not till after several months patient work of a special detective from Montana, that guilt was brought home to the driver, who was executed by the Denver Committee, on Cherry Creek. Eventually, it is probable that all of them will be captured, and meet their just doom.

The last offenders who were executed by the Vigilance Committee of Virginia City, were two horse thieves and confessed Road Agents, named, according to their own account John Morgan and John Jackson alias Jones. They were, however, of the "alias" tribe. The former was caught in the act of appropriating a horse in one of the city corrals. He was an old offender, and on his back were the marks of the whipping he received in Colorado for committing an unnatural crime. He was a low, vicious ruffian. His comrade was a much more intelligent man, and acknowledged the justice of his sentence without any hesitation. Morgan gave the names and signs of the gang they belonged to, of which Rattlesnake Dick was the leader. Their lifeless bodies were found hanging from a hay-frame, leaning over the corral fence at the slaughter house, on the branch, about half a mile from the city. The printed manifesto of the Vigilantes was affixed to Morgan's clothes with the warning words written across it, "Road Agents, beware!"

Outrages against person and property are still perpetrated occasionally, though much less frequently than is usual in settled countries; and it is to be hoped that regularly administered law will, for the future, render a Vigilance Committee unnecessary. The power behind the Throne of Justice stands ready, in Virginia City, to back the authorities; but nothing except grave public necessity will evoke its independent action.

The Vigilance Committee at Helena and at Diamond City, Confederate Gulch, were occasionally called upon to make examples of irreclaimable, outlawed vagrants, who having been driven from other localities, first made their presence known in Montana by robbery or murder; but as the lives and career of these men were low, obscure and brutal, the record of their atrocities and punishment would be but a dreary and uninteresting detail of sordid crime, without even the redeeming quality of courage or manhood to relieve the narrative.

The only remarkable case was that of James Daniels, who was arrested for killing a man named Gartley, with a knife, near Helena. The quarrel arose during a game of cards. The Vigilantes arrested Daniels and handed him over to the civil authorities, receiving a promise that he should be fairly tried and dealt with according to law. In view of alleged extenuating circumstances, the Jury found a verdict of murder in the second degree, (manslaughter.) For this crime, Daniels was sentenced to three years incarceration in the

Territorial prison, by the Judge of the United States Court, who reminded the prisoner of the extreme lightness of the penalty as compared with that usually affixed to the crime of manslaughter by the States and Territories of the West. After a few weeks imprisonment, the culprit, who had threatened the lives of the witnesses for the prosecution, during the trial, was set at liberty by a reprieve of the Executive, made under a probably honest, but entirely erroneous constitution of the law, which vests the pardoning power in the President only. This action was taken on the petition of thirty-two respectable citizens of Helena. Daniels returned at once to the scene of his crime, and renewed his threats against the witnesses, on his way thither. These circumstances coming to the ears of some of the Vigilantes, he was arrested and hanged, the same night.

The wife of Gartley died of a broken heart when she heard of the murder of her husband. Previous to the prisoner leaving Virginia for Helena, Judge L. E. Munson went to the capital expressly for the purpose of requesting the annulling of the reprieve; but this being refused, he ordered the rearrest, and the Sheriff having reported the fugitive's escape beyond his precinct, the Judge returned to Helena with the order of the Acting-Marshal in his pocket, authorizing his Deputy to rearrest Daniels. Before he reached town, Daniels was hanged.

That Daniels morally deserved the punishment he received there can be no doubt. That, legally speaking, he should have been unmolested, is equally clear; but when escaped murderers utter threats of murder against peaceable citizens mountain law is apt to be administered without much regard to technicalities, and when a man says he is going to kill any one, in a mining country, it is understood that he means what he says, and must abide the consequences. Two human beings had fallen victims to his thirst of blood—the husband and the wife. Three more were threatened; but the action of the Vigilantes prevented the commission of the contemplated atrocities. To have waited for the consummation of his avowed purpose, after what he had done before, would have been shutting the stable door after the steed was stolen. The politic and the proper course would have been to arrest him and hold him for the action of the authorities.

---

## BIOGRAPHICAL NOTICES OF THE LEADING ROAD AGENTS OF PLUMMER'S BAND, AND OTHERS.

### CHAPTER XXX.

#### HENRY PLUMMER.

The following brief sketches of the career of crime which terminated so fatally for the members of the Road Agent Band, are introduced for the purpose of showing that they were nearly all veterans in crime before they reached Montana; and that their organization in this Territory was merely the culminating of a series of high-handed outrages against the laws of God and man.

Henry Plummer, the chief of the Road Agent Band, the narrative of whose deeds of blood has formed the groundwork of this history, emigrated to California in 1852. The most contradictory accounts of his place of birth and the scene of his early days are afloat; upwards of twenty different versions have been recommeded to the author of this work, each claiming to be the only true one. The most probable is that he came to the West from Wisconsin. Many believe he was from Boston, originally; others declare that he was an Englishman by birth, and came to America when quite young. Be this as it may, it is certain, according to the testimony of one of his partners in business, that, in company with Henry Hyer, he opened the "Empire Bakery," in Nevada City, California, in the year 1853.

Plummer was a man of most insinuating address and gentlemanly manners, under ordinary circumstances, and had the art of ingratiating himself with men, and even with ladies and women of all conditions. Wherever he dwelt, victims and mistresses of this wily seducer were to be found.

It was only when excited by passion, that his savage instincts got the better of him, and that he appeared—in his true colors—a very demon. In 1856 or 1857, he was elected Marshal of the city of Nevada, and had many enthusiastic friends. He was re-elected, and received the nomination of the Democratic party for the Assembly, near the close of his term of office; but as he raised a great commotion by his boisterous demeanor, caused by his success, they "threw off on him," and elected another man.

Before the expiration of his official year, he murdered a German named Vedder, with whose wife he had an intrigue. He was one day prosecuting his illicit amours, when Vedder came home, and, on hearing his footsteps, he went out and ordered him back. As the unfortunate man continued his approach, he shot him dead. For this offense, Plummer was arrested and tried, first in Nevada, where he was convicted and sentenced to ten years in the penitentiary; and second, in Yuba county, on a re-hearing with a change of venue. Here the verdict was confirmed and he was sent to prison.

After several months confinement his friends petitioned for his release, on the alleged ground that he was consumptive, and he was discharged with a pardon signed by Governor John P. Weller. He then returned to Nevada, and joined again with Hyer & Co. in the "Lafayette Bakery."

He soon made a bargain with a man named Thompson, that the latter should run for the office of City Marshal, and, if successful, that he should resign in Plummer's favor. The arrangement became public, and Thompson was defeated.

Shortly after this, Plummer got into a difficulty in a house of ill-fame, with a man from San Juan, and struck him heavily on the head with his pistol. The poor fellow recovered, apparently, but died about a year and half afterwards from the effect of the blow, according to the testimony of the physician.

Plummer went away for a few days, and when the man recovered he returned, and walked linked with him through the streets. Plummer went over to Washoe and, joining a gang of Road Agents, he was present at the attack on Wells & Fargo's bullion express. He leveled his piece at the driver, but the barrels fell off the stock, the key being out, and the driver, lashing his horses into full speed, escaped. He stood his trial for this, and, for want of legal proof, was acquitted. He then returned to Nevada City.

His next "difficulty" occurred in another brothel where he lived with a young woman as his mistress, and quarreled with a man named Ryder, who kept a prostitute in the same dwelling. This victim he killed with a revolver. He was quickly arrested and lodged in the county jail of Nevada. It is more than supposed that he bribed his jailor to assist him in breaking jail. Hitherto, he had tried force; but in this case fraud succeeded. He walked out in open day. The man in charge, who relieved another who had gone to his breakfast, declared that he could not stop him, for he had a loaded pistol in each hand when he escaped.

The next news was that a desperado named Mayfield had killed Sheriff Blackburn, whom he had dared to arrest him, by stabbing him to the heart with his knife. Of course, Mayfield was immediately taken into custody, and Plummer, who had lain concealed for some time, assisted him to get out of jail, and the two started for Oregon, in company. To prevent pursuit, he sent word to the California papers that he and his comrade had been hanged in Washington Territory, by the citizens, for the murder of two men. All that he accomplished in Walla Walla was the sdeuction of a man's wife. He joined himself, in Idaho, to Talbert, alias Cherokee Bob, who was killed at Florence, on account of his connection with this seduction. Plummer stole a horse, and went on the road. In a short time, he appeared in Lewiston, and after a week's stay, he proceeded, with a man named Ridgley, to Orofino, where he and his party signalized their arrival by the murder of the owner of the dancing saloon, during a quarrel. The desperado chief then started for the Missouri, with the intention of making a trip to the States. The remainder of his career has been already narrated, and, surely, it must be admitted that this "perfect gentleman" had labored hard for the death on the gallows which he received at Bannack, on the 10th of January, 1864.

As one instance of the many little incidents that so often change a man's destiny, it should be related that when

Plummer sold out of the United States Bakery, to Louis Dreifus, he had plenty of money, and started for San Francisco, intending to return to the East. It is supposed that his infatuation for a Mexican courtezan induced him to forego his design, and return to Nevada City. But for this trifling interruption, he might never have seen Montana, or died a felon's death. The mission of Delilah is generally the same, whether her abode is the vale of Sorek or the Rocky Mountains.

---

# CHAPTER XXXI.

### BOONE HELM.

This savage and defiant marauder, who died with profanity, blasphemy, ribaldry and treason on his lips, came to the West from Missouri in the spring of 1850. He separated from his wife, by whom he had one little girl, and left his home at Log Branch, Monroe county, having first packed up all his clothes for the journey. He went towards Paris, and, on his road thither, called on Littlebury Shoot, for the purpose of inducing him to go with him, in which he succeeded.

Boone was, at this time, a wild and reckless character, when inflamed by liquor, to the immoderate use of which he was much addicted. He sometimes broke out on a spree, and would ride his horse up the steps and into the Court House. Having arrived at Paris, Boone tried hard to persuade Shoot to accompany him to Texas, and it is believed that he obtained some promise from him to that effect, given to pacify him, he being drunk at the time, for Shoot immediately afterwards returned home.

About 9 P. M., Boone came from town to Shoot's house and woke him up out of bed. The unfortunate man went out in his shirt and drawers, to speak with him, and as he was mounted, he stepped on to a stile-block, placing his hand on his shoulder, conversing with him in a friendly manner for a few minutes. Suddenly, and without any warning of his intention, Boone drew his knife and stabbed Shoot to the heart. He fell instantly, and died before he could be carried into the house. He spoke only once, requesting to see his wife. The murderer rode off at full speed. It seems that Boone had quarreled with his wife, and was enraged with Shoot for not going with him to Texas, and that in revenge for his disappointment, he committed the murder. Immediate pursuit was made after the assassin.

Mr. William Shoot, the brother of the deceased, was at that time living in the town of Hannibal, and immediately on receipt of the news, he started in pursuit of the criminal. Boone Helm had, however, forty miles start of him; but such good speed did the avenger make, that pursuer and pursued crossed Grand Prairie together, Shoot arriving at Roachport and Boone Helm at Booneville, within the space of a few hours. Telegrams descriptive of the fugitive were sent in all directions, and were altered as soon as it was discovered that the murderer had changed his clothes. Shoot returned to Paris, and being determined that Helm should not escape, he bought two horses and hired Joel Moppen and Samuel Querry to follow him, which commission they faithfully executed, coming up with their man in the Indian Territory. They employed an Indian and a Deputy Sheriff to take him, which they accordingly did. When ordered to surrender, he made an effort to get at his knife; but when the Sheriff threatened to shoot him dead if he moved, he submitted. He was brought back, and, by means of the ingenuity of his lawyers, he succeeded in obtaining a postponement of his trial. He then applied for a change of venue to a remote county, and at the next hearing the State was obliged to seek a postponement, on the ground of the absence of material witnesses. He shortly after appeared before a Judge newly appointed, and having procured testimony that his trial had been three times postponed, he was set free, under the law of the State.

He came to Calfornia and joined himself to the confraternity of iniquity that then ruled that country. He either killed or assisted at the killing of nearly a dozen men in the brawls so common at that time in the western country. In

Florence, Idaho Territory, he killed a German called Dutch Fred, in the winter of 1861-2. The victim had given him no provocation whatever; it was a mere drunken spree and "shooting scrape."

He also broke jail in Oregon, a squaw with whom he lived furnishing him with a file for that purpose. He escaped to Carriboo. He was brought back; but the main witnesses were away when the trial took place, and the civil authorities were suspected of having substantial reasons for letting him escape. He was considered a prominent desperado, and was never known to follow any trade for a living, except that of Road Agent, in which he was thoroughly versed.

Helm was a man of medium size, and about forty years old; hard-featured, and not intelligent looking. It was believed, at Florence that a relative, known as "Old Tex," furnished money to clear him from the meshes of the law, and to send him to this country. If ever a desperado was all guilt and without a single redeeming feature in his character, Boone Helm was the man. His last words were: "Kick away, old Jack; I'll be in h—l with you in ten minutes. Every man for his principles—hurrah for Jeff Davis! let her rip."

### GEORGE IVES.

We have only a few words to add to the account already given of this celebrated robber and murderer. He was raised at Ives' Grove, Racine county, Wisconsin, and was a member of a highly respectable family. It seems that life in the wild West gradually dulled his moral perceptions; for he entered, gradually, upon the career of crime which ended at Nevada, M. T. His mother for a long time, believed the accoent that he sent to her, about his murder by the hands of Indians, and which he wrote himself. It is reported that sorrow and death have been busy among his relatives ever since.

### BILL BUNTON

Followed gambling at his regular calling, at Lewiston, Idaho in the winter of 1861-2. In the summer of 1862, he shot a man named Daniel Cagwell, without provocation. There was a general fracas at a ball, held on Copy-eye creek, near Walla Walla. Bunton was arrested; but made his escape from the officer, by jumping on a fast horse and riding off at full speed.

The first that was afterwards heard of him was that he turned up in this country. In person, Bunton was a large, good-looking man, about thirty years of age, and rather intelligent. He had been for some years on the Pacific coast, where he had lived as a sporting man and saloon keeper. He was absolutely fearless, but was still addicted to petty theft, as well as to the greater enormities of Road Agency and murder. His dying request, it will be remembered, was for a mountain to jump off, and his last words, as he jumped from the board, "Here goes it."

Of Johnny Cooper we have already spoken. A word is necessary concerning the history of

### ALICK CARTER

which forms a strong contrast to the others. It appears that, for several years this eminent member of Plummer's band bore an excellent character in the West. He was a native of Ohio, but followed the trade of a packer in California and Oregon, maintaining a reputation for honor and honesty of the highest kind. Large sums of money were frequently entrusted to his care, for which he accounted to the entire satisfaction of his employers. He left the "other side" with an unstained reputation; but falling into evil company in Montana, he threw off all recollections of better days, and was one of the leading spirits of the gang of mauraders that infested this Territory. It is sad to think that such a man should have ended his life as a felon, righteously doomed to death on the gallows.

### CYRUS SKINNER

was a saloon-keeper in Idaho, and always bore a bad character. His reputation for dishonesty was well known, and in this country he was a blood-thirsty and malignant outlaw, without a redeeming quality. He was the main plotter of Magruder's murder.

### BILL HUNTER.

Probably not one of those who died for their connection with the Road Agent Band was more lamented than Hunter. His life was an alternation of hard, honest work, and gambling. That he robbed and assisted to murder a Mormon,

and that he was a member of the gang, there can be no
doubt; but it is certain that this was generally unknown,
and his usual conduct was that of a kind-hearted man. He
had many friends, and some of them still cherish his memory.
He confessed his connection with the band, and the justness
of his sentence just before his death. His escape from Virginia, through the pickets placed on the night of the 9th of
January, 1864, was connived at by some of the Vigilantes,
who could not be made to believe that he was guilty of the
crimes laid to his charge.

### STEPHEN MARSHLAND

was a graduate of a college in the States; and, though a
Road Agent and thief, yet he never committed murder, and
was averse to shedding blood. He was wounded in attacking Forbes' train, and his feet were so far mortified by frost
when he was captured, that the scent attracted the wolves,
and the body had to be watched all night.

Concerning the rest of the gang, nearly all that is known
has already been related. They were, without exception,
old offenders from the Pacific coast. The "bunch" on Ned
Ray's foot was caused a by wound from a shot fired at him
when escaping from the penitentiary at St. Quentin, California. This he told, himself, at Bannack.

### JAMES DANIELS.

This criminal, the last executed by the Vigilantes, it
should be generally understood, murdered a Frenchman in
Tuolumne county, California, and chased another with a
bowie-knife till his strength gave out. In Helana, he killed
Gartley, whose wife died of a broken-heart at the news;
threatened the lives of the witnesses for the prosecution,
and had drawn his knife, and concealed it in his sleeve, with
the intent of stabbing Hugh O'Neil in the back, after the
fight between Orem and Marley, at the Challenge Saloon.
He said he "would cut the heart out of the ————!" when
an acquaintance who was watching him, caught hold of him
and told him he was in the wrong crowd to do that. Daniels renewed his threats when liberated, and was hanged;
not because he was pardoned, but because he was unfit to
live in the community.

## CHAPTER XXXIII.

### CONCLUSION.

" All's well that ends well," says the proverb. Peace, order and prosperity are the results of the conduct of the Vigilantes; and, in taking leave of the reader, the author would commend to the sound sense of the community, the propriety of maintaining, in readiness for efficient action if needed, the only organization able to cope with the rampant lawlessness which will always be found in greater or less amount in mining camps.

At the same time, let the advice be well understood before it is either commented upon or followed. Readiness is one thing; intermeddling is another. Only on occasions of grave necessity should the Vigilantes let their power be known. Let the civil authority, as it increases in strength, gradually arrogate to itself the exclusive punishment of crime. This is what is needed, and what every good citizen must desire; but let the Vigilantes, with bright arms and renewed ammunition, stand ready to back the law, and to bulwark the Territory against all disturbers of its peace, when too strong for legal repression, and when it fails or is unable to meet the emergency of the hour. Peace and justice we must have, and it is what the citizens will have in this community; through the courts, if possible; but peace and justice are rights, and courts are only means to an end, admittedly the very best and most desirable means; and if they fail, the people, the republic that created them, can do their work for them. Above all things, let the resistless authority of the Vigilantes, whose power reaches from end to end of Montana, be never exerted except as the result of careful deliberation, scrupulous examination of fair evidence, and the call of imperative Necessity; which, as she knows no law, must judge without it, taking Justice for her counselor and guide.

Less than three years ago, this home of well ordered industry, progress and social order, was a den of cut-throats and murderers. Who has effected the change? The Vigilantes; and there is nothing on their record for which an apology is either necessary or expedient. Look at Montana that has a committee; and turn to Idaho, that has none. Our own peaceful current of Territorial life runs smoothly, and more placidly, indeed, than the Eastern States, to-day; but in Idaho, one of their own papers lately asserted that, in one county, sixty homicides had been committed, without a conviction; and another declares that the cemeteries are full of the corpses of veterans in crime and their victims.

Leave us the power of the people, as a last resort; and, where governments break down, the citizens will save the State. No man need be ashamed of his connection with the Virginia Vigilantes. Look at their record and say it is not a proud one. It has been marvellous that politics have never intruded into the magic circle; yet so it is, has been, and probably will be. Men of all ranks, ages, nations, creeds and politics are among them; and all moves like a clock, as can be seen on the first alarm. Fortified in the right, and acting in good conscience, they are "just and fear not." Their numbers are great; in fact, it is stated that few good men are not in their ranks, and the presence of the most respectable citizens makes their deliberation calm, and the result impartially just.

In presenting this work to the people, the author knows, full well, that the great amount of labor bestowed upon it is no recommendation of its excellence to a public that judges of results and not of processes; but one thing is sure; so far as extended research and a desire to tell the truth can effect the credibility of such a narrative, this history has been indited subject to both these regulations, since the pen of the writer gave the first chapter to the public.

If it shall serve to amuse a dull hour, or to inform the residents of the Eastern States and of other lands of the manners and habits of the mountaineers, and of the life of danger and excitement that the miners in new countries have to lead, before peace and order are settled on an enduring foundation—the author is satisfied. If in any case his readers

are misinformed, it is because he has been himself deceived.
As a literary production, he will be rejoiced to receive the
entire silence of critics as his best reward. He knows full
well what criticism it deserves, and is only anxious to escape
unnoticed. And now, throwing down his pencil, he heaves
a sigh of relief, thankfully murmuring, "Well, it is done at
last."